17

But What Comes After?

But What Comes After?

Ruth Leon

Constable • London

Constable & Robinson Ltd
3 The Lanchesters
162 Fulham Palace Road
London W6 9ER
www.constablerobinson.com

First published in the UK by Constable,
an imprint of Constable & Robinson Ltd, 2011

A copy of the British Library Cataloguing in Publication Data
is available from the British Library.

ISBN 978-1-84529-570-7

Printed and bound in the UK

PEFC/16-33-111
CATG-PEFC-052
www.pefc.org

This book is for my sister, Adrienne Landau, and for Sheridan's aunt, Sally Hardy.

It is also for my cousins, Mildred, June and Stephanie.

These remarkable women dispensed good advice, unselfish help and unconditional support when it was most needed and least deserved.

This book is also for all those who are caring for the sick; you are legion and you are not alone.

Cocktails and laughter,
But what comes after?
Nobody knows!

(from *Poor Little Rich Girl*, 1925)

Noël Coward and Philip Braham

Acknowledgements

First of all, I must thank the health professionals, the doctors, nurses, pharmacists, social workers and others who dedicated themselves to making Sheridan better. Professor Guy Goodwin who gave us hope at the blackest time, Professor Tipu Aziz who courageously operated on Sheridan, Dr Jeannie Speirs and Dr Leslie Morrish, the psychiatrists who worked tirelessly to allay Sheridan's pain, Dr Brett Kahr, the psycho-therapist who understood, Dr Colin Mackintosh and Dr Roberto Guiloff who saved his life several times. And my respect to all the nurses who, without adequate thanks and recompense, daily prove their indispensability to the patients they serve. Above all, in this category, my dear friend Dr Edith Langner who held my hand across the wide Atlantic and demystified all the contradictory medical advice.

My affectionate thanks to Michael and Alan Bennett-Law, who saved Sheridan's life by taking him to the hospital and who remained steadfast friends and colleagues throughout his illness. To his best friend, Christopher Matthew, who never abandoned him. To Hannah Kroma who taught me the meaning of patience. To Anne Bond and Becca Walton who held my professional life together when I could not and to Christopher Sinclair-Stevenson, my indispensable friend and agent, without whom this book would not be this book.

Where would I have been without my friends? On both sides of the Atlantic they supported and nurtured me, picked me up when I was down, and did anything they could to ease our situation. I learned to lean on them all, to exploit their generosity, to exhort their help. My love and thanks to Michael Arditti, Dan Avshalomov, Linda Blandford, Molly and Jurgen Brendel, Laurie Carney, Silvana Camiletti, Judith Flanders, Penny Gummer, Joan Harris, Penny Horner, Hilary King, Grace Lichtenstein, Hermine Nessen, Maureen Oxenford, Judy Rosenfeld, Eve Shapiro, Donald Smith, Don and Norma Stone, Daoma and Murray Strasberg, Stephanie Cooper and Howard Weinberg, Brian, Adele, Jessica and Matthew Winston, Debbie Wiseman. I am fearful that, in naming these, I am neglecting others who, with random acts of kindness, silly emails and serious talk, made life worth living in the darkest times. You will never know how much you all mean to me.

I need also to acknowledge those who died during the writing of this book but without whose help and support it could never have been written – Jo Durden-Smith, Peter Coller, and my parents, Rose and Sam Leon.

And my indispensable friend, Polly Dranov, who was there, in person or by telephone, every day and night, whenever she was needed, comforting, explaining, cajoling, joking, grieving and loving.

Thank you.

Introduction:
The Mother Teresa Gene

I lack the Mother Teresa gene. Most of us do. When you find yourself the principal carer of a chronically or acutely ill person you imagine that you're miraculously going to develop the gene that allowed the famous nun to be gentle and loving, warm and affectionate with the scraps of humanity she scraped off Calcutta's pavements. You tell yourself, if *she* can touch these filthy strangers, surely *you* can manage to be supportive to someone you love.

It doesn't always work that way. Sure, there are those among us who are born with patience, superhuman endurance, a loving heart and an endless sense of humour – I have a sister like that. She always knows the right thing to say, how to make someone feel better and what to do to get the best out of whoever she's with. I love her beyond reason and, sometimes, I hate her. She was born with the Mother Teresa gene.

I was not. I'm not a monster but an ordinary woman who, when called upon to take care of a chronically sick husband, found herself neither up to the job nor able to see a way out of it.

I learned a lot in the twenty years he was chronically ill and in the four years following his stroke when his illness became acute. I learned not to beat myself up for not being good enough.

I wasn't a very good carer but I was what he had, and that was, just about, enough. I did my best to make him happy and comfortable, knowing he was still sick and miserable and that, probably, someone else out there would have a better shot at it. My best wasn't, I always suspected, up to much.

But I wish someone had written a book that would have told me that I was all right, that what I felt was common to many others in the same boat, that what I was doing wrong was understandable and what I was doing right was commendable. Instead, your friends, secretly grateful that it isn't them, praise you for your fortitude without having any idea what you are experiencing and suffering.

When you find yourself in charge of two lives, there are many things that nobody tells you. One is that it's all right to be angry. You're entitled. Just don't let it paralyse you. Another is how boring it is. Depending on the illness suffered by your loved one, he or she is always going to be the one who gets looked after while you're always going to be the one doing the worrying. And the one who has to clear up the mess. Worse, when your friends are out having fun or at least having a pint, you're going to be changing dressings or pills or sitting by yourself while your charge sleeps or complains. A bit of organization will allow you an hour or two to read a book, go ice-skating, go to a concert or go to the pub. Learn how to find that hour.

One of the bits of advice I pass on to anyone with a chronic sufferer in their lives is: don't take this illness on yourself; it is theirs, not yours, so don't beat yourself up about it.

Another is to learn how to use other people. I remain constantly conscious of how incredibly lucky I am to have my friends and family. Had I been alone, I hope I'd have sought out fellow-sufferers online, in chat rooms, via the social services, in support groups or wherever they could be found. Over time, I learned to lean on others, as they once leaned on me, to ask for help and not to care about my carefully nurtured image as someone who is self-sufficient and available to care for others but who doesn't need that attention herself. I learned to talk straight about Sheridan's illness and my reactions to it. I tell my friends and sometimes others about what I did badly, about my inability to cope with the effects of the illness and about the occasions when I was ashamed of myself for shouting at him or not understanding that he couldn't help being infuriating because he was ill.

I've learned to forgive myself, at least a little, for being such a bitch, for snapping at him and manipulating and ignoring him. I did the best I could. It still seems to me that it wasn't good enough, he deserved better, but I was there when nobody else was. At such moments, while I was trying to forgive myself for making him even more unhappy than he already was, I was also trying to get rid of my anger. I know anger is a destructive emotion for me. Others can be fuelled and energized by anger; I am undone by it. It makes me weak and vindictive, two areas of my personality I can't afford to enter.

It's all right to resent the significant other in your life. It's not their fault that they're sick but they won't be doing much to make your life easier while your entire existence sometimes seems devoted to improving theirs. Bitching at them about the small things some-times helps you live through the harder stuff. Creative complaining makes you feel much better.

Illness is messy, dirty, unpleasant and, a lot of the time, it stinks. Literally. It is undignified, inelegant and militates against any kind of civilized life. Is this, you ask yourself, why I married (gave birth to, was born to, became friends with) him or her? Why did Mother Teresa do it? *How* did she do it?

I decided to write about all this following a party at the home of dear friends who always give very jolly Christmas parties with lovely food, good champagne, sinful desserts and an extraordinary guest list. At their gatherings you can either, depending on your personality, stand and gawp at the people and the paintings, or bounce up to someone you've always wanted to meet and start a conversation. If I can manage it, I never miss one of their Christmas parties and, that last year, when my husband was very sick and refusing to get out of bed at all, I planned to go alone. His darling aunt, Sally Hardy, arranged to come and sit with him while I went out.

To my astonishment, he insisted on coming with me. As we entered, we met an old friend and I left them chatting while I stole a few minutes to see who else was there. I sat down next to a woman I didn't know. As she made room for me on the sofa and we started to talk, I saw my husband turn from the buffet table, totally lost amid dozens of people, precariously balancing a champagne glass and a plate of food, both of which were clearly heading south. I shot up, rescued the comestibles, found him a seat and resumed my own. She looked at me with sympathy. 'I've got one of those,' she said, and we went back to our previous conversation about her recent retirement as Mistress of a Cambridge college, her elevation to the House of Lords and the books we were both writing at the time. Then, briefly, we talked about what it was like to see the man you have loved for decades turn into someone you don't know.

The following day, having exchanged addresses, she emailed me: 'It was wonderful to meet you and to know that I'm not alone.' This woman of achievement and power, this woman who, like me, had never faced a problem that didn't have a solution, this woman who was, like me, busy and privileged, was also, just like me, lonely and heartbroken.

The encounter made me wonder how many of us there are who feel isolated by our sudden exile, not by death but by illness, from what had been a close and interdependent marriage. Illness is no respecter of persons. It can strike any of us at any time and there's no point in the 'Why me?' question. As I broadened the net, talking with other people (mostly women, but some men) whose spouses, children or parents had dementia, Alzheimer's, strokes or crippling mental illnesses which made them not fit company for man nor beast, I began to break the silences which surround us.

One evening at a dinner I mentioned that I wished the man sitting next to me could meet my husband as I was sure they would like one another.

'Where is he?' he asked. 'Away on business?'

'No,' I told him, 'he's a severe depressive and he wasn't able to get out of bed today. Some days he doesn't talk at all. Today was one of them.'

'You're so lucky,' he said, wistfully. 'At least you can talk to him sometimes. My wife hasn't said anything sensible in three years and now she doesn't even know me.'

We often think we could cope so much better if we were rich. Then, we speculate, the illness would be just as bad but we could pay for help, get the smelly bits taken care of by someone else, live in a nicer place and not be so tired all the time. And, yes, money helps. But not much.

One of my closest friends is a woman who looks and behaves as though she has nothing to do but shop and take care of her appearance. She appears to have a perfect life. She is beautiful, charming, funny and rich. She has a house on a perfect garden square in Chelsea, two attractive and talented grown children, a flat in Rome within sight of St Peter's and an apartment in Miami overlooking the sea. Several years ago her equally perfect banker husband had difficulty with a tennis shot. His doctor had to break it to him that he had motor neurone disease and his nerves would atrophy, one by one, until he literally died of drowning in his own bodily fluids. Although they could easily afford round-the-clock care, he would allow nobody except his wife near him for the four years it took him to die and she took care of him every minute of every day. Finally, lying in bed next to her, he died.

She is a prime possessor of the Mother Teresa gene. I never heard her complain, and she never allowed her love for him to be ameliorated by the burden he placed on her. She still visits his grave, in the Italian manner, most weeks. Exactly five years later, her beloved daughter was diagnosed with another incurable wasting disease, this time of the muscles. See what I mean? Illness is no respecter of persons; money helps, but not a lot.

A man I know is so frustrated, following his stroke, with his inability to communicate with his beloved wife after fifty years of conversation that he routinely hits her. She says nothing, even to her children, knowing how he hates being locked in a body that no longer works. His anger imprisons her in their house and earns her the opprobrium of her children who think she is deliberately keeping them away from their dying father. She doesn't want them to think badly of him when he dies so she shoulders their anger instead.

A man suffering from severe depression no longer wants to do anything but stay in bed – the one thing the doctors say is worst for him – never speaks except in descending repetitious cycles about his misery, is suicidal and is angry with his wife for trying to keep him alive.

I was blessed with an extraordinary marriage, a true meeting of minds and lives. Until my husband's illness we lived in a symbiosis which is, I know, unusual. We did the same kind of work, usually in the same room at the same time. We stayed home together, we went out together, we travelled together, we ate together. We laughed, nearly all the time. And, when he became ill and the laughter stopped, I had no idea how to cope with him.

In every one of these cases, a marriage that was founded on love and friendship, and kept fresh by easy and stimulating communication, is reduced to silence, isolation and resentment.

And it isn't only spouses. The chronically ill are rich and poor, of every shade and religion, from everywhere. Tell someone, anyone, on the bus or at the Ritz, that you are caring for a sick person and they will tell you their story. Nearly everybody has one, and once the tidal gates open, the flood begins because almost all of us will, at some point in our lives, find ourselves taking care of someone we love and not knowing how to do it.

This is my story, just mine, nobody else's. I wanted to write about an amazing man and a rewarding marriage because you can't appreciate what you have lost without understanding what you had. I wanted to write for all the people who are trying to cope with someone they love who is no longer the same someone.

I know what they're feeling: I've been there. They feel alone, as I did. They feel inadequate, as I did. They feel trapped, as I did. And, as I did, they know there must be something that will make us feel less isolated.

Perhaps this book is it.

Chapter One

I was in New York on 21 November 2002, finishing my long overdue biography of George Gershwin, which was proving the easiest book I'd ever written so I was enjoying myself hugely. I had fallen in love with my subject and consequently found writing a pleasure, not a chore.

Before I got going that Wednesday, I followed my usual workday routine. I collected my morning coffee and the *New York Times* from Starbucks and called down to the maintenance department to fix the kitchen sink yet again. I had a quick conversation with my husband in London and checked in with our driver and assistant, Peter, also in London, about various minor crises. And, on that day, because tomorrow would be Thanksgiving, I called my friends, attorney Stephanie Cooper and her husband (who is my television producing partner, Howard Weinberg), about coming to their apartment as usual for the big annual dinner.

I worked, as I always do, office hours – 9.30 to 5.30 – as though I were still a secretary with a hard boss standing over me with a time clock to punch. On this day, there were few interruptions and I happily tapped away at my elderly laptop until I had to change out of my disgraceful but comfortable writing clothes into something acceptable for the theatre.

That evening, I went with my friend, David Staller, to see the latest Broadway incarnation of Rodgers and Hammerstein's musical *Flower Drum Song*. A critic for my day job, I wasn't reviewing that night so didn't have to rush back to the apartment to write. Instead, David, an actor and writer, and I made our way down to Pearl's restaurant in Greenwich Village for some of her delectable fried oysters and one of those equally delicious dissections of a show that theatre people cherish.

By the time we'd finished discussing *Flower Drum Song* there wasn't a song or a scene we hadn't pulled to bits. It was time to go home. David lives on the East Side in midtown and I live on the Upper West Side, so we separated and I made my leisurely way uptown on the bus. I wasn't in a hurry. I'd had a good day, and I had a book to read that engaged my attention all the way to 68th Street.

I walked into the apartment exactly at midnight and my answering machine was flashing excitedly. I briefly considered leaving it until the morning but I could see that there were five messages so thought I'd better check in case anything was really important. They were all from Sheridan's friend and cabaret partner, Michael Law, and they were identical. I was to call him back at his home in Kent, no matter what time I got the messages.

I thought immediately of my mother – Rosie was 93 then, and in a constant battle between her indomitable spirit and her failing body – and wondered why, if she had been taken ill or died, Sheridan hadn't called me himself. He must be with her at some hospital and unable to find a telephone, I thought, knowing his inability to make fiddly machines, such as mobile phones, part of his life.

I looked at the clock: 5.10 a.m. London time, and I knew Michael had been performing with Sheridan at a private party in Chelsea until late. I decided reluctantly to wake up Michael and his partner Alan. They were typically reassuring but their news was frightening. Sheridan had arrived two hours late for the show, unable to walk straight and lurching between the tables towards the stage. 'I'm not drunk,' he told the audience. 'I think I must be ill. I'm so sorry.'

Michael had already started the show but, having taken just one look at Sheridan, apologized to the audience, 'Ladies and Gentlemen, I hope you will excuse us but I think you will agree that Sheridan needs medical help.' Without waiting for an ambulance, he stuffed Sheridan into his car and drove him at breakneck speed to the Chelsea and Westminster Hospital Casualty Department in the Fulham Road where the highly competent staff went into top gear. Reassured that he was in the right hands, Michael and Alan drove home to Ashford and telephoned me in New York.

Alan's kind voice came over the transatlantic line, clear as if he were in the next room. 'We think that he may have had a stroke but, of course, they wouldn't tell us anything because we're not relatives.' Standing there, in my own New York bedroom, looking out at that astonishing and dearly loved Manhattan skyline, surrounded by the familiar books and papers of my craft, my world fell apart.

My bi-continental life had always been so easy to juggle. My two homes and my two lives – one married and London-based, the other alone in Manhattan – had meshed seamlessly. The Broadway and West End theatre communities were two halves of the same world and, after all, as we had always said to anyone who asked how we could so happily maintain a marriage like this, I was only six hours away by jumbo. Yes, six hours, and half a world. When something life-threatening happens to someone you love, six hours is more than a flight, it's an eternity, and the reassuring platitudes about airlines and hours become irrelevant. He is there, you are not, and that's all there is to it.

It was only 5.30 a.m. in London but not too early to telephone a busy teaching hospital's casualty department. Eventually, I located my husband and spoke to the staff nurse in charge of him. The shifts had just changed. She asked if I would call back when she'd had a chance to familiarize herself with Sheridan's condition. I asked what had happened to him; she didn't know but promised to find out. 'Was it a stroke?' I asked, unwilling even to use the word. She didn't know but would check. 'Could I speak with the doctor who had admitted him?' She was now off-duty. I wanted to scream at her but knew she was doing her best. The nurse was very kind. I learned nothing. I wouldn't get off the phone. I kept asking questions she couldn't answer. How had this happened? Would he make a full recovery? Was he conscious? Did he know what had happened to him? Who was looking after him?

Finally, she said, 'Your husband is awake. Would you like to speak to him?'

His voice was slurred and almost unrecognizable.

Chapter Two

I fell in love with Sheridan's voice even before I met him. It was the autumn of 1960 and I was visiting Brian Winston in his rooms at Merton College, Oxford. Brian was then, and remains, the cleverest person I've ever known. We had met at a Jewish youth club when I was twelve and he was fifteen, the kind of place in which neither of us would normally have been seen dead. He was short, dark, furious, funny; a boy with an enormous intellect and the curiosity to back it up; a working-class lad from Wembley Park. I was a Jewish princess from Regent's Park. We were an unlikely pair, especially as there was never a scrap of romance or sexual chemistry between us.

The first thing he said to me, having discovered how little I knew of literary oddities, was, 'My God, you're ignorant.' The second was, 'You mean you don't know anything about the Metaphysical Poets?', uttered with the kind of scorn magistrates reserve for miscreants caught peeing in the House of Commons gardens and with the lordly pretension of a fifteen-year old who had only just discovered them himself.

What either of us was doing in a Jewish youth club I can't imagine, but not a week has gone by for the past fifty years that I haven't blessed whatever instinct it took for the twelve-year-old me to overlook his contempt. I know, with absolute clarity, that I wanted to learn whatever this strange boy was willing to teach me.

He became my friend and mentor, making me read the kind of books and poetry I'd never heard of at my theatre school where literature meant speeches from Noël Coward plays and poetry was Shakespeare sonnets that would be useful for auditions. He gave me a recording of lute music, talked to me about the rise of technology and mass media, socialist principles and world politics. He made me hungry to know everything. In the course of trying to teach me everything he knew or thought he knew, Brian became and remains, after more than fifty years, my friend, my brother, my conscience, my counsellor and a large part of my heart.

By that afternoon at Merton he was about nineteen, I was sixteen, and he had polished what little intellect I possessed into a serviceable kind of confidence that allowed me to meet his friends without feeling too inadequate. And, of course, I was a girl and these were innocent times when the mere appearance of a girl among the boys was enough to set their hearts aflutter and allow me just a hint of sexual power.

Brian had arrived at Oxford with a week's supply of kosher food, dozens of books, almost no clothes and, courtesy of his mother, Nita, a complete set of milk dishes and meat dishes, two sets of cutlery and firm instructions to keep all the milk and meat foods apart. All that had, literally, gone out the window the moment his room-mate arrived.

The room-mate had settled in, without apparently having even thought of bringing food of his own. Feeling peckish after unpacking, he wandered into their shared kitchen area and, seeing some bread, butter and sliced meat, picked up a knife and made himself a sandwich. A sandwich, constructed of butter (a milk food) and cold cuts (a meat food), the two supposed never to come into contact with one another and to be handled, always, with separate utensils.

Brian returned to the kitchen, became horrified by what his mother would say if she knew her precious knife had been used to create treif, non-kosher food, and immediately threw the offending knife out of the window into the quad. At this precise instant, his new room-mate *returned, never having met an orthodox Jew before, became convinced that he had been assigned to share with a knife-throwing lunatic, and retreated to his own room.*

Sometime later, I was ensconced in the sitting room's only halfway comfortable chair, one of those which are easy to sink into but impossible to get out of without sacrificing modesty, and Brian was trying to make toast. As his mother had done absolutely everything culinary for him since the day he was born, this was not proving a great success and I was too deeply embraced by the armchair to help.

From the corridor came a voice. 'What's burning? Smells awful. Any tea going? Filthy weather. Got lost. Kept getting lost. Came back hoping for tea.' The voice was lovely – clear, modulated, full of mischief, confident, the kind of voice where you just have to meet the owner. It was pitched to carry, as though its owner was accustomed to being heard and understood. It was an actor's voice, although not the kind of upper-class showing-off sort of voice that repels rather than attracts. It was effortlessly comfortable with itself, its class, its education and its right to be in this place at that time. Nobody Brian nor I had ever known talked like that. This was one of those people he had come to Oxford to meet. By the time the stranger came into the room I was already in love.

'Ah,' Brian said, 'you're about to meet the room-mate.'

The nineteen-year-old Sheridan Morley, son of the famous stage and screen actor, Robert Morley, was a big boy – tall, with broad shoulders, slim hips and long legs. What was odd about his figure was that, like his father, he was egg-shaped, his body widening at the waist and narrowing at the hip. Unlike his father, though, he was terrifically good-looking, even without the beard he later grew and wore ever after. His face was wide, his lips in a permanent smile, his eyes tremendously alive.

He succeeded in giving the impression that I was the only person in the whole world he wanted to meet and he had come into that room at exactly that moment because he knew I was there. All nonsense, of course, but that expression of unalloyed joy on seeing me lasted for nearly fifty years.

Sheridan had, even at that first meeting, the quality of focusing with warmth on whomever he liked or wanted to know. There was no awkwardness about him, nothing gawky or teenage; there was only the pleasure of being in his company. He made me feel specially selected, even then, as someone he wanted to be with. It wasn't anything in particular that he said or did (he was happy to let Brian continue to wrestle with the toast) so much as the ease of being with him that made him someone I wanted to know.

I remember nothing of what we talked about that day – except that Sheridan and I discovered a mutual obsession with the theatre which gave us a bond that would never be broken – nor what made us curl up in helpless laughter over and over again. I remember a very tall boy called Jo Durden-Smith, with a grand accent and an amazingly fast wit, joining us and an American graduate student, Henry Fenwick, older than the rest of us, very good-looking and suave, who seemed to know everything about English literature, was suddenly making the toast, although whether that was that first day or a subsequent one is lost to hazy memory.

What is clear across the decades, though, is that we were all completely happy to be where we were, together. Other than Brian and me, none of us had known one another before and, although we made many friends after that time, these became the special ones, the lifers. Many vestiges of those days remain. Brian, Henry, Jo, Sheridan and I stayed more than friends throughout our lives, through the vicissitudes of jobs, emigration, immigration, marriages, children, divorces, even deaths. I met many eligible young men, some of whom asked me out, but I didn't need anyone else. When I needed a date for a ball or a picnic or a party one of them was always available. I listened to all their girlfriend angst, parent angst and studies angst, laughed at their jokes, marvelled at their brains and made chicken soup. I only married one of them but that was because I couldn't marry them all.

Chapter Three

'Darling, what happened?'

'Don' te' y' mudde,' he managed. 'I fine. No pro'lem. Fe' over. Sill' me. Tol' Mik'l no' te' ye . . .' From this I gathered that he was trying to tell me that he'd fallen over, it wasn't serious and I wasn't to tell my mother, whom he adored, in case it upset her. And he'd told Michael not to tell me because I'd worry.

'I'll be there as soon as I can get a flight out of here. I'm leaving right now.' I tried to make my voice loving and reassuring so that he wouldn't know how panicky I was but I needn't have bothered. There was no answer, he'd drifted off, and the staff nurse came back on the line.

'It's probably a stroke. Phone me again in thirty minutes,' she said briskly, 'I'll know more then. Wherever I am on the floor they'll find me.' It was that more than anything that alerted me to the seriousness of the situation. Nurses in my experience will do anything to avoid being called away from a patient to the telephone.

'I'll be there this afternoon,' I told her. 'Keep him calm and don't let him panic. He doesn't like hospitals or doctors and he'll be frightened by the word "stroke". If you can avoid telling him what's happened, please do. I'll tell him when I get there.' She said she would do her best but it was probable that the doctors would tell him when they came for rounds later in the morning.

I knew, from when I'd broken my knee, that Sheridan was really spooked by any medical atmosphere. He wouldn't go to a doctor and when I'd been in hospital he would only come to see me at the end of visiting hours and already be heading for the exit on his arrival.

I grabbed my passport and ran out of the apartment without locking the door, leaving all the lights on, in what I had been wearing when I came home from the theatre. I jumped into the first cab. 'Kennedy Airport, please.'

'Wha'?'

I jumped out again. It was now about 2 a.m. That morning I had no patience left over to direct a recently arrived Afghani or whatever he was to New York's main international airport. The next cab driver, a Sikh, was chatty.

'Where you go?'

'London.'

'Why you have no suitcase?'

'It's an emergency.'

'You run from police?' A typical New York question.

'No, I'm just in a hurry' (and shut up and drive faster).

After what seemed an eternity but was probably one of the shortest ever airport runs, we got to JFK. I threw some money at the driver and ran into the United Terminal.

It was deserted. Of course it was, it was the middle of the night. Eventually I located a United Airlines duty officer. 'Look, I've got to get on your first flight to London. My husband's had a stroke, I think, and I need to be there.'

He stared back at me without a hint of compassion. 'You must be kidding, lady. Today's Thanksgiving. Every flight's overbooked. Not a chance of getting out of here today.'

'Surely there's some way you can get me on that flight. It's a real medical emergency. Look, I'll call the hospital. You can speak to the nurse.'

17

The terminal was lit with that over-bright, yellow light and all the more uninviting for being unpopulated. I'd used up my best argument, the duty officer remained unmoved.

Over the course of the next few hours I tried British Airways, Delta, American, Air India, Air France, Alitalia, every airline that flew anywhere in Western Europe. Most had nobody on duty; those that did repeated the United's response. No available seats to London or Paris for three days.

I sat in a hard plastic seat near the check-in desks and wept. Only when every possibility had been exhausted did I go back to the apartment and turn off the lights.

Chapter Four

'*D*o you have a dress?' *Sheridan asked me one day. My parents owned a little boutique in Marylebone High Street, the kind of successful small business that flourished before the chains took over retailing. They sold beautiful imported clothes for upmarket West End ladies, Harley Street doctors' wives, high-class tarts with nearby mews houses and the few career women who could afford their impeccable taste. I grew up in the 'schmatta' business, the rag trade, second princess (my sister Adrienne was the crown princess) to the royal family of high street 'schmattas', Rose and Sam Leon. So, unlike many of my contemporaries, of course I had a dress. Several, in fact.*

My possession of a dress was therefore the engine of our first date. Quite early in his Oxford life Sheridan started writing profiles and reviews for The Times *and that day he had been to London to interview Noël Coward. They had hit it off so well that Coward, kind to young people, invited him to a concert that Sunday night.*

'Do you have a suit?' the great man enquired.

'Yes, sir.'

'And do you have a girlfriend?'

'Well, no, sir, I don't.'

'Well,' came the typically dry response, 'you'd better find one by Sunday. And make sure she wears a dress.'

I was, I think, the only girl Sheridan knew who had a dress. Actually, I was the only girl Sheridan knew. Just as I had escorts galore, all the boys had a girl who wouldn't give them a hard time, was up for any kind of loony scheme, wouldn't laugh at them and who made chicken soup. While they all looked longingly at other girls, and later got into all the scrapes and woman trouble that undergraduates get into, they usually ended up with me.

'Yes,' I responded rather haughtily to Sheridan, 'and high-heeled shoes to match. Why?'

That Sunday, I remember, I wore a full-skirted navy-blue eyelet summer dress with a fitted waist over a white lining. It had no sleeves, a scoop neck and was daringly (for a sixteen-year-old) lower at the back than in the front. My shoes were white with navy trim and I carried white cotton gloves. I felt very excited and very grown-up. Sheridan was late, the first of many, many occasions when he left me standing outside theatres, restaurants, houses and shops, worrying about whether he was going to make it.

Coward took us first to the Savoy Grill, an incredible treat, along with the rest of his party. I don't remember how many were in the party nor who the other guests were, but I knew them all by sight and name from the newspapers. They were famous. Sheridan was the only one I knew personally but I marvelled that he seemed to be so completely at home. He was, after all, only nineteen, but he looked comfortable in London's poshest restaurant, surrounded by stars, most of whom he seemed to know, giving as many theatrical anecdotes as he got. This was the advantage of being a film-star's son, I knew, but it was still a marvellous performance. I ordered steak, the only thing on the menu I recognized, and listened carefully.

By now I knew that I had somehow, unbelievably, scored a ticket to the concert of the century. Judy Garland had returned to London, bringing her daughter, Liza Minnelli, with her. She was making her London comeback at the Palladium in a late-night performance starting at 11 p.m.

I couldn't believe my luck. My father had been a refugee, a stateless immigrant from Eastern Europe. My mother, the youngest of seven children, grew up above a pub where her father was the first Jew to be granted a publican's licence in London. She had shared a bed with her sisters and gone to work at thirteen.

And on this night, Rose and Sam Leon's daughter was Noël Coward's guest at the world's hottest concert at the London Palladium. The first half was all Judy, from 'Born in a Trunk' to 'The Man that Got Away'. She had a full symphony orchestra behind her and she was out to make her comeback. I didn't know then that this was not the first Judy Garland comeback concert and would certainly not be the last, but it was the greatest.

Time and again she had put her miserable childhood and adolescence behind her and reinvented herself. She would straighten herself out, lose the weight that made her unrecognizable, get some new gowns on credit and go out to give a show that nobody who ever saw her would forget.

In the second half, Judy introduced her daughter, exactly my age, to London's biggest variety theatre. Liza was wearing a party dress very similar to my own with a full skirt and a tight-fitting waist with a ribbon down the back and her hair tied in a matching bow. I felt even closer to her then than I did years later when she became a friend.

She opened her mouth and a fully realized, natural voice and personality poured out of it. At sixteen, she was already Liza, complete with the instrument and the charm. She was a miniature Judy but she was also uniquely Liza. At the side of the stage, directly in our view from Noël's box, stood Judy. Her face, always too open for her own good, couldn't hide her feelings. As she watched Liza her expression was a symphony of conflicting emotions.

There was no hiding the pride, the sense of achievement which said that whatever mistakes she had made in her life she had done something right, and that something was standing centre stage and singing her heart out. There was no hiding either her real envy that Liza was at the beginning of her career, that she had it all to do ahead of her, that she, Judy, had already been 'washed-up' many times.

Many years later, when Sheridan and I were writing a book about Judy, Liza was both helpful and supportive. It was dispiriting to realize how very closely mother and daughter have shadowed each other's lives.

But I didn't know any of that then. It was one of the great evenings of my life and I've never forgotten it. What I remember now is how much Sheridan cared whether I had a good time. It was the first time I had met Noël Coward, whom I came to love, but Sheridan was almost apologetic; he was comfortable in the company of the luminaries we had dinner with but protective of me and most concerned that I was enjoying myself. It was the first time I understood how much he preferred the public to the private life.

Chapter Five

When Michael Law had sensibly taken Sheridan into the Casualty Department at the Chelsea and Westminster Hospital on the Fulham Road, his fast action had probably saved his life. He was lucky in that the neurologist on call was a top man, Roberto Guiloff, and the hospital's normal procedure for dealing with stroke victims moved swiftly. A simple blood test in the Emergency Room confirmed that Sheridan was a diabetic and Dr Guiloff immediately called in Colin McIntosh, an endocrinologist who is head of the Beta Cell Unit there, one of the best diabetes centres in the country. I spoke to them both within hours of the stroke, while I was still sitting at JFK airport waiting for a flight, and they were cagey but hopeful.

Dr Guiloff said, 'It's a stroke so not good. But he's in the right place and we're taking good care of him.'

'What's the prognosis?'

'I can't tell yet. We'll have to see how he is tomorrow. In twenty-four hours we'll have a better idea.'

'How could this have happened?' I asked Dr McIntosh. 'He was fine this morning. He was fine this afternoon. I spoke with him.'

'It can happen at any time. Especially with diabetes raging out of control like this. That could easily have been a factor.'

'What diabetes?' I asked.

There was a disbelieving silence on the transatlantic line. 'You didn't know?'

Well, I did and I didn't. Some years earlier, we had decided to buy a house in Chelsea Harbour which Sheridan loved but which was much too expensive for a pair of working writers. I wanted to buy a house for the money we had available between us but, for Sheridan, only this house would do and, for that, we needed a mortgage. As usual, he talked me into it. When Sheridan wanted something he utilized every scrap of charm and wit, every scintilla of persuasion and logic, to get it. I gave in, more or less willingly, but definitely against my better judgement. It *was* a lovely house.

To Sheridan's surprise, his bank manager insisted on a physical examination. Thinking he was being clever, Sheridan made an appointment with the doctor's surgery in Wargrave, Berkshire (where he and his family had been going for years), expecting a nice glass of wine and a signature on the form. He was none too delighted to be confronted by a youngish female doctor he didn't know who examined him thoroughly, told him tartly that he was much too fat and insisted on a blood test.

He told me later that he had been outraged when, as a result of the test, she sent him to a diabetes specialist in Reading who confirmed that he was at the beginning of what, if he wasn't very careful, would undoubtedly become Type 2 diabetes. If he would lose some weight and check his blood sugar level regularly, the GP informed him, she would sign the mortgage form. He gave her his best smile and promised. When Sheridan wanted something, he'd promise anything.

Careful with his diet and lose weight? Sheridan, who had weighed the same since he was thirteen and couldn't tell you what he was eating when it was on his plate? Check his blood sugar? Sheridan, who hated needles, blood and doctors in approximately that order? She obviously didn't know him very well.

Sheridan's relationship with food was a strange one. He loved the social aspects of eating but was instantly bored with the idea of food. He loved to eat out, preferably with other people, but didn't care what he ate. When I was away, no matter what I left for him in the refrigerator or freezer, he would eat out three times a day in a restaurant, just for the company.

If pushed, he would tell you that his favourite meal was sausage and mash followed by trifle, but he was just as happy with anything filling and full of carbohydrates, as long as it was followed by pudding. He fooled me by being appreciative when I cooked so it took me quite a while to work out that I could have fed him fried mouse droppings and he'd still have said, 'Delicious, darling.' But what he liked best was for me not to be what he called 'faffing around in the kitchen' but sitting next to him in the Ivy or the Caprice or Joe Allen's while he told his stories.

Anyway, the doctor signed the mortgage form, we signed away my peace of mind forever and bought the house, and Sheridan told me none of this story of the diabetes. Only several years later, when I walked into his study to ask him something, did I overhear him talking on the phone to someone. 'Yes, of course,' he was saying, 'I test my blood sugar every day. And it's fine.' There was only one interpretation to this. Sheridan was a diabetic.

He swore he was not, that he'd had a warning but there was no diagnosis. Technically, this was true. That he hadn't told me wasn't a surprise. Once I knew, he was aware that I'd feel compelled to try to deal with the condition. I would try to ameliorate his sugar-filled diet, get him to take some exercise and test his blood sugar. None of that fitted his image of himself. As long as he hadn't acknowledged it to me it couldn't possibly be true.

He flatly refused to let me test his blood sugar or to get him outdoors for some exercise. He wouldn't change his diet. The best I could do was covertly to move us away from the whatever-comes-first-to-hand theory of dinner to organic food prepared entirely from scratch. He wondered what had happened to sponge pudding and custard but, overall, didn't notice the changes much. In restaurants he always ordered dessert – two if I was sitting at the other end of the table and he thought he could get away with it.

When I wasn't looking he'd go round the corner to the newsagent on the pretext of buying the *Evening Standard* and return, usually without the newspaper, but smelling suspiciously of Cadbury's Dairy Milk. Initially I'd rationalize his excess eating by reminding myself that he wasn't a drinker, a smoker or a womanizer. He was just a shopaholic and an overeater. But, as his weight and his spending increased, I became worried and even more insistent. The bickering which had always been part of our marriage accelerated into rows.

Finally, after months of pulling in opposite directions, we had a long conversation. It was clear that in all the years we had known one another the only things we argued about were money and his health. Money was currently off the table. He was earning, I was earning, and if he spent too much I didn't mention it. But the possibility that he had, or would soon have, diabetes was killing me, not him.

The upshot was that he promised to pay attention to what he ate, to take one biscuit instead of the whole packet with his tea, one croissant instead of three with butter and jam, and to test his blood sugar once a week. In return, I was not to mention diabetes. At all. Ever. It was a stupid deal and it caused his stroke. Worse, I kept my side of it but he didn't keep his. I knew he wouldn't and because I knew it, in a way, his stroke was my fault.

The stroke, as it turned out, was the least of Sheridan's problems.

Chapter Six

*T*he Oxford years were, for Sheridan, among the best of his life.
His schooling up until then had been episodic, to put it politely.
*Having travelled with his parents to the United States and Australia
to follow Robert on long tours, Sheridan could barely read or write
until he was nine. Then, in Australia, he met a theatrically star-struck
teenager who volunteered to do whatever needed doing backstage at
Robert's play,* Edward, My Son.

*Casting around for jobs for this Sydney doctor's son, Robert sug-
gested that he might teach Sheridan to write since he hadn't had much
chance to go to school. The boy's name was Michael Blakemore, that
same Michael Blakemore who became one of the world's most distinguished theatre directors.*

*Many years later, when Sheridan had written a less than flatter-
ing review of a play Michael had directed, Michael wrote him a note
regretting ever having taught him to use joined-up letters. 'If I hadn't,'
he lamented, comically, 'you would never have been able to attack
me in print.'*

*On another occasion, when coincidentally but simultaneously
Sheridan had a play running in the West End and I had, more
modestly, a revue running off-Broadway, I bumped into Michael in
a theatre lobby in New York. First, with his usual grace and elegance,*

he congratulated me on the reviews for my show and enquired how the box office was for Sheridan's play in London. Then, with a broad smile that belied his words, complained, 'It's not that I mind you critics directing shows. It's your having hits that bothers me.'

On the Morley family's return to England Sheridan was sent to school at Sizewell in Suffolk where the rather odd Dutch headmaster only taught what he liked and he only liked English, French and History. This weird school was all Sheridan's pre-Oxford education amounted to. He had beautiful French, thanks to a hasty course at a South Kensington crammer college followed by a year at the University of Geneva, which yielded an impressive, gold-encrusted certificate that must have impressed the dons who interviewed him at Merton because they admitted him to Oxford to read Modern Languages with no other qualifications.

Once there, he was, for the first time, with people who loved and appreciated him. Having previously always felt ungainly, when he was at Merton and, more especially, at the Oxford Playhouse or with his fellow theatre enthusiasts in the OUDS (Oxford University Dramatic Society, of which he was secretary), he was considered handsome, charming and knowledgeable. He threw himself into productions of the classics, directed, produced, acted, painted sets and generally learned his craft.

There was never any question of his becoming a professional actor – he had neither the talent nor the desire – but, even then, I remember, he had an uncanny knack for identifying talent in others and he was invariably right about those in his circle of friends who would, and who would not, make it into the London theatre.

I'd had a weird school life too. For most of it I attended Arts Educational School (it still exists, I'm a trustee now), which was then a very peculiar institution where they sort of taught us things in between our dance, singing, acting and music lessons. I never wondered why, with the exception of my cousin Stephanie, I had no friends outside school, despite growing up in the West End of London, nor why I never did the things other little girls did such as riding bicycles or horses. I never even thought about the fact that I was never taught any maths except basic arithmetic, nor any science at all, nor sports of any kind.

The fact was that I was too busy. I could sing and read an orchestral score; I could play (not well but passably) two musical instruments; I could recite whole swathes of Shakespeare and other dramatic litera-ture; and I was a talented enough baby ballet dancer to have hopes of admittance into the forerunner of the English National Ballet, then called London's Festival Ballet.

And I had, which saved my bacon in the long run, a propensity for language, my own and other people's, that would provide me with an education and, eventually, a living.

By the time I met Sheridan I was no longer thinking of a perform-ing career but Arts Ed had done its job. I was only sixteen but the dedicated teachers to whom I had been exposed all my life had taught me, no, not much by way of conventional schooling, but commitment, discipline, confidence and the ability to learn anything fast. Just as important, perhaps, they had taught me how to make the most of a very small talent.

Brian, Sheridan and the other boys were like pets to me, easy to be with, cuddly and warm, an endless source of fun, needy without being insistent and an unalloyed joy, especially when, as happened frequently, I didn't understand something and one of them always knew the answer. I spent as much time as I could in Oxford with Sheridan and Jo, their admiration and appreciation bolstering my inevitable teenage anxieties about my unruly hair or the size of my backside.

The girls were a different matter. In the early 1960s they were frighteningly bright. I may have had a background knowledge of the arts, but the girls I met had been to the best schools and were properly educated as I demonstrably was not. They terrified me because they actually knew things. Having been the brightest girl at Arts Ed, I soon discovered, didn't qualify you to have tea with any one of them. Worse, they weren't just clever; many were pretty, too, much prettier than I, which mattered in those days.

I, the thickest and untidiest of the lot, took refuge with the drama bunch in the Oxford Playhouse and elsewhere. There I made myself useful – my choreographic skills were in demand as were my ability to copy music and read stage directions. I was never, as Sheridan was, centrally part of the action, but I hung around the fringes, grateful for the chance to do what I'd been trained to do.

Sheridan loved it all. Triumphs, disasters, muddles, fights, misunderstandings, feuds. He particularly relished the disasters which he later turned into wonderfully honed anecdotes for his after-dinner speeches. I never remember seeing him without a smile and his infectious laughter rang in every quad and every dressing room. Just being with him made life better. When I was scared (often) or confused (all the time) or in trouble (frequently) or had some good news to impart (rarely), it was to Sheridan I went. He had the gift, at Oxford, and intermittently throughout his life, of being completely happy. And his Oxford years were, I believe, the only time in his life when he was depression-free. Sheridan loved Oxford and Oxford loved him.

Chapter Seven

When it became clear that no matter what I did I wasn't going to get a flight to London that day I returned to the apartment I'd left in disarray hours earlier. The lights were still on but it already had an air of abandonment that said I wasn't going to be happy there for a long time. On the way to the airport I had telephoned my stepdaughters. I asked them to go, immediately, to Chelsea and Westminster Hospital and to stay there until I arrived. 'Don't let them do anything to Daddy till I get there.'

Some hours later, Juliet, his younger daughter, called me: 'Ruth, you've got to do something. Daddy's going into depression.' I believed her immediately because she had lived with a depressive father all her life and knew the signs. If she said he was going into depression, she was undoubtedly right and something had to be done even though, by any measure known to medical science, it couldn't be so.

I called Sheridan's psychiatrist, Dr Leslie Morrish, at his clinic in Berkshire and said, 'Please go to London as soon as you can. Sheridan's had a stroke and he's in depression.'

He said, predictably, 'It can't be depression unless he's been off his medication. Has he?'

'No,' I said, 'but please go anyway.'

When I eventually got back to London, I was shocked by Sheridan's appearance. Still in Chelsea and Westminster Hospital, he tried hard to appear normal for me. But his eyes were unfocused, his speech was slurred and after just a few minutes he lapsed into silence. It was obvious that, whatever else was wrong with him, he was once again in deep depression.

He was on enough daily medication that it should have taken at least three weeks to 'wash out' of his body. He had been without it for only forty-eight hours after his admission, when Dr Morrish had spoken with the neurologist and they had agreed to reinstate it – not enough of an interruption for there to have been any effect at all. It was not possible for him to have fallen into so deep an abyss so fast. Still, the fact was that he had.

This was the moment we missed. This was the indication that the depression into which he had fallen so precipitously was different from all the other bouts he had experienced for most of his adult life. And we missed it. The psychiatrist, the neurologist, the endocrinologist and me. Me, most of all.

I, who knew him so well and had gone through the highs and the lows with him so many times that I could recognize the symptoms from across the room. An irrational bark, a look, a gesture, a voice raised too loudly, a glance into his eyes, a refusal to listen or a shopping trip too many was sufficient to goose me into making an immediate appointment with the psychiatrist as soon as I could persuade Sheridan it was necessary. ('Hello, this is Ruth, Sheridan's wife, he's very manic. May I bring him in tomorrow?') His medication would be adjusted, followed by another week of mania and then a mini-crash, and then back to normal again.

My only excuse for not noticing that this time was different is that it didn't seem to be. His symptoms were just standard-issue depression. The sadness, the anger, the circular speeches, the self-pity, the unfocused eyes, the inability to get out of bed, the unwillingness to go out, the lack of interest, the repetitiveness, the irrationality – all the normal signs. Of course, there hadn't been the usual manic phase as far as I knew but, remember, I'd been in New York and Peter, our ever loyal driver and assistant, hadn't flagged anything odd. He used to describe Sheridan's manic phases as 'a bad case of the me-me's' due to Sheridan's inability to focus on anything outside himself, and he had been through enough episodes to recognize them when he saw them. In this case, he saw nothing out of the ordinary.

On the day of the stroke, Sheridan had been in Bath on a routine book-selling outing to stimulate the sales of his recently published memoirs, *Asking for Trouble*, making a speech and charming the literary luncheon ladies. He made a detour on the way back to see his mother in Berkshire, and gave Peter the evening off, saying he would drive himself. Peter said many times that if he'd had any inkling there was anything wrong, he would not have left him alone. I know this is true because, while Peter was fond of me, he adored Sheridan and would never have done anything to jeopardize him. Apart from anything else, Peter was terrified of Sheridan's driving and would never have let him drive himself if he had thought for a moment that he was unwell.

And, if Peter had the evidence of his own eyes, I had my own ears. Sheridan and I talked every day, sometimes two or three times if he had gathered a piece of news or gossip he wanted to share. Sheridan was an accomplished gossip, always out and about, always on the phone to someone or other, always full of titbits he could impart and so, inevitably, people told him things. Not things they wanted to hide, though, as Sheridan couldn't keep a secret to save his life. 'I hate secrets,' he used to say when upbraided for letting someone else's cat, or his own, out of the bag. 'They just lead to trouble.'

And, even if I was on the other side of the world, I was the person to whom he wanted to tell the secrets. Neither of us ever kept track of our telephone bills, and, although I would remonstrate with him when he called Directory Enquiries for the fifth time in a day instead of using the phone book, I never grudged the transatlantic communications that cemented our lives. It was too important to us to keep in touch.

We had talked that morning, very early New York time, before he left for Bath. I don't remember exactly what we talked about but it was probably the usual exchange of information about both our days, an enquiry from me as to whether he'd taken his pills (he had), an enquiry from him as to what I was seeing on Broadway that evening and with whom (*Flower Drum Song* with David Staller), a reminder from me about where his clean dress shirts were for his evening cabaret with Michael Law, regret from him that because of this engagement he couldn't get to New York in time for tomorrow's Thanksgiving dinner. Routine stuff, the kind of conversation every married couple has every day.

I wish I had known that it was to be our last every-day conversation. Maybe I'd have thought of something more profound to say than 'Don't forget to take a comb.' His voice, his beautiful captivating voice, was completely normal. He was not manic, he was not depressed, he was not angry, he was not sad. I, who knew that voice better than anyone, who could tell when he was feeling out of sorts the minute he said, 'Hello, darling,' had no doubt when we hung up that morning that we would talk again later in the day before he went to bed or early the following morning.

There was, therefore, no warning, not of the impending stroke nor of the killer depression that would embed itself into his being within twenty-four hours and never leave him again. We had both known, of course, that sooner or later there would be another bout of mania when he would buy too many books and CDs, be noisier than anyone has any right to be and make ridiculous, impossible commitments from which he would later have to be disentangled. We had known, too, that those periods of high living would be followed, with a horrid inevitability, by a long or short interlude in which he would want to kill himself, when he might think the telephone was going to burn him or that the doorknob would lock him in forever.

When these episodes were over we never talked about them, even if they had necessitated long or short stays in the Cardinal Clinic near Windsor where they stopped him from killing himself and adjusted his medication until he could bear to be in the outside world again. It would happen again, we knew, and when it did we would cope until it was over.

At the start of our life together, his depression had been very frightening. I knew nothing about the illness and I didn't recognize it when it reared its ugly head. I should have done. My father, usually a sunny character with a big personality, had a couple of days a month when you 'didn't bother Daddy', when changing the channel on the television would produce a torrent of fury, when he was sunk in a deep, dark place from which you interrupted him at your peril, but I never made the connection between my father's black moods and clinical depression.

With Sheridan, what I have learned to call bipolar disorder – manic depression by a less descriptive name – always started slowly so he was usually well into a manic phase by the time I noticed. Always much in demand at dinner parties, he would hold court but I would suddenly realize that nobody else had been allowed to get a word in and the 'conversations' consisted entirely of Sheridan talking. He managed this by the theatrical trick of raising his voice ever so slightly when someone else began to talk until he was speaking so loudly that nobody else even tried to cut in. Since he was so entertaining, and had such a fund of wonderful stories, those who didn't know him well weren't even aware that they had barely opened their mouths since they had sat down to dinner. His closest friends, those who had heard all the stories before, recognized this apparent egotism for what it was, a harbinger of trouble.

Sheridan loved shopping and would buy gadgets, CDs and books on an industrial scale. When he was manic he was a shopaholic who could spend thousands on absolutely nothing. He returned from a solo trip to California once with a suitcase so heavy that it took four of us to take it from the car boot. Peter, having collected him from the airport, rolled his eyes at me, 'He's been buying books again,' he humphed, struggling with the impossibly heavy case. Sure enough, when he opened it, it contained one sponge bag, one towelling bathrobe, no underwear, one pair of socks, and nearly 300 hardback books and CDs. I never did find out where he had jettisoned the rest of his clothes to make room for the books.

Sheridan had a prodigious capacity for work and he would take on almost any job he was offered. When manic, though, this was dangerous as he'd agree to write a book in a week, take on a new television series that had to be written by Friday, commit to different series of lectures in different parts of the country on the same day and get into all sorts of scheduling conflicts. Sometimes I could help (we could each write in the other's style and that got us out of a lot of self-inflicted scrapes) and sometimes I couldn't. Even if I could write like Sheridan Morley, I couldn't sound like him on the radio or look like him on the lecture circuit.

The purpose of the medication prescribed for bipolar disorder is to return the patient to an even keel. As the doctors have many times explained to me, everybody's even keel is at a different level so it is quite difficult for a psycho-pharmacologist to gauge exactly how much and what to prescribe for each patient. Sheridan's 'normal', for instance, was at a much higher level than most so his treatment was especially complex – he often appeared to be 'high' when he was just being Sheridan.

His lows, though, were unmistakable. When he was depressed he was the sorriest specimen you've ever seen unless he had a public appearance and then, if you didn't know him, you'd never know there was anything wrong. It's not an unknown phenomenon among show people. It's known as Doctor Theatre. When under the lights, he could entertain the audience without a misstep or a missed beat, but as soon as he got offstage, he'd revert to being suicidal.

On several occasions, he disappeared completely. On one occasion, he was appearing at the Pizza on the Park in cabaret with Patricia Hodge and Steve Ross. He would tell funny stories about Noël Coward or whoever the subject of the cabaret was, Steve would play the piano and he and Tricia would sing the songs of a bygone era. I was the director of these shows and wrote the scripts that Sheridan never stuck to, so I was there, too.

On this particular night, though, he simply didn't show up. Sheridan, the most professional performer in the world, wasn't there at 'the half' (all performers have to be in the theatre a minimum of a half-hour before the curtain goes up), wasn't there for the fifteen-minute call, wasn't there at curtain time. Hysterical with worry, but not wanting to panic Tricia and Steve just before they had to perform, we had a quick confab and agreed that as he'd been unavoidably delayed, I would go on for him. I knew the stories, could get away with the patter, and had done it before when he'd been stuck in a television studio.

Just as the performance ended, more than two hours after the half, I saw Sheridan wander in and go into the tiny dressing room at the back that they all shared. As soon as I got off the stage I opened the dressing-room door. He looked up at me, bleakly. 'Don't be angry with me. I've been sitting at Charing Cross trying not to throw myself under a train.' I didn't even ask him why he hadn't called me; I got on the backstage telephone and called Dr Morrish at the Cardinal, who said, 'Go and lock him in the dressing room, now. Then call me back.' When I did he said to get Sheridan into the car, however I could, and bring him at once to the clinic in Windsor. It took about six of us to get him into the car. Sheridan cried, screamed and shrieked all the way there, insisting that I was trying to lock him up, sure that if I left him there he would never get out again. It was a nightmare drive with Sheridan trying to grab the wheel at every turn. I still remember the relief I felt when the clinic appeared out of the darkness and Sheridan's favourite Filipina nurse opened the door and took the responsibility away from me. I sat in the dark and cried.

Chapter Eight

*O*xford had to end sometime. At the end of his three years, with his third-class degree clutched firmly in his hand, Sheridan reluctantly went down. He applied for a BBC traineeship but didn't get it and instead was offered a job as a writer at the nascent Independent Television News (ITN). First, though, before he got down to real life, Sheridan wanted a little time off and one day spied a small advertisement on the front page of The Times for a teaching assistant in the drama department at the University of Hawaii and applied. They must have been desperate, or else impressed by the idea of an Oxford graduate, because his ticket came by return of post.

'Hawaii????' we all chorused. 'Where's that?' We had barely even heard of it – something to do with grass skirts and pineapples, we thought – but Sheridan had fond memories of childhood stays with his parents on Waikiki Beach when the only hotel there was the Royal Hawaiian, the chic pink one now dwarfed by skyscrapers.

He spent a happy year there although it culminated in the assassination of President Kennedy in Dallas, on his way to visit the University of Hawaii. While there, Sheridan directed a then sixteen-year-old Bette Midler in her first stage appearances, and he met his first wife. Margaret Gudijko was an American graduate student from a Polish and Irish family in Boston. To the amazement of all his friends, Sheridan came home from Hawaii engaged to be wed, the first of our gang even to contemplate such a grown-up plan.

They married in a Catholic ceremony in Boston and honeymooned on a luxury liner crossing the Atlantic. Once home in England, they set up house first in a London flat and then in a little house in Dulwich. Eventually they moved to a large modern house not far from Sheridan's parents in Berkshire. Hugo, their son, and Alexis, their elder daughter, arrived in rapid succession.

We all drifted off into our own little worlds at this time. Brian went to the BBC and then to Granada Television where I eventually followed him. All Sheridan's friends tried to stay in touch with him but he was now living a very different life of husband and father which was, I think, something of a strain for a man who was not designed for domesticity.

Although the idea of hearth and home was attractive to Sheridan, the reality was not. He was an urban not a rural character, comfortable not at a fireside but in a theatre. He was bored in the country but, because he sought always to emulate his father, the ideal had seemed to be the house in Berkshire, the wife and three children. He could never understand why, having achieved this ideal, he couldn't wait to escape it, to go to London, to the office and to the theatre. It wasn't, I suppose, so different from millions of other commuting husbands but for a man of his nature it was surprising that this was what he had deliberately chosen.

But if his home life wasn't exactly bliss, his professional life certainly was. ITN was as good as its word, hiring him as a staff writer on the then fifteen-minute news bulletin. He was soon promoted to newsreader, taking his place alongside Andrew Gardner, Reginald Bosanquet, and Peter Snow. I have often wondered how Sheridan, whose interest in politics and current affairs was precisely zero and whose knowledge of world events was even sketchier, survived, indeed thrived, in that hothouse of news that was ITN. But they loved him *there, recognizing in his easy on-air personality a presenter of genius. No matter what he was talking about, the audience believed and trusted him. He was classless, an actor's son with a fine but not posh voice, perfect for the less formal thrust of the new commercial television. He became a great favourite with audiences all over the country and it was a blow to his bosses when he decided to leave to become Assistant Features Editor of* The Times.

In retrospect that, too, was an odd choice for a man who was bleakly uninterested in both the form and content of newspapers. He worked for a marvellous woman called Margaret Allen whom he revered as a 'real newspaperwoman'. She taught him the craft of writing features, how to shape an article, what a 'lead' is (the all-important first sentence of a story), what to leave out and how to write a tag. He had talent, certainly, but it was Margaret Allen who made him a journalist. He was, I expect, hoping that the job would lead to his being allowed to write about the theatre, always his main interest, but the theatre critics' jobs were already taken and he satisfied himself by writing profiles, every Saturday, of whoever was in town and interesting.

Dozens of these interviews for The Times *survive in his scrapbooks. He would have lunch with everybody who mattered in the theatre and film world and in each case he unfailingly discovered the one fact or titbit of information that these stars had told no other journalist. He made and kept many friends from these interviews and one day he went back to our old friend Noël Coward who, charmed by what Sheridan wrote about him, had an interesting proposition.*

Chapter Nine

My first impression of Dr Roberto Guiloff, the neurologist who had saved Sheridan's life, was of an important bat on a night mission. On closer examination he was a black freighter hurrying towards harbour. He sailed down the hospital corridor towards me wrapped in a flowing black cape, with his pitch-black hair slicked back, and he was almost vibrating with vitality and the air of being too busy to be on the same planet with us lesser mortals. He was attended, always, by a flotilla of medical students and junior doctors who regarded him with a mixture of awe and attention as, indeed, I learned to do myself. That first time, though, I merely registered his presence, thanked him for having been there when Sheridan was admitted, and launched into my list of questions, compiled on the long, sleepless, transatlantic flight.

Sheridan had not only lapsed into a depressed silence in which, as usual, he was more asleep than awake, but, more worryingly, he was weak all down his left side and, worse, his voice was now so slurred that he was impossible to understand. 'Do you know yet how serious a stroke he had?' I asked.

'Yes. Not a massive stroke, not a mild stroke, but a pretty fair crack and we'll have to see how well he recovers.'

'But his voice. It's so slurred. Will that recover?'

'I hope so.'

'What do you mean, you hope so?'

'Sometimes it comes back, sometimes it doesn't.'

'What happens if it doesn't?'

'Sometimes speech therapy helps.' And he sailed off down the corridor, his cape flapping, his small ships dutifully bobbing in his considerable wake, promising to return the following day, by which time we might know more.

On the next day Sheridan's left hand was strong enough to hold mine but his voice was just as bad. When Dr Guiloff arrived, I was ready for him. 'His voice is no better. What can we do?'

'Nothing. He'll either get it back or he won't. We'll have to see.'

Sheridan was now sunk completely into depression, slept almost all the time, stared into space when he was awake. I knew the symptoms but it was still his voice that worried me. Not that he was showing any inclination to use it. By the third day I was nearly hysterical. 'His voice, Dr Guiloff. It's still unrecognizable. Will it come back?'

Dr Guiloff had had enough. 'Mrs Morley,' his slightly accented voice thundered at me, 'all my other patients' wives want to know whether their husbands will ever walk again. All you seem to care about is whether he'll ever speak clearly again.'

Unforgivably, I uttered that question that nobody should ever ask, 'Don't you know who he is?'

For a moment, Guiloff looked confused. Then he looked back into the room where Sheridan lay and saw him, really saw him, for the first time. He had been so focused on saving Sheridan's life that it hadn't occurred to him that he was treating a professional broadcaster, a man whose voice was his job, and, to his credit, he realized that if Sheridan could never walk again it would be very sad but if he could never talk again he couldn't earn a living. 'I am so sorry, Mrs Morley, I do see now why you have been asking so urgently. But I'm afraid the answer is still the same. I don't know. We'll have to wait and see.'

Sheridan was giving every impression of not caring a damn if his voice came back or not. He didn't even look at either of us.

It did come back. Not ever as strong or as flexible as it had been, whiny at times and querulous, but recognizably his. Within a week the left-side weakness had gone and by the time, ten days later, I hauled myself into Chelsea and Westminster clutching chocolates and flowers for the nurses who had taken care of an almost coma-tose and unresponsive patient, the doctors – Guiloff and McIntosh – had decided there was nothing more that could be done for him as an in-patient.

Colin McIntosh, quiet and authoritative like a Scottish bank manager, had put Sheridan on insulin for the diabetes; Roberto Guiloff had him on a cocktail of drugs for the stroke; Leslie Morrish, tall and mercurial in his country cashmeres, was concerned that he had gone into depression so fast and had reinforced his usual anti-depressants with something else. It was clear that if he were to take all of this stuff I was going to have to administer it. Sheridan practi-cally fainted the first time he was confronted with a do-it-yourself syringe for the insulin and although he assured the doctors that he would take all this, I knew he wouldn't. The responsibility became mine and remained mine until he died.

Don't underestimate it. At various times during the ensuing four years he was on upwards of twenty-five pills a day, plus insulin three times a day. The medications and the dosages changed all the time, and the various medicines could interact and cause adverse reactions. Just watching him to ensure he was not overdosing was a full-time job. Every Saturday morning I would sit at the kitchen table with piles of pills and divide each into individual daily pill-boxes for the coming week.

I had a computer-generated chart which told me what he had to take at what time each day and I had to adjust the chart every time one of the doctors changed any of the medications. It would have been easy to get it wrong – on the only two occasions on which I wasn't watching him actually transmit the pills into his mouth he took them twice in the same morning and ended up in hospital.

I was also worried that his doctors, good and caring though they were, were not talking to one another. Sheridan was so depressed and sleepy that I wondered aloud whether the individual medications – each correct in their own right – were interacting and having a deleterious effect.

I tried to set up a meeting with all three doctors before Sheridan left the hospital but the most I ever managed was two at a time. Doctors don't, apparently, like communicating with one another. They've never heard of email, telephones haven't been invented in their universe. Instead, they all write letters to one another. It's a slow and cumbersome process in which the doctors cover themselves but the patient and, by definition, the patient's carer, has to wait until the postal dance is completed and that often takes days if not weeks.

Consequently, Sheridan was discharged from the hospital long before the three primary doctors ever actually shared their worries about his rapidly improving physical condition and his rapidly deteriorating mental one, although they all shared their fears with me. Nurses, of course, are not trained in pharmacology, and the hospital pharmacist would sooner die than gainsay the word and prescription of a doctor. We left the hospital loaded with medications and headed for home.

Home was, by this time, a big house on the river in Battersea. Every time we moved house we did so not to accommodate ourselves and our cat, Byline, but to make space for a library which, like the plant in *Little Shop of Horrors*, was always threatening to consume us. When I gave it away, two years after Sheridan's death, it comprised 22,000 items – books, records, CDs, manuscripts, plays, scripts and memorabilia.

This was our last move. We couldn't fit into our Chelsea house any longer and, worse, there wasn't a single surface not covered in books and papers. Sheridan was furious that we were moving. ('I don't see myself as a Battersea kind of chap'; 'Hard luck, that's what you're going to be.') He loved the Chelsea house but we couldn't afford it any longer as he had 'forgotten' to pay the mortgage and the bank was threatening to foreclose. As it happened, the Battersea house, while not as prestigious an address as Chelsea, was far better suited for our needs. Constructed out of an old wharf, we were able to make ourselves a separate library which didn't encroach on the living space upstairs.

We had a common space filled with books and desks for our PA and our indispensable driver/fixer, Peter. The two of them didn't get along but Sheridan and I had a separate book-lined study for when we wrote solo, as well as an office we shared for when we wrote together, so we couldn't hear the mayhem.

Sheridan went straight to bed (despite Guiloff's warning that he had to keep moving in these early stages to avoid another stroke) where he slept twenty hours out of twenty-four. I could barely wake him to take his medication and when I did he would launch into an endless litany of complaints that lasted sometimes for hours. Above all, he didn't want the BBC or the publications where he was theatre critic to know he had suffered a stroke. 'I'll never work again,' he whined, 'nobody will hire me. Nobody will want me. My professional life is over.' I assured him that his BBC job was secure. Jim Moir, then head of Radio 2 where Sheridan presented the 'Arts Programme', was wonderful. 'We'll wait for him. Just get him better,' he told me and I told Sheridan. Over and over again.

I hadn't told his print editors anything. I wrote his columns under his name and his colleagues protected him. Critics from the other papers knew that he wasn't in the theatres at night. Nobody gave us away. But getting him better was harder than it looked. He continued to sleep all day and whine all night. Always wondrously verbal, now when he was awake he couldn't stop talking. His complaints took the form of circular arguments which began and ended in the same place, usually the end of his career. Nothing mollified him. He barely ate. He rarely got out of bed. He wouldn't take a shower or let me change his sleeping robe. He had been home from the hospital for less than a week when I realized that I couldn't cope. I struggled on for three weeks, a lifetime, and then I took him back to the Cardinal Clinic.

Chapter Ten

*I*n 1964, over lunch at the Ivy, Noël Coward, following his recent
triumph directing a revival of his play Hay Fever at the National
Theatre, suggested to Sheridan that he might like to write his biography.

'Me?' stammered Sheridan. 'But I'm the wrong generation. I wasn't
even born when you had your greatest successes. I don't know enough,
I've never written a book, never mind a biography, and I'd make the
most terrible mess of it.'

'No, you won't,' calmly responded Noël. 'I'll help you. I want someone with a fresh eye who isn't part of my history in the theatre. I'll
give you a list of my friends and tell them they must talk to you. More
importantly, I'll give you a list of my enemies and their telephone
numbers. Talk to them first, they'll have the best stories.'

So naive was Sheridan about publishing that he had no idea that
the advance for a biography – the money paid by the publisher in
anticipation of sales – went to the author rather than to the subject.
Although he was immensely flattered by the suggestion, he had no
idea how he was going to find the money or the time to write a book
while still fully employed by The Times. In addition to his day job, he
was fully occupied with as many freelance articles as he could drum
up, frequent BBC Radio jobs and a burgeoning extra career as host
for various events that his familiar television face had made possible.

He had a non-working wife, two children and an enormous house to support, and, like his father Robert, he hadn't a clue how to manage money. Still, he knew this was too good an opportunity to miss.

He had been mad about Noël Coward at a time when he was deeply unfashionable and never lost his enthusiasm, even when the rest of us were listening to the Beatles and the Rolling Stones. Sheridan was not very musical, he had no knowledge of or interest in melody or rhythm. I spent years trying to talk with him about my own passions for chamber music, jazz and opera without any real effect. The only time he willingly came to the opera with me was when the Metropolitan in New York premièred an operatic adaptation of Tennessee Williams' A Streetcar Named Desire. He didn't like it but at least he understood who the characters were and what the plot was about.

He came with me once, only once, to Aspen in the Colorado Rockies where the world's best music festival takes place every summer. I thought the beauty of the surroundings and the welcome and warmth of the musicians might lull him into an appreciation of what they do. But he said, 'Your friends are very nice but they keep playing violins at me and there's no theatre here.' And, despite my annual pilgrimage to Aspen, he never came back.

Where we intersected musically was, not surprisingly, in show tunes. We both adored musicals and, although he was more interested than I was in British musical theatre, it was in the American shows that we found our musical common ground. The Great American Songbook – the songs of Cole Porter, George Gershwin, Rodgers and Hart, Irving Berlin, Oscar Hammerstein, Lerner and Loewe, Jerome Kern and their contemporaries – was my playground, whether the songs were written for the theatre or for cabaret, whether romantic or comic. Sheridan's great love was the patter and list songs of the great songwriters and the apparent gentleness of the British show songs where the deceptively simple melodies barely concealed the rapier-like sharpness of their lyrics.

The master at this, The Master, even, was, of course, Noël Coward. Coward represented everything Sheridan most loved about England and what he most admired in a man. In the songs, the poetry and the letters, even the autobiographies, Sheridan saw a kind of ideal Englishman that he wanted to emulate. In Noël's insouciance, his social ease and his ability to live his life exactly as he wanted through his own work, Sheridan saw what he wanted to be. This is why he loved him, studied him and made himself unquestionably the greatest living expert on his work.

What Sheridan loved was to get inside a lyric such as 'Mad Dogs and Englishmen', 'Mrs Worthington' or 'Nina' and expose both its brilliance and its viciousness while laughing uproariously at its comedy. We were familiar with the plays, of course, as obsessive playgoers we had seen them performed in the West End and at the National but it wasn't until we started going to the theatre for a living that we focused on the extraordinary craft of Coward. The big plays – Private Lives, Design for Living, Hay Fever, Present Laughter *– were so perfectly calibrated to work that it is very difficult to manufacture a bad production of them. Difficult, not impossible.*

While Sheridan was working on the biography, Noël was always available to answer questions, to clarify a point, to insert a wicked aside. Sheridan shuttled between London and Noël's houses in Jamaica and in Switzerland, somehow fitting it all in. The poetry, the diaries, the letters – Sheridan drew on them all to find out how he did it, to discover the core of this great English showman and, in the end, produced A Talent to Amuse, *as one critic said, 'one of the best show business biographies ever written in English'. He found the title in one of the songs Noël wrote for* Bitter Sweet. *'For I believe, that since my life began, the most I've had is just, a talent to amuse.'*

Noël said he didn't want to see the book until it was published but that everything about his life was fair game except his homosexuality. Sheridan begged Noël to let him at least touch on the subject, feeling that the book would be incomplete without it. Noël refused. 'When I'm dead you can rewrite it,' he said, firmly, 'but while I'm still here I have to make a living and while I'm not in the least ashamed for myself, my audience wouldn't like it. They know I'm queer, I know I'm queer, they know I know they know I'm queer but they won't like having their noses rubbed in it.'

Sheridan sent Noël the first published copy and held his breath. By return came a telegram: 'Darling Boy, I am simply mad about me. Stop. Love, Noël.' In appreciation, he sent Sheridan a small and sunny painting of some stick figures on a beach, which faces me as I write. On the back he has scrawled, 'A little something from my touch and Gauguin period.'

Chapter Eleven

Sheridan was home from the hospital for only a day when it became clear that he had descended into the worst depression of his life. His eyes were clouded, he wouldn't get out of bed, he cried non-stop. He was almost entirely silent but, when he did talk, he locked into a set of repetitive downward spirals.

One was a bizarre demand that we move to Miami (or Hawaii or Australia or the south of France) where he could live on a beach and nobody could find him. Another was a riff on the employers who hated him and were trying to get him to kill himself. (His employers at the time – BBC Radio 2 and the *Spectator* – were, in fact, great to him and covered for his absences whenever they could.) Another was a long lamentation about how we were going broke and he had to get more work immediately so we wouldn't starve to death. Over the course of the ensuing four years he would return to these subjects and invent several more obsessions, each of which had its own vocabulary and syntax.

Silent for most of the day, in the evening when I returned from the theatre he would embark on one or more of these verbal spirals and continue for hours until he fell asleep or I did. Usually he would be crying when I came home. The crying, initially genuine, became a weapon he used to beat me with because he knew I found it terribly upsetting. If I left the room he would follow me, even into the bathroom. It was as though he didn't feel real unless I was there to reflect him back at himself. It didn't matter how I reacted. I tried everything. Brisk, no-nonsense matron worked best but even that didn't work awfully well. I tried responding with warmth and sympathy; he merely cried harder. I tried anger, which went straight over his head. I tried reasoning with him – 'I'm really tired, darling, I've been working since eight this morning, I've filed your review and mine, I've made breakfast, lunch and dinner for you, I've been listening to you for three hours, it's two a.m.' – but he simply went on talking.

'Yes, yes, you're tired, but so am I and you wouldn't be tired if we lived in Miami.'

'Why on earth would you want to live in Miami? You hate Florida,' – silly question, this, it was just somewhere with sunshine and a beach where he thought he could hide.

'Nobody could find me there, I wouldn't have to work, I could just live on the beach and swim all day.'

'You don't have to work. You can stay here at home quietly until you're better and then, when you feel like it, you can go back to work.'

'I'll never feel like it and, anyway, nobody will hire me ever again. Nobody wants a broken-down theatre critic.'

'Of course they will. You're Sheridan Morley; they'll always want what you have to offer. Look how everybody's filling in for you now because you're ill. They wouldn't do that if they didn't want you.'

'They're trying out new people so they can replace me.'

'Nobody is even thinking of replacing you. It's all in your imagination.'

'You don't understand anything. You're not ill.'

And so on. And so on . . .

When I did leave him to go to sleep in the spare room, he would go to his trusty old electric typewriter and write it all down for me in a letter that would be waiting for me on my dressing table in the morning. He was inexorable. A man who has used words as his only weapon, as his only defence, as his friends and companions for a lifetime, could not help but call them into service when all other anchors were out of his reach.

None of this was very different except in degree from the way he had been each time he had fallen over from mania to depression but it was much worse this time. Because the symptoms were familiar, it never occurred to me that the illness might be different. I knew, or thought I knew, that sooner or later the torrent of words would stop, the storm would be over and things would return to normal. In the meantime, it was horrible but, I thought, temporary.

If I had known it was not, I'm not sure I could have gone on. I was hardly sleeping, doing two people's work and taking tremendous verbal abuse from Sheridan which lasted for hours every day. All his articulate tsunamis had a germ, just a trace, of truth in them. Of course, his employers *were* worried about how to cover for him if this illness turned out to be long term but they were bravely carrying on by reassuring me (and, through me, him) that they would wait indefinitely, if necessary. Disentangling the germs of truth from the masses of hyperbole and sick imagination was taking more energy than I thought I had.

I was waiting for the anti-depressant drugs to kick back in, assuming that the few days when the hospital had stopped him from taking them after the stroke had caused this extreme depression. It would soon lift. When it didn't, I took him back to the Cardinal. He had been out of hospital for three weeks.

Dr Leslie Morrish, who owned the clinic, took him in and his wonderful staff of psychiatric nurses and social workers calmed Sheridan a little but couldn't seem to get a handle on the depression. When I asked why it seemed so intractable this time, I remember now that Morrish said something about the stroke having possibly changed the pathology of Sheridan's brain.

'He's had a bad stroke,' Morrish told me, 'and we don't yet know what the effects might be.'

'Oh, but Leslie, we *do* know. We've been so lucky. The weakness down the left side of his body has gone away and, although his voice isn't back to normal because of the depression, the slurring has gone.'

'Those,' said Dr Morrish, gravely, 'may not be the only consequences. We'll have to wait and see what insult there has been to the brain.' I heard him but didn't take in the import of what he was saying and he didn't push it.

I didn't want to know, not really. If I had focused then on the possibility that Sheridan would never recover, might never again lose the depression that he had fought all his adult life, would never regain his memory or his sense of humour, or his confidence, or the life he had known before the stroke, and if I had had any idea what was ahead of us, I don't know what I might have done. Divorce? Suicide? Both unthinkable. But something.

Fortunately, I chose subconsciously not to hear him. Of course, Sheridan would recover. We had been lucky, after all. Sheridan was not paralysed as so many stroke victims are. Any physical effects that had been there for the first few weeks, his slurred voice, for instance, had vanished, although his wonderful voice had now been replaced by an unpleasant and self-pitying whine which was only to disappear when he was performing and, sometimes, not even then. There was no reason he should not make a full physical recovery; indeed, he had already made it. There was nothing he needed to do – walk, stand, sit, eat, etc. – that he couldn't do and the slight left-side weakness which had manifested itself in his first few days in hospital had by now completely gone. Yes, we had been lucky.

But there remained the worrying fact that he was more deeply depressed than ever. There had been no manic phase this time. He had gone from being 'normal' for him, in other words, a bit 'high', to being sunk into blackest fog. Even the vigilant nurses at the Cardinal couldn't keep him out of bed; the moment their backs were turned he headed for his room and they described to me the 'game' of trying to head him off before he reached there.

I spoke to him or to Kate, the nurse in charge, several times a day. 'No change,' she would report. 'Dr Morrish is trying something else.' I went to Windsor whenever I could get away or when I didn't have a play to review. It didn't seem to matter whether I was there or not. Sheridan didn't seem to notice. I called the BBC. 'Don't worry,' they said, 'we'll fill in for him for a few weeks. More, if you need it.' They were great and, I suspect, quite glad not to have to deal with him while he was ill. As it turned out, he was in the Cardinal through Christmas. He wasn't getting any better.

It still didn't occur to me that what was wrong with him wasn't the same depression he had always had. The symptoms were identical, perhaps a little worse but exactly the same, and he was in the best possible hands. If anyone could have cured him it would have been those wonderful women at the Cardinal. One tiny Filipina nurse was especially good with him, 'You're safe,' she kept saying, when his irrational fears got the better of him and he couldn't stop crying, 'I won't let anything happen to you. You're safe here.' There was something infinitely touching about this enormous man sitting with the little nurse, holding her hand and sobbing as though his heart was already broken.

I bashed on. He'd be fine. He always was in the end.

Chapter Twelve

*T*hrough the 1960s, while Sheridan was getting married, having his first two children and writing his first book, I was moving in a different direction. I followed Brian Winston to Granada Television in Manchester where I started as a secretary and, over several years, progressed through a number of jobs from news to light entertainment to drama, until I was a script editor and sometime producer in the drama department. Granada taught me my craft and I was properly grateful although I hated living in Manchester. In those days, a girl who wasn't a typist was something of a misfit, and with my London accent and my professional ambitions I was more of a misfit than most. Eventually, thank heaven, they let me come back to London and I had a happy year or two at the offices in Golden Square.

I met a handsome American, married him and moved to Washington, DC where, in short order, largely thanks to my English accent, I suspect, I became head of arts programming in public television, while my husband, a third-generation Washington journalist, joined NBC News. Since my first trip to New York at age 17, I had always wanted to live there but, for the moment, Washington, DC was exciting enough.

In retrospect, I married Michael, a journalist then working for the international news agency United Press International (UPI), because *he was reassigned from London's Fleet Street to Brussels to cover what was then the Common Market. Living in different countries, we found, was difficult although we took ourselves all over Europe on long weekends. On one weekend in the forest of the Ardennes he asked me to marry him. I said 'yes' but I had actually given it little thought. Michael wanted to leave Brussels, and I think I was his excuse to return to the United States. For my part, I thought, rightly, that there would be far more opportunities in America for an ambitious young woman. Besides, he was arguably the best-looking man I had ever met.*

So, we were engaged. We loved each other dearly, still do, come to that, but we mistook compatibility and friendship for passion. There was no heat between us but much warmth. For a long time that was enough. We rarely argued, never fought, agreed on values and politics. Our personalities were complementary, we were perfect travel companions, we liked the same food and the same people. It was a good marriage.

Sheridan and I remained friends, writing letters, talking on the telephone, gossiping shamelessly, and when he and his burgeoning family (by now they had a third child, Juliet) came to Washington, DC or when Michael and I were in England we saw each other en famille. *Michael liked Sheridan enormously and accepted that our relationship predated my marriage.*

Meanwhile, Brian Winston of the Oxford group became a BBC producer in New York but soon realized that he was better suited to academic life and became a professor at New York University. He had already met Adele in London and married her. They subsequently became parents to Jessica and Matthew, the first of my dearly loved godchildren. Jo Durden-Smith married a New York Mafia princess and Henry Fenwick married a ravishingly beautiful African-American actress and was appointed features editor of Playboy *magazine in Chicago. All of us, then, except Sheridan, were happily living in the United States.*

Only in retrospect do I realize how privileged I was. Michael and I moved into a beautiful apartment near Georgetown where we entertained regularly. Through his job we had access to the political, diplomatic and journalistic worlds, and made friends among the many Congressional aides and diplomats who came in and out of Washington. Through my job we enjoyed meeting the artists and performers as they came through town. We were invited to embassy parties and private receptions. We worked hard, long hours but we loved our jobs and it didn't seem like work at the time. We were young and successful and we were both doing work that got us noticed within our own industries.

Somehow, I persuaded my bosses that what the Public Broadcasting Service (PBS) needed was live performances – operas, ballets, jazz – from various high-profile venues and, as a result, became a pioneer in the field of performance programming. I still hankered to live in New York but I made regular, often weekly trips to see a new artist or a play and that kept my New York obsession at bay.

We stayed in Washington, DC until I received an offer I couldn't refuse. One of the United States' biggest corporations, Allied Chemicals, was accused of polluting the Charles River and was being pilloried in the press for its indifference to the environment and public safety. I met the executive in charge of corporate public relations at exactly the moment when his company was in desperate need of some good PR. I went to see him with a proposal to make live performance programmes from one of the world's great concert halls.

I liked him, he liked me and he liked my proposal. On a handshake and the promise of three-quarters of a million dollars, I walked out of his office with everything I needed to produce a series for public television which would be known as 'Tonight at Carnegie Hall'. This would make me an independent television producer with my own company, my own staff and my own little empire.

I gave my notice, gleefully accepted the accolades at a farewell office party and moved to New York. For me, this was heaven. Proximity to the music and musicians, the actors and writers, the theatres and dancers of New York would be wonderful and, indeed, for me, it was. I became what I had always dreamed of being, a New Yorker.

Oddly enough, unlike so many dreams, the reality surpassed the fantasy. I found an apartment which overlooked Central Park on one side and the Hudson River on the other near Lincoln Center for the Performing Arts. I had told the estate agent that I wanted to be within walking distance of Carnegie Hall and close to Zabars, the great delicatessen. She found me one that was equidistant. I said yes as soon as I saw it and only then called my husband to tell him that I'd found us the perfect New York home.

What I didn't realize at the time was that he didn't want to leave Washington, DC. He was doing it for me and selfishly, in my own excitement at seeing my dreams realized, I didn't understand how great a sacrifice it would be for him to abandon, albeit temporarily, his own dreams. For Michael, it was too big a leap from the job he loved at NBC to . . . what?

To my surprise he announced his intention to become a freelance magazine writer like his best friend, the medical writer Paula (Polly) Dranov, with whom he had worked early in his career. Privately, Polly had misgivings which she shared with me although not with him. 'Michael loves structure. He likes to work with a team. He likes to see the results of his work fast. And he thinks New York's a great place to visit. A freelance writer works alone, sometimes writing months before publication, and he has to be willing to work in an unstructured set-up which changes from editor to editor.' She thought he wouldn't like it and he didn't. If he had, or if I'd been more flexible and willing to return to Washington, DC, we might still be married.

Michael tried several jobs, including the editorship of a local family newspaper in Connecticut where we rented a little house, keeping our apartment in Manhattan, and I commuted to and from New

York every Monday morning and every Thursday evening by bus. We played a lot of tennis, we made good friends there, and I loved the opportunity to sample rural American life, but the pull of big-city political journalism was too much for Michael and stories about bake sales and local Little League baseball games couldn't keep his excellent newsman's brain from hankering for Washington, DC and world events.

I, meanwhile, was blissfully happy, with my eyes fixed on New York and the hard but rewarding life of an independent producer on the world's most demanding stage. I wallowed in music from jazz to opera, from avant-garde dance to ballet, from cabaret to lieder. I worked with everybody – Dizzy Gillespie, Aaron Copland, Mikhail Baryshnikov, Leonard Bernstein, Sarah Vaughan, Beverly Sills, Rudolf Serkin and, most often and happily, the violinist Isaac Stern. I loved New York.

Eventually, the inevitable happened. Michael was offered his dream job back in Washington, DC as a producer on the best news show on television, the 'MacNeil/Lehrer NewsHour', and there was no question but that he should take it. We went down to Washington together, bought and furnished a flat for him (we had sold our apartment when we left for New York), in the colours of the American southwest that he loved, and agreed that I would come to DC every weekend that I could get away. It was the only answer for a couple who had ambitious but conflicting plans. And, for a long time, it worked.

Chapter Thirteen

The antidepressants weren't working. Dr Morrish, while Sheridan was still in the Cardinal, again raised the possibility that the stroke had changed the pathology of Sheridan's brain, thus rendering ineffective the drugs he had been taking for some years. He changed them. This is always a difficult process. First, the patient has to be slowly weaned off the current drug. This takes about three weeks. Then he has to begin to take the new medication, slowly increasing the dosage until the optimum is arrived at. This takes another three weeks. Then you wait to see if this one is working, watching the patient closely to ensure there are no disastrous effects, such as an increase in suicidal or psychotic symptoms. If it's not, the whole process begins again. Over these four years, Sheridan was on ten or twelve different combinations of drugs. There are a lot of antidepressants. All of them work for many people. None of them worked for Sheridan.

He – we – had been lucky. He appeared to have recovered physically from quite a serious stroke. Now, if we could only get a handle on the depression, which we all still assumed to be a mental condition, he'd be right as rain again. Better, in fact, because now, thanks to Dr McIntosh and his Beta Cell Unit, his diabetes was under control.

I took him home again. There wasn't any point in keeping him in the Cardinal when he was sleeping most of the time there. Sometimes the nurses won and he went to group therapy or lunch. Other times they lost and he escaped them to go back to bed. They thought that perhaps he would improve when he resumed some elements of his regular routine. He was obsessively worried about his BBC presenting job. When awake, one of his most insistent circular rants, often accompanied by tears and hysteria, was that the BBC wouldn't want him anymore. No amount of reassurance from the doctors, the nurses, me, or even Jim Moir on the telephone from Radio 2 would assuage his ongoing panic.

Once home, he went straight to bed but now I could often get him up in the evenings to go to the theatre with me. He felt slightly better as the day progressed, his mood lifted a bit, and he would occasionally read the arts sections of the newspapers at the dining table. At the theatre, in contrast with his lifelong habit of bounding into the lobby, talking to everybody, exchanging gossip, picking up titbits to tell me on the way home, he kept his head down. When one of his colleagues, Charles Spencer from the *Daily Telegraph* or Benedict Nightingale from *The Times*, would drop by to tell him how happy they were to see him back in his usual seat on the aisle, he mumbled something and wouldn't look at them.

Usually, he didn't look at the stage much either, being apparently asleep, and he still couldn't write his own reviews, but he would often say something so blindingly perceptive about the play, the production or the performance on the way home that I could base an entire review around it. He still knew his theatre and had something wonderful to say about it even if he couldn't exactly say it himself. He would sit in the car on the way home, his chin on his chest, only the top of his head visible, while I tried to stimulate some response to what we had seen. Then, very occasionally, he would mumble something.

'What? I can't hear you.'

'I said, the first act is like a tightrope that pulls the play taut but in the second, it breaks.'

This broke my heart. Sheridan had spent a lifetime learning to write about the theatre and nobody, absolutely nobody, did it better. But he couldn't do it. He wasn't blocked, it wasn't that he had nothing to say or even that he had a problem saying it. He was simply so depressed that he couldn't bring himself to do what he was obviously longing to do. I, who wasn't fit to clean his literary boots, was his mouthpiece. My words, not his, encouraged the actors, analysed the plays, delivered the appreciation. His would have been so much better. I did my very best, writing at a level I'd never achieved on my own through several books and hundreds of columns, but I knew I wasn't Sheridan, even if no one else did.

Fortunately, almost nobody noticed. The editors were concerned with getting the right number of words in their publications on time and as long as they got their columns at the correct word-count, by deadline, they didn't look too closely at their content. Those who did notice – most of his colleagues and his friends – loved and admired Sheridan enough to make sure that nobody questioned him or me about the obvious anomaly of his sometimes not having been present at plays he'd reviewed. I always knew what he thought or would think about a production as we'd been going to the theatre together for the best part of forty years, so I never used his voice to praise a play that he would have hated nor criticized an actor he loved.

What was missing, of course, was Sheridan himself. Our earliest conversations were about the theatre – what we wanted to see, what we saw, what we had seen and what it meant. My theatre-school education and his lifetime of living backstage around actors took us into realms of analysis and synthesis that seemed natural to us. He was visceral, his father and grandmother and just about everybody he knew were people of the theatre. I was intellectual and emotional, my entire life had been spent looking at, reading and trying to understand the theatre. Our theatregoing had always been, in a way, an extension of our lovemaking, an ongoing relationship-defining miracle that made us collectively more than either of us was separately. And, suddenly, I was alone.

From that first day in Brian's room, long before we were lovers or even friends, we had recognized one another. I was interested in many things but theatre was pre-eminent. Sheridan was interested in nothing else. We could say anything to one another, and did, but our conversations about plays and musicals were really one conversation, one that lasted for nearly fifty years. It was the thread that held us together, the glue that stuck together many different thoughts and values. We were of different classes and different religions; we had different ambitions and very different backgrounds. But we saw in one another the only person on earth who understood what we thought and felt about the one thing that mattered more to us than any other.

And, suddenly, it was gone. He was gone. The warm, loving, maddening, irresistible centre of my world was gone. When he talked, which was for several hours a night, the only hours when he was awake, he talked only of himself and his demons. When I attempted to talk with him about those things that had for so long been his lifeblood, he would turn the conversation to himself. If I said, 'There's going to be a new Hamlet,' he'd say, 'Hamlet's depression wasn't nearly as bad as mine.' I would say, 'It's a beautiful day. Let's walk by the river,' but he would respond, 'You go, I'm going back to bed.' I told him I was lonely without his company. No response. One day I was so miserable and so fed up with watching him sleep that I went to the local cinema on my own. When I got back he was awake and frantic. 'Where have you been? I thought you'd left me. Don't leave me. I love you. Do you still want to go for a walk? I'll come, I'll come.' It was pitch dark outside. And inside.

Nothing outside himself touched him, not the death of a friend ('Wish I were dead too') nor a deserved knighthood awarded to an actor he admired ('Nobody's going to make me a "Sir"') nor even the birth of another grandchild ('They don't want me around'). He became paranoid, convinced that his colleagues were after his jobs, resentful of any assignment that had gone to anyone else. That he couldn't have written the book or made the broadcast or done the interview in his current state of health never occurred to him; only that someone else had done it, stolen it from him.

His negativity wore me down. And I was so damn tired. My life was bounded by the pills that had to be given to him three times a day, the injections, the doctors' appointments, the difficulty of getting him out of bed, to wash, to dress, to go to the theatre. I was doing his work, and mine, and writing, writing, writing. Then I had to file both reviews, ensuring that I sent the right one to the right publication and then, only then, making and eating dinner. Most nights it was midnight before either of us ate. Sheridan had been asleep all day, I'd been working, so he wanted to stay up and tell me what was wrong with his life. 'I'm so ill. I'm so unhappy. Nobody understands. There's no future. You've got a life. I haven't. I'm so ill . . .' As I've mentioned, when I would finally walk away from the endless stream of consciousness, he would follow me and then he'd go to the typewriter to write it all down again. Once I was so fed up with his endless whining that I locked the bedroom door on him. He kept hitting the door until he broke the lock.

One night I realized to my horror that, while I loved him to bits and was worried about him down to my soul, I didn't like him anymore. And that was the cruellest revelation of all. We had been through so much to be together and now our life was reduced to pills and drudgery. There had to be a way back. And there was.

Chapter Fourteen

*M*y New York life has always been more carefree than my life in London. I always knew that I'd been born in the wrong place. London is a wonderful city and the best place in the world if you happen to write about the theatre but, despite my being born and brought up there, it has never felt like home to me. New York, on the other hand – even when it was dirty, dangerous and expensive before Mayor Rudy Giuliani cleaned the city up in the late 1990s – always has.

From my first visit, aged seventeen, I always knew that someday I would live in New York. Because I knew that, there wasn't any great urgency about it. When I married Michael and lived in Washington, DC, I happily moved to that white-marbled city of monuments and intrigues because I knew that New York was only a train-ride away.

I was very happy working in public broadcasting. PBS, a loose association of university and non-profit stations based all over the United States, was just being born when I arrived. Unlike the BBC which was, from the very beginning, intended as a public service, American television until now existed only to sell soap powder and cigarettes. It was Commercial with a capital C.

PBS was a non-commercial service from the start, funded by the federal government and by grants from private corporations who got

nothing more for their money than an announcement at the begin-
ning and end of each programme. PBS was different to mainstream
stations. Its aspirations were nobler. It wanted to give Americans good
music, drama, documentaries and thought-provoking in-depth cover-
age of the news – all the content that the major networks had either
never had or had jettisoned. Arts programming was what I knew and
loved and public television waited for me with open arms. For nine
wonderful years I toiled in the PBS vineyard in Washington and I
loved it. But I always yearned for New York and independence.

So now, seemingly, I had it all. Except that I was living in New York
and Michael was living in Washington, DC. Our marriage became
hard work. One of us was always on a plane to visit the other. We
were beginning to have separate friends and interests. As an inde-
pendent producer I was the prisoner of my various shooting schedules
and he would suddenly have to fly off to Cairo or Atlanta to cover a
story. Our lives were beginning to diverge.

I was busy in my New York eyrie but not too busy to develop my
long-held love of the American popular song. I had always loved the
Great American Songbook, but now I had time and the freedom to
study it. I made friends with the singers who specialized in singing
those tunes and whenever I had a free evening I could be found
squashed into a tiny chair in one of the many clubs where cabaret was
the fare. I started to write about cabaret and its practitioners, and
some of the singers began to ask me to help them to put their shows
together.

Michael liked cabaret but his musical tastes tended towards more
contemporary music. He always found my New York friends too
theatrical but was too nice a person to say so. When he returned to
Washington, though, I could give full rein to my theatrical and musi-
cal interests and whenever I wasn't in the theatre or working, I was
at a cabaret. Life was very full. Our marriage wasn't, and it was this
disjunction between us that caused us to go in different directions.

In the mid 1980s, one afternoon at about 2 p.m. the telephone rang in the Manhattan apartment. It was a voice I knew well and cherished. I hadn't seen Sheridan for months, not since Christmas. Michael and I always went to England for Christmas with my family and sometimes stayed to celebrate New Year at Sheridan and Margaret's annual party. When we were in the same country Sheridan and I always tried to get together: if the timing worked, great; if not, there would be a next time. I was used to his turning up and disappearing again like the White Rabbit.

'Hello, darling, I'm in New York, promoting my David Niven biography. Are you free for dinner?' I was. Michael was in Washington, I was rough-editing a documentary, and my time was my own. 'Pick you up about eight?'

'Not necessary,' I responded, a bit surprised. He'd never picked me up before. 'Tell me where we're eating and I'll meet you there as usual.'

This time, though, he insisted. 'Wait 'til you see,' he promised, mysteriously.

I knew he'd be late. Twenty-five years of shivering on street corners told me so. But this time, I could just stay home until he arrived. Sure enough, at 8.45 p.m. the doorman rang from the lobby. 'Gentleman in a limo here to see you,' he announced. A limo? At the door of my apartment building a beaming Sheridan enveloped me in the usual bear hug.

'Look what I've got. The publishers hired it for me so I wouldn't be late all the time.'

'Well, that was a great success,' I said with heavy irony and a meaningful look at my watch. 'Less than an hour late. Not bad. For you.'

The enormous black vehicle, more a bus than a car, drove us in great style to an ornate Italian restaurant on the East Side, where the food was mediocre but the service so ridiculously attentive that you wanted to spin the waiters around, point them towards the kitchen, and yell, 'GO AWAY!' Every time we got into conversation, someone appeared with more bread, or water, or a query about the food. We became giggly. Finally, before dessert, we thought that we should beat a retreat before we disgraced ourselves completely.

'Come back to the apartment,' I suggested. 'I'll make you a coffee and I'm sure I've got some ice cream in the freezer.' I knew my customer; Sheridan had been an ice-cream addict since early childhood. He'd rather have an ice cream than tea with the Queen, especially if there was some hot chocolate sauce and a brownie to go with it.

We piled into the limo, still giggling, and Sheridan told the driver to go the long way around Central Park, not wanting to relinquish the unaccustomed luxury, past the lighted trees of the Tavern on the Green and past the fantastical lights of midtown Manhattan. Like fascinated teenagers, we explored the limo. There were cut crystal decanters with various spirits in them and matching tumblers. Also, there was a small refrigerator with an ice bucket and a small bottle of champagne.

With great ceremony, Sheridan opened the champagne, found a couple of flutes and a jug of fresh orange juice, and poured us each a Mimosa. 'My grandfather invented this drink,' he told me airily, 'putting orange juice into champagne.' I was used to Sheridan's grandiose assertions.

'Nonsense,' I said, 'you can't invent a Mimosa.'

'Ah, but it's not a Mimosa. It's called a Buck's Fizz and my grandfather was Captain Herbert Buckmaster, founder of Buck's Club and inventor of the Buck's Fizz.' This was one of his assertions which turned out to be dead true.

Still giggling, and clutching our elegant champagne flutes from the limo, we had by now arrived back at my apartment building. Sheridan asked his long-suffering driver to come back in an hour and gave him some money so he could have a bite to eat in the meantime. We fell into the apartment with the inelegance of puppies and I went into the kitchen to make coffee and dessert, leaving Sheridan, still chuckling, looking out of the picture window in my living room at the amazing light show that is Manhattan.

When I returned, some five minutes later, with cups of coffee and bowls of ice cream, he was still standing there, back to me, no longer laughing. 'Do you have any idea how much I hate my life?' he asked, quietly. I thought I had misheard him.

'What?'

'I hate everything about it. I hate England, I hate Margaret, I hate Berkshire, I hate that there is no escape from it, and I hate not being in New York with you.'

'What?' I asked again, stupidly. He was still looking out the window and not at me.

'I love you,' he said, with a finality so complete that I couldn't doubt his sincerity. He was not looking for an effect, there was nothing theatrical about his delivery. 'I have loved you for as long as I can remember and I just decided I don't want to die without telling you that.'

I had no idea how to react. This was my dear friend, my lifer. This was the man who had introduced me to Noël Coward, the man who would take me to any social gathering no matter how boring, just because I asked him. I could not imagine my life without him and what he had just said had changed our friendship forever. This was someone I didn't want to lose but I couldn't see any outcome but disaster for us. We were both married, he had three children, I lived in New York, he was a London broadcaster. I didn't even know if he was serious or whether he would be embarrassed in the morning when the champagne wore off.

'Oh, I don't expect you to do anything about it,' he continued, despairingly, 'but you had to know. I love you, I always have, I always will.'

I was close to panic. A number of men have told me they loved me and a few of them actually did. It is not difficult to deflect these declarations. One can either laugh it off or take them to bed. But when it's one of your best friends, neither of those is an option.

'Darling, of course you don't,' I said, feebly. 'You're tired. You've been running around selling the book, tasting the kind of freedom you think I have here and looking out of this window at the kind of cityscape that you believe personifies my life. But you're wrong. Everybody's marriage is imperfect. My life is interesting but insecure. Michael's away a lot and there's no money. You couldn't possibly live on my knife-edge. In England you have a wonderful job, fame, the admiration of the public and the critics. If you came here you wouldn't have any of that. America is a daily struggle and, believe me, you are not a man for a struggle.'

'If I could have you, live with you, spend my life with you, none of that would matter, but I know I can't. It's not the children, they'd be better off without me, and Margaret likes it better when I'm not around. I'm a coward or I would have asked you to marry me years ago when we were both single. But I knew you'd refuse and I couldn't have borne being rejected. I have always felt like an outsider except when I'm in front of a camera or a typewriter. This evening proved it; only with you am I myself. You know everything about me and you still love me.'

I was at sea, I couldn't work out what I could say that would put this genie back into the bottle without inflicting harm on this generous, misguided, damaged soul. 'Of course I love you,' I told him, 'and I will love you no matter what, as I always have done. You don't have to live with me or come to New York for us to love one another. We have been friends for twenty-five years, we will be friends for another fifty but you would hate yourself if you left what you have in England – Margaret and the children and the house and your parents – and after a while you would start to hate me too.'

He stood, framed in the window with a background of New York, still looking out over Central Park. 'I already hate myself,' he said, sadly. 'The only thing in the world I love is you and by telling you that I'm afraid I've cut myself off from you too.' Throughout this entire *conversation he had neither looked at me nor touched me. We'd had twenty-five years of hugs but we had never kissed.*

Somehow I coaxed him on to the sofa, made him eat his ice cream and drink his coffee. Within minutes, he was Sheridan again, back to telling stories of the television interviewers he had met that day and about the bookshop keepers who had never heard of his book or of David Niven and I wondered if I had imagined the whole episode. I hoped so. Half an hour later, I bundled him out of the apartment towards the limo and the hotel. Tomorrow he was flying to Michigan on the next leg of his publicity tour. I was shaken but managed to convince myself that nothing untoward had happened.

I called Michael before I went to bed. 'I had dinner with Sheridan this evening,' I told him.

'How was he?'

'He seemed very tired and a bit weird,' I said. We talked for a few minutes and said goodnight. I went to bed but I didn't sleep.

I didn't hear from Sheridan for a month, which was not unusual. Sometimes a year went by without either of us being in the same country at the same time. But this time, instead of a postcard, I got a letter. Pages long, it was a deeply passionate outpouring of love and longing, detailing his feelings for me over more than twenty years. For all of that time, I had had literally no idea of his love for me. I didn't share it and I had no idea how to cope with it.

Now, all these years later, I recognize that, while his feelings and emotions were real, the extravagance with which they were expressed was a consequence of the manic phase of bipolar disorder. Had he not been ill he would probably never have said anything at all to me. But, of course, I had no idea he was bipolar, couldn't have identified the signs if I had known, and took what he was saying at face value. So I was shocked at the violence of his emotion and just assumed that, having kept it bottled up for all these years, it was bursting out of him in extravagant and theatrical ways.

I wrote back immediately, still hoping to diffuse this torrent of feelings or, at least, to channel it back into our friendship. I reminded him that we were both married. More importantly, to me at least because I have never held a particularly high opinion of sexual fidelity, I said that while I could probably find a dozen lovers, I could never find another friend like him and that I had no intention of letting him subvert our friendship into something far more superficial – an affair.

His response came by return of post – he feared he hadn't made himself clear. He didn't want an affair, he wanted to marry me. He was going to leave Margaret, he said, and then we could be together. By now I was totally panicked but I believed him. It never occurred to me that he was ill.

I couldn't call him at home, naturally, but I had his number at Punch *where he was arts editor and I called him there. No longer trying to let him down lightly, I told him in no uncertain terms that he had made a terrible mistake. The assumption that I wanted to leave Michael and/or that I wanted him to leave Margaret was entirely erroneous. I couldn't have been clearer. Neither could he. He heard me out and then simply repeated what he had said in his letter, which was that he didn't want an affair, he wanted marriage. I hung up on him.*

I didn't hear from him again for several months. It later transpired that he had 'fallen over the edge' into depression and had been in the clinic but I thought he had regretted his approach to me and now couldn't work out how to get himself back into my good graces.

I don't know what really happened but this is Sheridan's version: he was behaving erratically, shouting a lot, repeating himself, displaying a number of what we came to know as symptoms and which were odd enough that Margaret noticed. Apparently, she decided one morning that he couldn't be trusted to drive a car, especially not on to the M4 motorway, and that he was sick enough that immediate medical help was required. Because Sheridan was insisting on leaving the house to drive to London and his office at Punch, *she threw a full cup of coffee over him and his clean white shirt to detain him. While he went upstairs to change his shirt, she called the GP, who recommended a local psychiatrist, and somehow she got Sheridan to the Cardinal Clinic in nearby Windsor.*

For obvious reasons, I know next to nothing about that first hospitalization. I don't even know how long he was there, except that at some point he was given ECT (electroconvulsive therapy), also known as shock treatment, which worked to the extent that Sheridan was able to leave the Cardinal Clinic with part of his prodigious memory impaired but better able to observe that the clinic's doorknobs would not burn him if he touched them.

Another exchange of letters followed. I don't know what he did with the ones I sent him but I still have all of his to me. His at that time were calmer and sadder but still insistent. It was the first time I came across the circular arguments of bipolar disorder where the sufferer returns again and again to his original thesis. In this case, it was that he was going to marry me. He knew what he wanted and he was determined to get it, no matter what the cost.

Chapter Fifteen

Clearly something had to be done or we would lose each other forever, lost in the morass of the daily routine of illness. Sheridan was by now completely dependent on me. He couldn't get up in the morning, shower, dress, breakfast, take his pills or even sit at his computer without me. The main ordeal was just getting him out of bed. The doctors had told me that the worst thing he could possibly do was to sleep all the time and that's all he wanted or was able to do. Some days it took three, four, even five hours of shouting, cajoling, begging and insisting to rouse him. Even if I got him as far as the bathroom, he would inevitably wait until my attention was distracted and creep back to bed. Some days, if I was really busy with work, I'd just let him get on with it but I knew how bad and dangerous it was for his heart and that the possibility of a second stroke loomed large so mostly I went with the yelling routine.

It was horrible. For him and for me. But it was a measure of his iron will that, much as his conscious mind wanted to please me, to do what I asked and rejoin the world, he still was unable and unwilling to make his body follow. And so he slept, through days and weeks and months, waking only at night to go to the theatre occasionally and to rail against everything – his life, his work, his children, his fate and, of course, me. Me, most of all. I was, he told me over and over, stupid, insensitive, thoughtless, cruel, and wicked. He thought that I wanted him ill so that I could control him. I wanted him well because he was the biggest earner. I wanted him dead so I could inherit all his money.

On these occasions I pointed out, quite unnecessarily, that as he didn't have any money there was nothing for me to inherit and that I wanted him well for the simple reason that nobody wants the person they love to be ill. Why I tried, and kept trying, to get through to him I still don't understand. The doctors told me again and again that it wasn't Sheridan speaking, it was his illness, and that I should simply ignore him when he started to rant at me. Somehow, I just couldn't.

I have hundreds of letters he wrote me during these years of long nights after I had gone to bed, exhausted by his irrationality. Many of them are truly vicious and, because he was a great writer, beautifully written accusations about my cruelty, my lack of understanding, my mendacity, my indifference. These would be waiting on my dressing table most mornings when I dragged myself from sleep to start yet another day of yelling. There is no question but that, at the moments when he wrote these, he believed what he wrote. When he woke up the following evening he would ask whether I had read his letter and whether, therefore, I now understood what I was doing wrong.

When I would burst into tears and suggested that, if he was really so unhappy with me he would be better off if I went back to New York, he was quick to console me. He didn't mean it, he'd been angry, he loved me, he didn't want me to leave, what would he do without me? It was true. He didn't mean it. He was just so upset and frustrated that nothing we did made him feel better about himself. He needed to blame someone. I just happened to be there, the only one who always was.

Blame avoidance was a basic tenet of Sheridan's character. He was terrified of being blamed for anything, no matter how trivial – 'Darling, this cup appears to have got itself broken.' Fine, I would say, it's a cup, a thing, it doesn't matter. But it did to Sheridan. His automatic response to a query about anything that went wrong was, 'It wasn't me.' And nobody had said or suggested that it was. This led me to wonder what on earth he had done in his childhood that was so horrendous that owning up to it had brought dire consequences. Maybe nothing. Maybe it was just a personality trait. I, who was brought up to say, 'Yes, I'm sorry, it was me,' found all this incomprehensible.

He never admitted that anything, no matter how trivial, was his fault. Ever. And so his illness – for which there was no fault, no blame to attach to anyone or anything, it was simply there – had to be someone's fault and, inevitably, it had to be mine, just as it had previously been Margaret's. Letter after letter said so, said that if he weren't married to me he wouldn't be ill. Then he would retract them, full of remorse. But the next night he'd write another.

Sheridan was now falling down a lot. The medical term is 'postural hypertension'. Always a bit clumsy, because of his size, he had no physical tools to help him remain upright when he got up too fast and his blood pressure dropped precipitously. This caused him to faint and several times he hurt himself badly. It was caused by the combination of medications he was taking for the stroke, the diabetes and the depression. When it happened, it was terrifying. This very tall, large man would, without warning, simply fall like a tree, forwards on to his face or, on several occasions, backwards, hitting his head. There was never enough warning for him even to stretch out a hand to break his fall or for me to try to catch him.

The faints would usually last only a few seconds, a minute at most, but once down I couldn't pick him up. And because of his size, drug-hazed state and general physical debilitation, once he dropped, he couldn't get up by himself. Then the only thing I could do was to call an ambulance, even though I knew he didn't need to be hospitalized. The local ambulance service got quite used to showing up and getting him on his feet. Often, of course, he would hurt himself in the fall and then they had to clean him up and then take him to the Chelsea and Westminster Hospital to be checked out.

I remember a nightmarish birthday lunch with my cousins. He had dragged himself out of bed for the celebration but, as I parked the car opposite the Ivy, Sheridan, knowing we were already late, got out too quickly and fell face-down on to the concrete floor. Somehow I got him on to his knees and into a sitting position and, eventually, on to his feet. I should have taken him straight home or to the nearest casualty department but he insisted he was fine and wanted to continue with the outing. 'I'm hungry, darling, and I'm okay. Besides, what will Mildred say if we don't turn up?' Cousin Mildred would, of course, have understood but I let him persuade me, probably because selfishly I wanted to see my family and was keen for a day out.

Everyone oohed and aahed over his incipient black eye and the cuts on his face but we ordered lunch and everything went fine until my cousin Stephanie and I went off to the loo before dessert. We came back to chaos. Sheridan had set off for the men's room but never got there. He had fallen again amid the tables and it had taken half the staff to get him up and on to a chair. There was a doctor lunching at a nearby table and she was very kind to him. By the time Steph and I returned from the ladies', the paramedics were on their way. They patched him up but by this time nobody was in much of a mood for pudding. I sent the ambulance away and took Sheridan home.

What should have been a happy family day had turned into yet another horror scene starring Sheridan. I was worried about him, frantic that he might have hurt his head in the falls, upset for Mildred because her birthday had been ruined, feeling guilty about causing such a fuss. And, although I'd never admit it, and repressed the thought as soon as it surfaced, I was resentful that the blameless Sheridan had once again inadvertently made himself the centre of attention. 'It's always about you,' I muttered to myself. 'Always about you.'

Chapter Sixteen

'No' wasn't in Sheridan's vocabulary. Time and again I tried to send him back to his marriage and his children. When Sheridan wanted something, he would let nothing stand in his way and what he wanted was me. His insistence was frightening. He made himself ill several times out of sheer frustration. I went to London. He wouldn't leave me alone until I escaped to my work in Germany and Holland. I went back to New York. He followed me. I tried cutting off all communication with him. He simply called and called and called, sometimes ten times a day, from Punch, where nobody kept track of international telephone calls. I even offered him an affair, a quiet affair that wouldn't upset any apple-carts in either marriage. He didn't want that, he said, he wanted to marry me.

He went to see my parents to tell them that his intentions were honourable. This, about a forty-year-old woman. They had known him since he was nineteen and had watched his success and increasing fame with the delight of insiders. Over the preceding twenty-five years, whenever he had passed their flat or shop he would pop in with a bunch of flowers just to say hello. This big, sweet boy who had always been their daughter's friend was a man they now saw on television every evening. But this naked declaration of love and intent was different, new and dangerous. I don't think my parents gave a damn about his intentions, they were too worried about my marriage. They loved both my men and didn't want me to hurt either of them. They were far more worried about them than about me. They could see the storm on the horizon. Sheridan couldn't. Michael was oblivious.

I was discreet but had no idea how to deal with any of it. Here was I, an almost middle-aged woman who hadn't wanted to be married to anybody, in the middle of a triangle with two men who weren't all that interested in taking me to bed but both of whom wanted to be married to me. I wanted to run away from both of them but I had a job I loved and I took the position that I was damned if I'd let this pair of idiots run me off. My sister and my girlfriends warned me that I'd end up with nobody if I allowed this situation to continue. I couldn't see a way out of it. I didn't want to end my marriage and I couldn't get Sheridan to return to his.

Eventually, Sheridan resolved his situation in a very Sheridan way: he left enough evidence of his obsession around his house that Margaret couldn't ignore it. I don't know exactly what, probably unfinished letters to me and telephone bills. He called me in New York and announced, without a trace of regret or compassion for the pain he was causing, 'She knows.'

'What does she know?'

'She knows about you.'

'What about me?'

'She knows I'm in love with you and that we're going to get married.'

'But we're not.'

'Of course we are.'

And we did. Not, it's true, for another ten years but Sheridan always got what he wanted in the end.

I was still living in New York, happily working for PolyGram Classics, coordinating the video for all of their classical labels – Deutsche Grammophon, Philips Classics and Decca – and commuting *to Washington, DC most weekends because by this time Michael had landed his new job. Deutsche Grammophon was based in Hamburg, Philips in Eindhoven in the Netherlands, and Decca in London so I was constantly travelling. The last thing I needed or wanted was a divorce and an upheaval of seismic proportions.*

Amid much Sturm und Drang Sheridan left Margaret and moved into my Regent's Park flat which PolyGram had rented for me because, though still based in New York, I spent so much time in Europe that it was cheaper than a hotel room. At the time, it was just a way of helping out a friend because Sheridan, as usual, hadn't thought through where he might live if he left Margaret. His friends were appalled at his defection from hearth and home so none offered him a temporary home with them, and his finances were, as usual, in such chaos that he couldn't rent a place of his own.

That Christmas, it all came to a head. Sheridan was in Mexico with his elder daughter but the London flat was full of Christmas cards addressed to 'Sheridan and Ruth'. I hadn't even noticed. But Michael did, as soon as he got to London for our annual Christmas with my family. Although he knew, of course, that Sheridan was living there temporarily because his marriage had broken down he had not focused – neither had I – on the obvious 'couple-ness' of the flat until he arrived there, looked around and realized that, unless things changed radically, our marriage was over.

He wanted to return to Washington immediately but I persuaded him to stay so we could talk things through. It was a difficult and uncomfortable few days but there was no shouting, just a lot of sadness. He returned to Washington, as planned, on New Year's Day. The following day he called and said, 'You've got to choose. Either you come back to Washington, DC, stop all this running around the world and be my wife again, or I want a divorce.'

I was stunned. I shouldn't have been. It had been coming for a long time and it was my fault. I hadn't paid attention to Michael's needs for years, hadn't understood how passionately this third-generation Washington journalist loved his hometown with its constant political turmoil, diplomatic spats and community of hacks, hadn't given him enough credit for his sacrifice when he agreed to come to live in New York with me.

That was when I knew that I should never have married anyone. I wasn't any good at it. And I certainly didn't want to marry Sheridan with all his baggage.

Slowly, over the next year, we were both divorced. Mine was sad, not noisy. Michael and I pretty much agreed about how to split up what we had – he kept the flat we'd bought in Washington, while I kept the lease on the rent-stabilized apartment in New York; he took all the abstract paintings and drawings, and I kept the figurative ones. Once I had accepted the inevitability of hurting everybody around us, the worst splitting-up moment was walking back into the New York apartment after a trip to Europe and finding Michael had been there and removed all his books from the bookcases which lined every wall. The shelves looked moth-eaten, with gaping holes throughout. More than anything else, it was the missing books that symbolized the end of twenty years of my life, many of them productive and happy, married to a good, kind man whom I liked and respected more than anyone else I knew.

Amicable as it was, it was horrible, as all divorces are. While it was going on, I took a break from PolyGram and went to Connecticut to write my first book. In fact, I went to hide myself away while I recovered from the unexpected trauma of separation and divorce. There, in a little apartment my parents had bought from the estate of Michael's cousins, I could cut myself off from all outside interruptions and, most importantly, I could escape from Sheridan's inexorability. I didn't see or speak to him throughout this time because he didn't know where I was and he couldn't reach me.

Oddly enough, the only people I did see were new friends although they treated me as family. The previous year, the University of East Anglia had set up the Arthur Miller Centre for American Studies with an inaugural seminar which both Sheridan and I attended. Miller and his beautiful photographer wife Inge Morath were there and, improbably, we became friends. Not close friends, but friends all the same.

When they were in London Sheridan and I always saw them whenever they could fit us into their schedules, even if it was just a cup of tea at my flat, and when we were on different continents Inge and I kept in touch via postcards. When Inge heard that I was to be writing my book in Southbury, Connecticut, only ten minutes from the Millers' house in Roxbury, she insisted that, once a week, I had to have a proper meal.

For months, I wrote all day and night, spoke little and barely left the flat. But on Friday evenings, when the Millers were in Roxbury, I spruced up a bit and went to talk to another human being, one who didn't judge but was always ready with a wise thought or an amusing anecdote. Often it was just Inge and me; Arthur would join us sometimes and occasionally there was another guest. Inge fascinated me. She had lived through some terrible times, met and photographed everybody, come out of every experience with her morals and values intact. She was elegant, charming and endlessly kind. Over those relaxed kitchen-table suppers, she helped heal my troubled spirit and I loved her until she died in 2002.

During this time, back in London, Sheridan had his first big theatrical hit. Noël and Gertie is a delightful entertainment based on the writings of Noël Coward which Sheridan wrote for an appearance at the Hong Kong festival. Over the years, it has had more than fifty productions and two West End runs. The first West End appearance was at the old Donmar Warehouse in 1986 and starred Patricia Hodge.

Reluctant at this time to take any medication for his severe depression and entirely rejecting any other kind of therapy, it was inevitable that Sheridan would sink back into what was becoming a chronic illness – manic depression – and would once again end up in the Cardinal Clinic.

Over the years, I have learned more than I care to know about this killer illness. Sometimes it kills people, more often it kills marriages, jobs, relationships with children and friends. Above all, it kills joy. It is impossible for those of us not ill with this appalling malady to understand how truly terrible it is for the sufferers. We can only look on helplessly, knowing that nothing we can say or do will help. It has no cause, only triggers; it has no cure. One day the world looks like a black and bottomless pit. The next, it will simply lift. Suddenly, they can hear a bird sing or a child laugh.

There have been some wonderful books written on this subject by sufferers from William Styron to Sally Brampton, and many works of art designed to show the rest of us what is going on in a brain sick with hopelessness but none of them work for the patient who is in depression. After they recover, and there are very few who don't, they can read the books, attend the plays and look at the paintings and say, 'Yes, that's what it's like,' but at the time nothing helps. Sheridan was one of the few, the very, very few, for whom it didn't lift and whose recoveries were partial and fleeting. At the time I'm writing about, his illness still followed the usual course: he was high, he was low, he was better.

His divorce from Margaret was bitter and painful. I took no part in it at all except to urge Sheridan to give her anything she wanted because I could see even from a distance of 3,000 miles that denying her would lead in the long run to untold grief for Sheridan.

He wouldn't listen. He had convinced himself that he had to keep their family home, T'Gallant House, because it was the only place he could write. All nonsense, of course, he could write anywhere but he hated change, even when he had instigated it himself. Having caused this upheaval he now wanted Margaret to move out of

T'Gallant House, leaving it for him. Fat chance. She didn't and why should she?

Eventually, the house was sold but not before the rancour between them had soured all his future dealings with his family. Forever afterwards, Margaret remained at the centre of the Morleys as the wronged and deserted wife while Sheridan was edged out as the adulterous and uncaring husband who didn't deserve to be part of his own family. As his father said to him when he told him he was leaving Margaret because he was in love with me, 'Dear boy, keep her as your mistress by all means. You don't marry them. Mistress, yes, wife, no.'

As I've said, I didn't want to marry him, or anyone, anyway. I was perfectly able and willing to support myself, I loved my job at PolyGram, I had been married all my adult life and I was looking forward to a freer transatlantic life. And, in addition to that, what sensible woman wants a man with a furious ex-wife, three divorce-damaged children, a family which blames her for his defection and a chronic mental illness? I am not Mother Teresa and I had, even then, a healthy instinct for self-preservation. Love? Absolutely. Marriage? Absolutely not.

Chapter Seventeen

The longer Sheridan's depression continued, the surer I was that somewhere there had to be a cure. Living for thirty years in the United States has given me an American attitude towards trouble of any sort: if there's a problem, there must be a solution and if there's a solution, it's my responsibility to find it. Only much later could I face the reality: to some problems there is no solution no matter how devoutly you search for it. And, there are some problems, many, in fact, that I can't solve. This knowledge was very hard won. The impetus for the search was my inability merely to survive his illness without at least trying to eliminate it.

How he withstood the misery in which he was mired I still don't know. As difficult as he was on a day-to-day basis he was often gallant in his pain. 'I hurt,' he would say, 'everywhere.' As you would to a small child I would say, 'Show me where it hurts,' and watch his wounded face as he sobbed, 'You don't understand, it's not a place, it's a *thing*. The *thing* hurts.' And then he would drag himself to a radio studio or a theatre when all he wanted was to lose the *thing* in sleep. The only place he felt safe was in bed, the only way he could avoid the pain was to be asleep and yet he persevered. He did all the work he could manage. His struggle to have his depression not show in front of strangers was superhuman. His stage fright was so extreme that it was like another character in his personal drama. He was terrified of all the things he had most loved – microphones, typewriters, audiences and the act of writing. On the 'Arts Programme' mornings before the car arrived to take him to the studio to record he would scream in terror, crying hysterically. The animal sounds would stop as soon as the driver rang the doorbell.

His radio producer was understanding, giving me the running orders in advance so I could write Sheridan's script and rehearse it with him, over and over again, until he could deliver it without stumbling. Sheridan, who before his stroke and depression could ad-lib an entire show without a single 'er' or 'um', now had to be rehearsed in a script someone else had written and force himself into a studio to deliver it in small pieces when he was so afraid he could hardly walk.

One morning when he had a show at Broadcasting House, I put his pills on the breakfast table in front of him and went off to get his script for just one more run through. When I returned a few seconds later he said, 'Where are my pills?'

I said, 'There, on the table.'

But they weren't. I knew he'd taken them but he was convinced that he hadn't.

At about 11 a.m., I got a stricken call from his producer, 'Ruth, we hate to worry you but Sheridan has collapsed in the studio and we can't wake him. We've called an ambulance and they're taking him to University College Hospital. Will you go under your own steam or should we send a car for you?' I knew immediately what had happened. I said, 'Don't worry. He'll be fine. Sorry to give you all this trouble. Silly sod, he's taken his pills twice.'

And so he had. When I got to the casualty department of the hospital, they had him in what they call a 'crash' room, where they only put the worst traumas, heart attacks and strokes – patients in danger of imminent death. No matter what they did, they couldn't wake him. The doctors and nurses were, I think, somewhat shocked by my cavalier attitude. I told them exactly what he was on, a cocktail of antidepressants, antipsychotics and anti-everything else in dosages that were already well in excess of the drug companies' recommended amounts. They didn't believe me, didn't believe the amounts he was taking and didn't believe that the coma-like reaction they were seeing could have been caused just by his taking his pills twice.

Sheridan was a big man, even antihistamines for hay fever had to be taken in industrial quantities, and he was already resistant to the drugs he had now been taking for most of his adult life so the doctors had worked out that his body absorbed medication to the extent that overdosing was the only way they could work. As a result, he was at the limit of how much he could take and still function even at a minimal level.

Now he'd taken twice as many, almost all at once. Sheridan had taken the following day's pills rather than leave himself vulnerable to the possibility that he would be without the crutch that would get him through the show. By the time I got to the hospital they'd already given him an MRI and were embarking on a series of diagnostic tests. They took all day. I waited patiently while they panicked and then looked at my watch. 'He'll be fine,' I kept saying to the nurses. 'Just let him sleep it off. I'll be back later.' And they stared disbelievingly at my disappearing back, appalled that a wife could be so callous as to leave her seriously ill husband without a diagnosis when he was nearly dead.

But the fact was that I had a show to review for us both and had already delayed long enough that I was in danger of missing it. I'd seen the overdose before and knew that unless his heart gave out under the strain of all those drugs, which would have happened much earlier if it was going to happen at all, he'd be back to what passed for normal by morning.

I returned to the hospital after the play and he was still asleep. No change there then. All the tests had proved negative. They had to keep him in overnight because he still wouldn't wake up. When I arrived at 8 a.m. the following day to pick him up he was munching toast and complaining that they'd woken him much too early. The staff of the casualty department at University College Hospital were, I think, happy to see the back of both of us.

I couldn't bear watching his misery, seeing him suffer was pain I hope never to repeat. So I dragged him from quack to quack, shrink to shrink, but also from fine doctor to fine doctor with massive reputations. I'd have willingly transported him to Mars if I'd heard of a little green man who knew how to cure depression. They all tried, including a daft collection of well-meaning NHS therapists in an assortment of dreadful cardigans, who watched us from behind a two-way mirror and then had us listen to them as they discussed us, earnestly but with total incomprehension, before reversing yet again to watch us. Sick and miserable though he was, even Sheridan thought this game of non-musical chairs was hilarious and it lightened the depression for several hours as, back home, we tried to work out what they thought they were achieving.

He went to each doctor willingly enough, convinced that each would be the one with the miracle cure. I had read enough to know that the patient needs to have a direct relationship with the doctor so each time I tried to get him to go alone or at least to let me wait outside but he wouldn't go without me and I had to be there with him when he talked to the doctor. 'You can explain it so much better,' was his excuse but the truth was that he wanted them to know how much he hurt without having to tell them.

When he did speak to them it would be one of his endless circular stories, whichever one he was using that day. 'I wouldn't be ill if I could live on a beach where nobody could "get" to me,' or, 'The BBC is going to fire me because I'm ill,' or, 'They want me to work

91

too hard, don't they know I'm ill?' or, 'I've got to retire, I don't want to work anymore,' or, 'I've got to work harder, I'm just wasting time being ill,' or, 'I don't want to write journalism anymore, I just want to write books,' or, 'I only want to write journalism from now on, no books, it's too hard.'

There was another set of rants, even more contradictory and personal. 'I love my children but they hate me because I left their mother,' or, 'I hate my children because they only love their mother, they never loved me,' or 'God [the same one he didn't believe in] is punishing me for loving Ruth and leaving Margaret,' or, 'God is punishing me for not being a good father,' and then back to 'I want to live on a beach . . .' So it went on, words pouring from him, each sentence perfectly formed and articulated like the first-rate broad-caster he was, making sense only if it wasn't attached to the one that came before or after.

I had heard it all before. Many times. The truth is that, much of the time, I was bored to screaming point. It would have been lovely if I could have had an hour off while he was in the consulting room to read a book or go shopping but he wouldn't let me off, I had to be there, as back-up, I guess, while he reiterated everything he had now been saying for several years. Once, I actually fell asleep during a session with one of the psychiatrists. I didn't doubt that, each time, he believed what he was saying, but the doctors didn't see him later when he would say exactly the opposite, meaning it just as much.

The months merged into one another until now I can't remember who he was seeing when or which events happened in which years. It was endless and seemed set to continue for the rest of our lives.

The doctors in turn listened, said very little, prescribed more drugs. Sometimes, on those nights when he frightened himself so badly with his ceaseless fears and torments that I couldn't calm him, I would buy myself a few hours of peace by giving him half a

Lorazepam that knocked him out for the night and most of the following day. One of the doctors, I forget which, had prescribed them and I used them sparingly, but I used them. Another prescribed an antipsychotic which worked but which turned him into a zombie, unable to function or respond. It is a measure of how sick he was and how tired I was that we were grateful for both.

Once, in desperation, Dr Morrish had reluctantly prescribed Dexedrine for Sheridan to try to jar him out of his depression. For two weeks, two blessed weeks, it worked. Sheridan went overnight from depressed to manic and, believe me, manic was preferable. For a week he answered his own phone, went willingly to the theatre, wrote reams of articles, took on new work, talked to me, to our staff and to everybody else, ate properly and was able to wash and dress himself without incident. The only fly in the ointment was that he didn't sleep. Not at all. Not one hour.

And then, as Leslie Morrish had warned that he might, he crashed again, worse than ever. Now he was really suicidal and almost totally non-functional. Dexedrine is a dangerous drug, on a restricted list, and was never intended to be a long-term solution but it had been worth a try. At that point, anything was worth a try. However, the commuting to and from Windsor to see Dr Morrish was becoming impossible. Of course, Peter could have taken him but he wouldn't go without me so, without cutting him off from the Cardinal, we needed a doctor closer to home for regular visits.

We were recommended to one with a pristine reputation who worked in a pretty Chelsea townhouse and was affiliated with the Priory. Elegant, birdlike and tiny, her cut-glass voice is precise and she wastes neither movement nor words. She is a psycho-pharmacologist, a specialist in treating mental illness with the judicious application of different drugs in different dosages. It's like a recipe – every cake requires butter, sugar and flour, but too much flour and the cake won't rise, too much sugar and it's too dense, too much butter and it won't adhere. Each patient is different so the dosages are as much a matter of art as science.

Her job was to find not only the right drugs in the right combination but also in the right amounts. It's incredibly difficult and she worked with Sheridan for months, trying to find the appropriate medications for him. She was cool and professional, withstanding the worst excesses of Sheridan's long perorations, listening to him for the whole session with patience before dealing with the medication which was, after all, what she was there to do. I don't know how many different drug therapies she tried. Nothing worked.

Had I been less upset I might have found his latest obsession amusing. Sheridan suddenly decided that he should be living in her pretty Chelsea townhouse and went on and on about how he wouldn't be ill if he could live there and so, obviously, since he couldn't afford to buy it because all his employers hated him, she should give it to him. I don't remember whether he ever mentioned this to her but he wrote many pages of letters to me on the subject. After the first few times, when this turned into another regular rant ('*Why* won't she give me the house? She knows I'm ill, she's my doctor, you'd think she'd do it without asking.'), I no longer bothered to tell him that, in common with many other doctors, she didn't own her consulting room and merely rented it to see patients in a couple of times a week.

He became convinced that, since electric shock treatment had worked for him when he was first in the Cardinal, all those years ago, he should have it again. His psychiatrist was not in favour but, to my surprise, she was not entirely against it, as I was. She explained that, although it was now administered in a hospital in the safest possible circumstances, medical professionals still don't know how it works and it is akin to kicking an old-fashioned television set. Sometimes the 'snow' clears, sometimes it doesn't. If it does, the patient thinks it's a miracle.

Sheridan became so insistent that she agreed to send him to another doctor at the Priory for a second opinion on the ECT question. The other doctor, who I sensed was also not very keen on the therapy, nonetheless agreed that it was another avenue to try to lift the depression since nothing else seemed to work. I tried hard to talk Sheridan out of it because the most common side-effect of the treatment was memory loss. In a business where almost everything is carried in your head – who starred in what play in which year under which director, or which anecdote goes with which actor in what scenario in which location – and where all these facts have to be produced on the spur of the moment, on live radio, for example, or on the lecture platform, the memory is in some ways the most important organ of the body.

I knew that there had been some minor memory loss when he had gone through the treatment at the Cardinal although most of his memory had returned. But he had been much younger then and there had been less to remember. My worry was that Sheridan's prodigious recall for all things theatrical would be severely impaired and with it his confidence in his ability to do his jobs.

I had never had an exceptional memory and, once a fact had been used for its intended purpose in an article or book, I routinely forgot it, knowing I could look it up again if I ever needed it. Married to Sheridan, though, I got worse, not bothering to commit stuff to memory because he remembered everything and everybody. Following his stroke, though, he had suffered some lapses where he hadn't known who someone was or what they had recently appeared in. I sharpened up so I could fill in the gaps. My fears about what would happen if ECT destroyed his ability to recall what he needed when he needed it proved only too prescient.

Chapter Eighteen

*W*hen Sheridan went to live in my little rented flat in Regent's Park, I was mostly in New York or haring off across Europe for PolyGram and we saw very little of one another. But we spoke often and wrote letters. They varied enormously depending on his mental state at the time. Most were loving and warm, full of theatre news, jokes, gossip, reviews and the kind of writing that made the readers of his books love him forever. Some, though, were full of darkness and fear, self-doubt, anger and his conviction that nobody loved him.

As it happened, I loved him. Very much. Despite all my protestations, my conviction that Sheridan was 'just' a friend, albeit a very good friend, was swept away. After twenty-five years of friendship, I finally fell in love with him, although it took another ten years before I agreed to marry him. I realized that beneath the theatricality, under the bravado and apparent confidence, there was a good and loving man struggling not to show it. He wanted simply to be loved and simply, I loved him. Not, I think, as he loved me.

Sheridan had an enormous capacity for love and he lavished it on me. He begged me to let him look after me. I knew that he had no more idea of what he was promising than our cat. Our relationship was complex and profound. We had hurt a lot of people, not least *our first spouses, and we both had a sort of desperation to make our relationship 'worth' their pain. He wanted love and I gave it to him without clearly understanding what it was I was taking on.*

Sheridan needed a level of reassurance all his adult life (and, for all I know, all his childhood, too) that it was impossible to give. He needed to be told over and over again that he was right, that he was good, that his work was worthwhile, that he wasn't boring, that his jokes were funny, that he was liked. Sometimes I got through to him on those grounds but it was my failure that I could never convince him, no matter how often I told him so, that he was loved.

When his self-esteem dropped below critical mass he went manic or 'high', which is what the psychiatrists call it. They mainly describe a 'chemical imbalance' which can be corrected with drugs but it's more than that. Or it was in his case. His view of himself, always shaky, would take a beating in some way. Maybe he had lost a job he thought he should have had or been at odds with his colleagues about a play or been snubbed by someone for whom he'd done a kindness. On one occasion an unscrupulous producer had used a line from a review he had written of a song composed for an upcoming show as the marquee advertisement for the show itself. When the show opened it turned out to be dreadful, albeit with some good songs. Several of the other critics ribbed him about it. Instead of laughing, Sheridan was distraught: 'I'll never work again. Nobody will ever believe my reviews. I'm finished.'

Sometimes it was a slight, invisible to the human eye or, at any rate, to mine, but he felt things so deeply that it was enough to send him over the edge, especially as his public persona and his essential Englishness would not allow him to complain to whoever had insulted or ignored him.

Publicly, he just bashed on regardless, hiding the hurt, pretending everything was fine, his apparent insensitivity and obliviousness to insult masking a nature so sensitive that sooner, rather than later, his demand for reassurance would take him 'high'. He would tell his jokes too loudly, begging for the reassurance that he had entertained us, he would go on a present-buying spree he couldn't afford, hoping to be recognized as the generous-hearted man he was, and he would take on more and more work just so that he could demonstrate how diligent he was and how professionally worthwhile.

When we finally did get to live together in Regent's Park his problems regarding his self-esteem, mismanagement of money and desire to be loved began to emerge. His misplaced energy and need for reassurance was tiring to be around. He would be up all night talking, at me, rather than with me, or writing his long letters to me. Sometimes this phase lasted a few days, usually a couple of weeks before he crashed into deep depression. I didn't understand what I was looking at and just thought he was being particularly annoying.

It didn't occur to me that these 'highs' were anything other than Sheridan being Sheridan. He was, during this period, having a hard time with his ex-wife and was feeling very conflicted about his children with whom he was constitutionally incapable of discussing any part of his decision to leave their mother. These seemed to me good and sufficient reasons for him to try to forget his troubles in work, excessive shopping and storytelling so I didn't weigh in at all. I thought that he had to sort out his family relationships himself, believing too that my interference would do nothing but harm to his children who I thought, more than he did, needed to feel protected by him rather than by us. All bad decisions on my part, as it turned out. As a result, early in our relationship there were several bouts of severe manic depression that I simply failed to recognize until it was too late and he'd fallen from high to deepest low.

I blamed myself. I still do, because I could perhaps have saved him a lot of pain if I'd been looking in the right direction and not working so selfishly hard. On the other hand, as a veteran of dozens of these episodes, I now recognize that I neither caused this illness nor could cure it. *It actually had nothing to do with me and I wish I'd known this then.*

Fortunately, at that time he always recovered, due to a succession of good doctors and psychiatrists who listened to him for hours and then prescribed the antidepressants. One of the best was the chief GP at the Marylebone Health Centre opposite our London flat. Patrick Pietroni was not just a physician, he was also a major practitioner in homeopathic medicine and a trained psychiatrist.

After having treated Sheridan for some time, it was he who first told me, 'He is like a sponge. He has never had enough attention and now nobody, not even you, can give him as much as he needs.' There were many times in the next twenty years when I repeated that to myself like a mantra, usually after I had left Sheridan, still talking after hours of insistence on my undivided attention, to grab a few hours' sleep. He could never get enough attention or enough approval or enough reassurance. But I did try.

I have often wondered whether this chronic need for more and more attention was inherited from his father, Robert, or just a consequence of being Robert's son. I saw for myself how, when Robert was home at Fairmans, the floor was always his. Those Sunday lunches were ruled by Robert and everyone else had to wait their turn to speak, including, perhaps especially, his children. Sheridan admired Robert immoderately, believing, wrongly I think, that Robert lived his life on his own terms and according to his own choices. Sheridan, until quite late in his life, certainly until after Robert died, wanted more than anything to emulate him, to be him. That may be why he married so young, why he moved to Berkshire near his parents, why he had three children when he had so little interest in and connection with them. Maybe he was just trying to become his father.

It infuriated him that fame and fortune, which he thought Robert achieved effortlessly, eluded him. In fact, Sheridan was as successful in his own fields of broadcasting and journalism as his father was in films and in the theatre but he always felt he was trying and failing to catch up with Robert.

The recurring bouts of depression notwithstanding, Sheridan and I settled into our life together and it was, when he wasn't ill, wonderful. We wrote, we travelled, we lectured, we broadcast. We saw friends and colleagues, gave parties, ate out, ate in. We lived. We laughed. We completed one another. One of our jokes was that I was broad and he was deep. In many ways, it was true. I knew a little about a lot of things – history, science, languages, painting, politics, economics. It was a sketchy but wide-ranging grab-bag of bits and pieces which served us well in that I could usually get us out of whatever scrapes he got us into.

What Sheridan knew, he knew everything about. He was more than an expert in his fields of theatre, film, books and journalism: he was a master. He read the arts pages of five daily newspapers and could remember everything he read on his subjects. He amassed the best theatre library in private hands but rarely had to consult any of his books as their contents were embedded in his brain. On the other hand, he was the single most unworldly person I have ever met, and this led to financial problems.

We were always broke. Sheridan consistently spent more than he earned, on presents for me and for his children, on CDs and books, on gadgets and on souvenirs, never on anything with lasting value. Four times he nearly bankrupted us. He spent every penny I had earned in a lifetime of working and saving.

I've always been quite careful with money and by that I don't mean cheap. I earned well from the time I first went to the United States, and Michael and I almost never needed to talk about money. We arranged our finances fairly between us and, while there was no extravagance, we never lacked for anything we really wanted. In Washington we both had cars, travelled often and comfortably, and entertained lavishly. I started my life with Sheridan with a good job and substantial savings. I can never remember being broke until I was living with him. He spent like a drunken sailor, thought nothing of taking ten friends or acquaintances to the Ivy, had no concept of what anything cost. He once told me, when informed that he didn't need whatever it was he had brought home because he already had one, 'Darling, you don't understand. If I want it, I need it.'

He kept asking me to marry him and I kept refusing until nearly ten years later, in the mid 1990s, in California. We were sitting in our rented car outside the beautiful house his grandmother Gladys Cooper used to have in Pacific Palisades, talking about the latest of our perennial financial crises. Sheridan had shown me the house by the simple expedient of walking up to the front door and ringing the bell. A very nice Englishman, a dealer in grand cars such as Rolls-Royce and Jaguar, had bought it and was chuffed to meet Gladys' grandson. He invited us in and showed Sheridan all the renovations he had made to return it to its original state in Gladys' time. He gave us lunch and the grand tour and it was nearly dark when we left him.

Why, demanded Sheridan as we walked back to the car along the path between the orange trees that Gladys had planted, hadn't he done something sensible like deal in used cars instead of becoming a journalist and being 'poor'? If he'd done that, he moaned, we'd be rich and we'd be able to afford a house with orange trees in Pacific Palisades. I pointed out, for the millionth time, that we weren't poor but broke, that we'd be an awful lot richer if he'd stop spending all our money on houses we couldn't afford and other rubbish, and that in any case he'd have loathed being a second-hand car dealer, no matter how posh the cars. I reminded him that London theatre critics can't live in Pacific Palisades, with or without orange trees, and that we were quite happy as we were but that it would be nice if we didn't have to be broke forever.

That evening, for the first time, instead of changing the subject, he talked about money as though it were a real and necessary commodity.

We had no savings. We had no pensions. When he and Margaret had divorced he had made over to her his pension rights and his life insurance. What money came from his share of T'Gallant House went into the flat he insisted on buying in Chelsea Harbour and into which we had moved from the flat in Regent's Park. Now he had moved us into a house in Chelsea Harbour that we couldn't afford and took all his money and all mine, as well as a mortgage. It was an idiotic purchase for a couple of working journalists.

This time, Sheridan was asking me to marry him because he had worked out that we couldn't take care of one another if we weren't married. There had been several occasions on which doctors and hospital staff had refused to give me information about his condition when he had been an in-patient because I wasn't a relative. He was worried that one day perhaps life or death decisions would have to be made and that medical personnel would not let me make them if I were not his wife.

Also, he had belatedly realized that I had put all my savings into the Chelsea Harbour house at his insistence and that if he died tomorrow, the house, our only asset, would go to his children and I would be destitute. It is not very romantic to admit that this purely pecuniary and practical argument was the one that convinced me to marry him when all his love and loyalty had not, but there it is. So there, on a beautiful California evening, we got engaged, some ten years after we became lovers, and more than thirty years after we had met.

Chapter Nineteen

There was no question of Sheridan returning to the Cardinal for his ECT as his doctor of record was affiliated to the Priory. Besides, I rationalized, the Priory was close to where we lived and it would be much easier for me to go back and forth if I didn't have to drive to Windsor each time.

Sheridan was now in a state that can only be described, not medically but functionally, as catatonic. He didn't get out of bed for days or weeks unless I was able to convince him over several hours of yelling and cajoling that he had an appointment that could not, absolutely could not, be missed. I did what I could about his personal hygiene but I could rarely get him out of bed long enough to change his sheets and he would only shower if he was getting dressed, which was rare. I moved into the spare room most nights but every time he turned over I heard him and ran back into the bedroom to ensure that he was still breathing. When out of bed he would sit with his head bowed, unmoving and unseeing. He spoke only to tell me (and anyone else present) how sick he was, a fact that was blindingly obvious to everybody.

Eventually, despite my misgivings and hers, his doctor and I agreed that we might as well give in to his demands for ECT and admitted him to the Priory. His stay there was a horror story from the first moment to the last.

The room which Sheridan was assigned stank of stale smoke so strongly that he burst into tears immediately. 'Take me home, don't abandon me here,' he begged me, sobbing. Only when his doctor arrived and asserted her authority did the room clerk agree to move him. The second room was better but unclean and without basic amenities. He was to start his twice-weekly ECT the following Monday and needed preparation, so taking him home until there was a more suitable room wasn't an option.

When I left him with his doctor, he was crying piteously, and I reluctantly drove home, terribly distressed. She thought he might settle better if I left because then there would be no possibility of his going home. There was nobody around in the wing to which he was assigned, no nurses, no aides, no patients. In the garden outside his window were a few lost-looking souls, wandering unattended, smoking. Nobody seemed to be in charge. But this, after all, was the famous Priory and I reasoned that they were just having a bad afternoon. I'd be there again the next day and on Monday the highly trained staff would take care of him.

I can't do better than to reproduce here two of the letters I wrote to the director, one when Sheridan was still a patient and undergoing treatment, the other after I had removed him.

Dear Sirs

My husband, Sheridan Morley, has been a patient in the Priory for the past four weeks and his doctor, — thinks he should remain there for another two weeks to complete the course of ECT that he has started.

I have, since his admission, been concerned about his care in the Priory. I emphasize that I do not, of course, mean

his medical care, but the level of indifference and carelessness on the nursing and administration side has given rise
to considerable worry. My husband is suffering from acute
and profound depression. He is left, for hours every day,
simply to lie on his bed untended, no therapy – physical
or mental – is offered (except for the ECT). There appears
to be no stimulation, little personal interaction, no exercise
and no encouragement for him to participate in his own
recovery. He is now so weak that he can barely walk.

When he arrived, frightened and seriously ill, he was
taken to a room that reeked of old cigarettes. Physically
nauseated, he begged to be taken home. He was moved
to a dimly lit room with a broken wardrobe, a distorted
bathroom mirror, and old Blu-tack on the walls where,
presumably, pictures once were. In the garden, things are
not much better. There are no ashtrays anywhere on the
grounds which are carpeted with cigarette butts.

He was admitted on a Friday. The admitting nurse asked
a number of questions and filled out her form, but nobody
offered to show him around or to point out the facilities
(if there are any) then or at any other time. This simple
act of kindness might have alleviated his fears and made
him less upset to have been 'abandoned' there. Over that
and all subsequent weekends the wing has appeared to be
mostly deserted and staffed with agency nurses who take
care of the most basic duties and do not, obviously, know
the patients.

On Monday he had his first ECT and a therapist left a
schedule in his room which gave him activities on Monday
and Friday, the days of ECT, suggesting that there is no
coordination between the staff. At no time has this therapist or any other come to his room to encourage him to

participate in any activity at all. Without professional involvement, as I'm sure you know, a deeply depressed person will not have the volition to do anything which could be of value to himself.

Until I insisted that he be accompanied to the dining room, my diabetic husband was left to fend for himself among the fatty, sugary, carbohydrate-laden foods on offer. His blood sugar levels went up and his stable diabetes became temporarily unstable. This is a man who, as his key nurse knew, had already had one stroke as a direct consequence of unstable diabetes. Surely this should have been addressed before I asked?

After four weeks, nothing has improved and his doctor agrees that my husband is not responding to treatment as we had hoped he would. As a social being and a public man, he needs and craves company, is at his best when he has someone to talk to, at his worst when left alone, and too ill to seek that company himself.

This week, during ECT, someone made a mistake and my husband's tongue, inadequately protected, was almost bitten through. It turned black and it has been painful for him to talk all week. This seems to me emblematic of the carelessness with which this patient, in your care, is treated. This, on top of everything else, and the illness itself, has brought him to a level of despair which is frightening . . . he is always asleep, unwashed, undressed, his room untidy. The nurses assure me that he is up in the mornings and I am sure it is true, but my own experience is that he returns to bed as soon as he can and stays there. Surely somebody on your staff should be addressing this rather than treating him as a parcel to be warehoused and protected but not cared for?

I believe that my husband is neglected in the Priory, not deliberately but because that is just the way you do things. I am sure that you too do not want my husband's final weeks in the Priory to be as miserable as the first weeks. Please let me know what you are doing to redress the situation.

Sincerely

Ruth Leon Morley

Dear Mr Smith

When I met with Dr — and Mr — to address some of the concerns I raised in my letter to your office they did try to reassure me as to the care of my husband. As a result of my various complaints, voiced regularly to the staff from the start of the five weeks that he was in your charge, Mr — agreed that more personal care was required and it was somewhat provided during the time he remained with you. Does it not seem to you symptomatic of precisely the lack of attention that I complained to you about that, despite having voiced my concerns from the beginning, this meeting with the Ward Manager of my husband's wing was the very first time I had ever laid eyes on Mr — or even heard his name?

I decided to remove my husband from the Priory, partly because he had become appreciably more ill there, partly because I was not convinced that his insurance would continue to cover him indefinitely at your rates, and partly because he was so terribly unhappy there. He is now recovering at another facility, having been considerably traumatized by the experience at the Priory.

Your assumption that 'all the concerns you raised in your letter were addressed to your satisfaction' is unfounded.

Dr —, for whom I have nothing but the greatest respect, and Mr — were trying to step up the care for my husband only, care that should have been offered from day one. You have many other patients. For the sake of your reputation and particularly the well-being of the other ill people at the Priory, I hope you will take a less complacent attitude to very real systemic care problems in your facility, or at least, in the one wing where I was an anxious and interested observer. Treating one patient slightly better because his wife complains does *not* amount to addressing the concerns I raised. And certainly not 'to my satisfaction'.

Yours sincerely

Ruth Leon Morley

There was no response at all to this second letter. I should, of course, in the interests of the other patients, have carried this Priory story further. I should have sued them for neglect or at least written a series of articles exposing the real story of Sheridan's time there but I didn't. My only excuse is that I had a terribly sick husband and he was my priority. Everything else came a long way behind his needs.

His doctor thought he should complete the course of twelve ECTs and, in the event, he had eleven. It didn't work. He emerged with his memory permanently impaired, his tongue damaged from being burned by the probe, his confidence shattered, his diabetes at crisis level and his depression intact. He was no longer making sense at all. He was either asleep or in tears. I knew that if I took him home he would attempt to kill himself if he could summon the energy and I couldn't take the chance that he wouldn't when my back was turned or I'd gone to the loo. Trying to look after him at home was a gamble I couldn't take. I called Dr Morrish at the Cardinal Clinic, explained the situation, and asked if he would admit him. I told him frankly that Sheridan was at the very end of his BUPA benefits, having used them up in the series of doctors and clinics over the past year and that I didn't know how I was going to pay for his care. I said I could pay for the out-of-pocket costs such as the doctors and drugs but that his room and board were beyond me. 'Don't worry,' came the reassuring words. 'Bring him here. We'll look after him.'

I drove Sheridan directly to the Cardinal where the nurses cleaned him up, got him dressed in clean clothes, fed him something nourishing, and, most importantly, talked gently and reassuringly to him until he stopped crying and began to respond. At the Priory the staff had never even made him take a shower, let alone talked to him, and although his Aunt Sally and I had wrestled him into the bathroom once or twice he would just stand for a minute in the hot water with his eyes closed and go back to bed, wet and soapy. Slowly, after several weeks in Windsor, he returned to normal – a very low and depressed normal, to be sure – but recognizably Sheridan.

Back home, he wouldn't go back to see his doctor in Chelsea – he blamed her quite unfairly for his frightening and unhappy experience in the Priory. He was beyond reasoning. He took the pills that Leslie Morrish had prescribed and he did whatever work he could manage, including his radio show more often than not. He was valiant.

There was even a grisly fortnight where he and Michael Law performed a sold-out run at the King's Head Theatre in Islington. Dan Crawford, who ran the theatre and who was a good friend of Sheridan, had somehow acquired an odd little man who claimed to be a producer and who wanted to programme a season of cabaret starting with Michael and Sheridan's Noël Coward show.

Sheridan was virtually non-functional in what was laughingly known as real life but he could, with the help and support of Michael, me, and Michael's long-time partner, Alan, just about function onstage. In fact, that was where he was most alive. Knowing this,

I agreed – frankly, we needed the money, which was pretty good. Inevitably, there were some mishaps. One day Sheridan fell off the stage and hurt his back, on another he went out for a newspaper and came back to a frantic Michael several hours later because he had become disoriented and lost. Michael said later that the worst part would have been having to admit to me that he'd lost Sheridan on his watch. Somehow they got through the fortnight, fulfilled their responsibility to Dan and waited for the cheque. Which never came.

It turned out that the dubious producer took the money from the Noël Coward box office to pay for a Jacques Brel show which was a total failure. At another, earlier, happier time, Sheridan would have roared with laughter, said, 'That's show business', and picked up another lucrative job the following week. As it was, he didn't even notice, not even when Michael took the producer to the Musicians' Union on a grievance and got him banned for life

Sheridan became angrier. He realized that he had not only lost his short-term memory due to the ECT, he had lost himself, his sense of who he was and had been. Worse, for me, was that he had lost his sense of humour, the most priceless gift he had. His humour, so singular, so off-the-wall, had saved us throughout our life together, the subtlety of his sideways looks at the world and the quickness of his reactions had been at the heart of our marriage. I've always maintained that all a man needs to captivate and hold a woman is brains and humour. If he's smart and can make me laugh, I'm his. I was still Sheridan's and he was mine, but his brains were buried deep inside his misery and his sense of humour had gone forever. If he was angry, so was I, just not as angry nor so unable to control it.

Something about the pills affected his appetite and it was now difficult to get him to eat. He lost a huge amount of weight, nearly three stone, and, although he was by now completely dependent on me, he was furious that he was so needy and consequently fought me every inch of the way. If I said we had to be somewhere at seven o'clock he'd deliberately delay us so that we would be late and I would have to make excuses when we arrived. Then he'd use me for a verbal punching bag whenever he was awake and we were alone. His passive aggression at every level increased and he was working against us at every turn.

The letters he left on my dressing table got more vicious, more accusatory. They hurt, every one of them, even though I knew it was his illness talking. The fatigue which now accompanied me everywhere was deepening into despair. I couldn't make him better, I couldn't make him more comfortable, I couldn't stop his pain. I was useless. I was still dragging him from doctor to doctor, sure there was a cure somewhere; it was just that I hadn't found it yet.

He was becoming impossible to live with and so, I expect, was I. All 'conversations' ended with disputes or out-and-out rows. I would promise myself at the beginning of every day that no matter what he said or wrote to or about me, I would not react, I would not become upset, I would not shout, I would not let the argument deteriorate into a row.

I failed with every one of these resolutions. Sheridan always knew how to push my buttons and he did it now compulsively and reflexively. If there was no disagreement he would invent one and then berate me for it. I should have known better, I was the one who wasn't ill, but I never learned not to let him provoke me and he never learned not to do it. He seemed only to feel alive when he was expressing his resentment and anger at his situation. There was nothing coming back from him except waves of misery and anger.

Occasionally, I would suggest an outing, more, if I am honest, to get myself out of the house than for his benefit. They always ended in one kind of disaster or another. If we went out to eat, he sat with his head down and he never spoke at all. After staring at the top of his head for an hour-and-a-half I would inevitably say something like, 'Can't you make any kind of effort? I might as well be here on my own.' He would raise his head briefly, try to focus his eyes and ask whether we could go home. Guilt for me, misery for him.

I organized a trip to the Victoria and Albert Museum because they had an exhibition of art nouveau, one of the few visual arts periods he really liked. He wouldn't look at anything in the exhibition but while I looked he went into the museum shop and spent hundreds of pounds. He then put his purchases in two carrier bags which he placed carefully behind the dining table and never opened again. It was the shopping he liked, not the purchases. Perhaps I should have been more sympathetic: if the shopping gave him ease, even temporary ease, maybe I should just have let him get on with it but money was tight and I knew he didn't want the things he bought.

We were occasionally invited to his friends, the Matthews, for Sunday lunch. There, he made a sort of effort but his exhaustion when we got home would sometimes last for days. They were very kind to him – Christopher Matthew really loved him – but Sheridan's difficulty in focusing made visiting a problematic operation. Only with my sister and cousins, and his Aunt Sally, did he seem able to relax a little but it was obvious to everybody that he was not well. What stood him in good stead in public – his ability to put on a show no matter how he was feeling – operated against him in private company so that even with his best friends, and Christopher Matthew was certainly that, he felt the need to entertain.

Sheridan had now been continuously depressed for more than two years, except for the brief period when Dr Morrish had put him on Dexedrine. I was so sad and discouraged that I didn't know how I was going to go on. I couldn't bear seeing him so unhappy but I was on duty twenty-four hours a day, seven days a week and I had no choice but to watch him deteriorate into a person I didn't know.

This man I had loved and laughed with, this wonderful man I had worked and played with, this amazing man who had changed and enriched my life, was a stranger.

And I was turning into a shrew. Strain and hopelessness were making me bad-tempered, critical and unpleasant. I made Sheridan's life even harder than it already was by trying to force him to return to some degree of normal behaviour in the hope that if he behaved as though things were normal, they would slowly become so. If I didn't recognize him, it was also true that I didn't recognize myself in this nasty rat-on-a-treadmill that I had become.

Proactive as I am by nature, I had run out of things to try.

Chapter Twenty

*W*e found out we could write together quite by accident in 1998. Our house in Chelsea had five floors. On the very top was a big room (which Sheridan predictably called 'the big room') that was Sheridan's domain. It had a lovely view of the Thames, a balcony on either end, lots of windows and books from floor to ceiling. June Mendoza painted a stunning portrait of Sheridan sitting at his desk, feet bare, hair tousled, in front of his beloved elderly typewriter, surrounded by books, papers, records and the other tools of his trade. In the painting, a copy of which hangs over my New York desk, he looks happy. He looks as though he's where he's meant to be. He loved that room.

My study was on the floor below, light and cheerful, and full of my much-loved electronic equipment – televisions, screens, editing machines, computers – and lots of books. I rarely ventured upstairs to the big room because Sheridan would often wander down to mine, on his way to his own room or to the kitchen, three floors below. Thus it was that he was able to write a book a year without my really knowing what his working method was.

Then, one day, after a particularly frantic period of work and travel, when I hadn't paid enough attention to his shopping or talking levels, I realized that he had crashed, this time very badly. I called the *psychiatrist as usual, bundled Sheridan into the car, and set off for Windsor over his loud protests. I wasn't listening to what he was actually saying – I never did when he was sick – and just prayed that this hospitalization would be brief because we had a lot to do that winter.*

I returned from Windsor through the traffic, furious with him that he'd got sick at just the wrong moment (as if there's ever a right moment). Sheridan's telephone was ringing as I entered the house.

'Sheridan Morley!' demanded an imperious female voice.

'I'm so sorry, he's not here. May I give him a message?'

'Where's my manuscript?' demanded the same voice. 'It's already a month late. The printer's waiting. If we miss this slot God knows when I'll be able to get another. So where the fuck is it?'

I genuinely had no idea who she was or what she was waiting for and was too scared to ask. She was truly terrifying. 'If you'll give me your number, I'll check and get back to you.' I hung up only a little wiser. I called Mike Shaw, Sheridan's agent, a lovely man of a certain vintage, who had been handling Sheridan's books ever since A Talent to Amuse.

'Who is she?' I stammered.

'She's Penny Phillips from Bloomsbury,' he said, naming one of Sheridan's publishers.

'What does she want?' I asked. 'Only Sheridan's had one of his turns and I've taken him to the clinic and it'll be a while before I can ask him myself.'

'Christ!' said this gentle, sweet man who has never been known to swear. 'But it's Penny.'

'Yes', I said, reasonably, 'but he's too sick to talk to at the moment and I don't know what book he's working on, do you?'

'Well,' he said, cautiously, 'it could be the biography of Dirk Bogarde but he's supposed to be finished with that.'

I told him I'd look in Sheridan's study for the finished manuscript and made my way upstairs to the big room. In the middle of the floor, not far from his desk, was an enormous pile, the size of a tepee. It contained books, manuscripts, videos, transcripts, cassettes, all the detritus of researching a book. Everything I picked up from the periphery of the pile related in one way or another to the British film industry circa the 1950s: no question about it, I had located the raw material for the Bogarde biography. The typescript, though, was nowhere to be found in the big room though I looked for the rest of the afternoon. While I searched, the telephone rang and the machine picked up increasingly irate messages from Penny Phillips.

I called Mike Shaw back. 'Well, I've got good news and bad news. He was clearly working on the Bogarde. I've got all the research material in front of me. That's the good news. The bad is that I don't think he'd actually started writing it.'

'Oh, Christ,' he mumbled, 'and I already got him an extra month. She'll skin him alive. If she can't find him, she'll skin me.'

'She's already trying,' I informed him, bringing him up to date with the messages. Wondering whether to ring her back or not, I asked, 'What do you suggest I do?'

'I suggest,' he said, with exaggerated courtesy, 'I strongly suggest you start writing.'

'But,' I spluttered, 'I write about dance and music and drama. I don't know anything about the British film industry circa 1950.'

'In that case,' he said, gently, 'I suggest you start reading that pile. If, that is, you value your life or Sheridan's or, well, mine.'

In the end, I agreed at least to start on the book if he would call Bloomsbury and get me another month from the Dragon Lady.

There was no question of my writing anything on Sheridan's old electric typewriter and the pile was much too big to drag down to my study so I hauled my computer up to the big room, sat on the floor and opened the first transcript. I remembered having had a wonderful English teacher at Arts Ed, Mrs Jack, who stepped into the breach when our monsieur went missing once by staying just one step ahead of us and reading the French lesson she had to teach us just before class. I put her method into practice. Sorting the pile into some kind of chronological logic, I began, to quote The Sound of Music, *at the very beginning, a very good place to start*. I would read the material about his early life, then quickly write it before I forgot it. Then the schooldays, reading first and regurgitating it into some kind of readable prose. And so on.

It was hard graft, and hell on my back, but it worked. Sort of. By the time Sheridan came out of the clinic, some ten days later, I was deep into the Rank Organisation and wondering whether Dirk would ever come out of the closet (he didn't). It was as exciting to me as I hoped it would be to the reader since I literally had no idea what he would do next. When I picked up Sheridan he was still pretty low but I was desperate to involve him in the book. For my sake, not for his. I still didn't know anything about the subject I was writing except what I read five minutes ahead of putting it on the screen. Sheridan, who knew the territory inside and out, was sorely needed.

I wrapped him in a blanket like an Indian chief and sat him on the sofa in the big room. Then I hauled the computer on to a small table in the middle of the pile so I could sit on a proper chair instead of the floor and carried on, only this time I spoke the words aloud as I typed them. He didn't speak at all. Nothing happened for a couple of days and then, on the third, typing furiously, I said something like, 'The cameraman invented a new kind of light to illuminate the left side of Dirk's face which was known as "Dirk's bar",' and from the sofa came a voice.

'He used to call it, "little boy looking at God".'

I stopped typing. 'What?'

'That's what Dirk used to call the left side of his face. The right side, he said, was what they used when he was playing a villain.'

He was back. And better. But, what to do? The first third of the book was now on my computer which Sheridan had not yet learned to use. It was too late for him to start again alone on his typewriter. Also, I had reorganized his tepee pile of research materials and he didn't know where anything was. The following day, without really discussing it, he moved from the sofa to the floor where the pile was, I stayed at the little table typing away, while he found the next piece of the jigsaw to add to the picture of Dirk. When we got to the end we went back to the beginning so that Sheridan could add his own flavour to what I had written, and correct my mistakes and errors of emphasis. He knew so much more than I did about cinema and its history. We took it roughly in turns to speak the book as it was being typed, and whoever was typing would edit as we went along. Editors always commented thereafter about how little editing our books required.

Although we did sometimes write our own single-byline books after that – such as Sheridan's memoirs, Asking for Trouble, his classic biography of John Gielgud, my biography of George Gershwin and my book about New York theatres – we wrote all the other books together. One of us would be on the floor with the research, the other on the keyboard (Sheridan did eventually learn how to type on a computer) bashing away, speaking it out loud, correcting as we went along. We wrote extremely fast, believing that the speed added energy to the book. Also, because Sheridan was a deadline writer, he didn't even start until the deadline began to frighten him and I'd moved from yelling at him to terrified silence, but then he was too professional to miss it by much. Far from setting up conflict within our marriage, writing books was one of the best things we did together, our rhythms matched, as did our sense of what was important to include and exclude. Most days the books moved along on gales of laughter. When the laughter stopped, in a way, so did we.

We were having fun. We were screamingly busy with our regular writing and broadcasting gigs and we would deliberately complicate our lives with various additional projects, things we wanted to try or events we thought would be amusing. We both liked to scare ourselves *professionally by taking on jobs we thought were on the edge of our competence and seeing whether we could do them.*

Sheridan had been commissioned to write a major authorized biography of John Gielgud and was in no hurry to finish it. Sir John would try to chivvy him along by phoning occasionally and I would hear that inimitable fluty voice from across the office, 'How old am I now, dear boy?'

'You're eighteen, Johnnie, and you've just gone to drama school.'

'Oh dear, I'll be dead before you finish this book. Come and have dinner on Thursday at the Garrick and tell me what everybody has said about me.'

That last comment turned out to be prophetic. Sheridan had found that everybody he wished to interview about Sir John wanted to know whether it was going to be published in his lifetime. If 'yes', they'd give him a bunch of clichés; if 'no', they'd tell fascinating, sometimes salacious, stories about what it was like to work and play with the greatest actor of the century. The book went slowly. I don't think Sheridan actually intended not to publish it until after Sir John's death but, in the event, that's what happened.

One day, a famous actor who was one of Sheridan's sources called him to complain that another theatre writer had been asking for an interview about his time with Gielgud, insisting that he was authorized by Sir John to speak with his friends and colleagues. 'I thought you were doing that, Sherry, and now I'm confused as to who I should talk to.'

Sheridan was furious, especially as the publisher of the second biography was one of Sheridan's own publishers. It turned out that Sir John, by this time getting rather forgetful and keen for a quiet life, had agreed to a careerography. So, although he didn't intend to authorize two books the fact was that he had. Although Sheridan's book, John G., got lots of attention and was a bestseller, he felt bruised and betrayed by both his fellow writer and his sometime publisher,

Methuen. He soon got over it – Sheridan never carried a grudge. He was, without a doubt, the least malicious person I ever knew.

There was a spectacular bash at the Theatre Museum in Covent Garden for the launch of John G. *the day after my sister and I had returned from a trip to China. I had bought a bright red and gold Chinese jacket in the Forbidden City to wear at the party. I probably looked like a traffic light but I loved that jacket and it seemed somehow bright enough and theatrical enough for the by now late Sir John Gielgud.*

At some point during the party I saw Sheridan deep in conversation with his friend Dan Crawford from the King's Head pub theatre. Over dinner at the Ivy he told me what they had been discussing. 'Darling, would you object if I wanted to direct a play? One of Noël's?' Other than his already-jammed schedule I not only had no objection, I was enthusiastic. Nobody on earth knew as much as Sheridan about Coward and we'd recently seen several appalling productions of Noël's plays. It was time someone who knew them and loved them directed them.

Sheridan was not a first-time director. He'd done his own Noël and Gertie *in several versions and had enormous fun directing* The Jermyn Street Revue *for his friend Penny Horner who runs the Jermyn Street Theatre. But in every case he had been working with actors who were friends – Annabel Leventon, John Watts, Frank Thornton, Judy Campbell, Thelma Ruby and others – and who would gently correct him if he tried to make them enter through a window or forgot from what side of the stage they had exited. Now he was discussing not a revue but a grown-up production of a grown-up play with grown-up actors who wouldn't give him the benefit of the doubt.*

The play he chose was one of a set of three in which Noël himself had starred with Lili Palmer and Irene Worth in 1966. They were his last plays, which hadn't been done since. Two were simply unplayable, too old-fashioned and too full of attitudes nobody would recognize today, but A Song at Twilight *was different. It was a heartfelt three-hander about a successful writer whose late-life peace is shattered by the arrival of an old girlfriend threatening to drag him unwillingly out of the closet.*

Noël always said that the central character, Hugo Latymer, was based on W. Somerset Maugham and his tortured homosexuality but it was also undoubtedly about Noël himself; it was an open plea for tolerance from a time when 'deviant sexual behaviour', as it was known, was still illegal. I read it, liked it very much, and we started to think about casting.

Obviously, the role of Hugo was the important centre of the play but the two women – his wife and his old girlfriend – had to be played by major actors, too. In a play with only three characters, all must be strong and able to hold their own or the performance is unbalanced. Naturally, Sheridan immediately suggested his old friends, those actors he had worked with before and had known since Oxford. Dan Crawford vetoed that. He said that the prospect of a 'new' Coward play was not a sufficient draw to bring the West End critics to an Islington pub theatre unless there was a 'name' actor in the leading role.

The casting process was really fun, a game in which we were the only players. Every night at the theatre we scoured the audience for stars to see who might make a good Hugo, sorting and rejecting them as though we had the pick of theatre royalty. Dan had some very impractical ideas too – at one point he suggested Sir Anthony Hopkins, who hadn't done a play in years. 'Yeah,' we jeered, 'Hopkins is definitely going to return from Hollywood to work in an Islington basement.'

We were having such a good time blue-skying actors that Dan started to get worried that rehearsals were nearing and we didn't have a cast. I suggested that we start from the other end and cast the women, while continuing to think about the man. I had seen Kika Markham in several plays and always admired her chameleon-like ability to become her character without imposing her own ego. She is a fine actor and physically right for Hilde, Hugo's long-suffering wife. I knew, but had forgotten, that she was married to Corin Redgrave, the only brother to Vanessa and Lynn, and once she had been cast, she asked, rather shyly, who we were considering for Hugo. Sheridan told her honestly that he had many ideas but that so far no one had pushed his buttons. To his amazement, she asked whether he might consider Corin.

Corin was by some stretch a cut above the actors Sheridan had realistically thought of casting. The King's Head was, though home to us, hardly the Theatre Royal, Haymarket. Corin was a leading actor, having made the transition to middle age without losing either his exceptional good looks or his reputation for not suffering fools. His extreme socialist politics had worked against his professional achievements but he was such a good actor that he still got film and television parts galore. That he would even consider being directed by an inexperienced director such as Sheridan and, having spent a lifetime in the West End, on Broadway and at the National, would work for peanuts at the King's Head, had simply never occurred to us.

But Kika said he had read her copy of the play and asked whether Sheridan would talk with him about it. That night, while Sheridan was still reeling from the possibility of having a real star in his play, Corin rang. Sheridan hung up with a bemused look on his face. 'Darling, I can't quite believe that conversation. Corin said he loves the play and really wants the part. And you'll never believe this: Corin Redgrave is asking if I'd let him read for the role of Hugo. Imagine, he wants to read for me.' Instead, they arranged to meet for a drink in the bar at the Royal Court. By the time Kika and I joined them several glasses of wine later it was a done deal. We had two fabulous West End actors as Hugo and Hilde and something about the warmth of our meeting said that the four of us would become great friends. That left only the role of Carlotta to be cast.

This wasn't as easy as it sounds. It had to be a woman of a certain age, still beautiful, able to hold the stage with Corin and Kika, and believable as the mistress of a successful author and subsequently of other successful men. She would have to be a consummate actor to be able to navigate the many different pathways Noël leads her through without giving herself away to the audience before the denouement of the play. Somebody who hadn't been on a London stage for years would be ideal.

One person of whom we thought was Leslie Caron who had recently written the preface to our book about Gene Kelly. She was the right age, she was still beautiful and she still worked. Another was Claire Bloom. We asked them both and they were unavailable. Maybe they'd seen the King's Head.

A few nights later we were at a dinner for the Olivier Awards. Across the room I spied a face I thought I knew. I said to Sheridan, 'Do you remember 'The Forsyte Saga'?' Of course, he did. 'Do you remember the character of Irene?'

'Yes, of course, why?'

'Well, she's sitting over there.' And so she was, the ravishing and ethereal Nyree Dawn Porter, slim to the point of transparency and so beautiful it was hard to believe that it had been some thirty years since she captivated Eric Porter's Soames Forsyte.

Within seconds, Sheridan had made his way, with commendable celerity, through the Olivier Award crowds, had knelt by her table, introduced himself and asked her to play Carlotta. By the time the waiters had served dessert, he had his cast. Dan introduced a lovely couple, Roger Braban and Nicola Lyon, who would serve as producers with him and Sheridan was charmed by them and by the good-looking young actor, Mathew Bose, who auditioned to play the only other role, the small part of a hotel waiter.

Rehearsals didn't play out exactly as Sheridan had imagined. He had expected Kika to be a pleasure to work with and so she was but, from his reputation, had persisted in the thought that Corin might not like being directed by him. Not only was Corin not difficult to work with, he was a joy, and Sheridan met me after rehearsals every evening at whatever play we were reviewing buoyed and excited by all he was learning from his cast. But poor Nyree was fighting illness all the way through rehearsals and one day, just before they opened, she didn't show up at all. For three days one-third of his cast went missing. No call, no reply to her telephone, nobody answered her doorbell, she had simply disappeared. Dan was ready to cancel the show.

Then, at the last minute on dress rehearsal day, Nyree reappeared, without any more explanation for her presence than she had given for her absence. That evening there was a press night at the National and an exhausted Sheridan was telling Maureen Lipman about how rehearsals were going. 'Has Nyree done her bolt yet?' she asked, genuinely interested. We gaped at her. 'Only usually she disappears and it's only even money whether she comes back or not.'

Song at Twilight *(Sheridan had dropped the 'A') opened with a full complement of actors to a house packed with national newspaper critics. All our colleagues had turned out to support Sheridan and because this was a spectacular cast by any standards. It didn't hurt that it was a Noël Coward play that even the Coward experts didn't know. The reviews were ecstatic, surprising us with their warmth and enthusiasm, and within hours the entire King's Head run was sold out. On the first Saturday of the run, I found myself standing at the back, squashed tight against Sir Peter Hall, Sir Trevor Nunn, West End producer Bill Kenwright and a number of other theatre luminaries who hadn't been able to get seats. A tall, blue-jeaned woman was jammed into the opposite corner and only at the interval did I recognize her as our leading man's sister, Vanessa Redgrave.*

At the end the applause was sustained and excited. I'd lost track of Sheridan who I assumed had gone backstage into the minuscule single dressing room to congratulate the actors. I waited in the pub. Dan appeared and beckoned to me. He led me to his little office where what looked like the whole of theatrical London was assembled. 'Fantastic news,' he whispered. 'Bill Kenwright's taking us into the West End.' I was thrilled. 'All Vanessa's doing,' he continued as we joined the meeting. 'She told Bill that if he'd take it into the West End, she'd play Carlotta.'

This is a classic demonstration of both the kindness and the cruelty of the professional theatre. This was the best thing that could have happened to Sheridan, Corin, Kika, Dan, Roger and Nicola, everybody involved with Song at Twilight. *Everybody, that is, except Nyree who was almost casually jettisoned to make room for a better and more famous actor. She took the news with the grace and elegance she had displayed throughout rehearsals and wished the other two luck. She played until the end of the King's Head run and then, like the White Rabbit, disappeared again.*

My husband, though, had added another achievement to his long list – he was now a West End director. I was so proud of him. His courage, his willingness to try anything no matter how difficult, to put his work where it could have been pilloried by his colleagues, to risk his reputation on a new venture – all this was the real achievement, rather than the success he had found. Mind you, the success wasn't half bad either.

Chapter Twenty-One

After the West End success of *Song at Twilight* in 1999, Sheridan had got the directing bug. For years, he begged Bill Kenwright to let him direct *The Chalk Garden*, the melodrama his grandmother Gladys Cooper had been performing when she died. I could never understand what Sheridan loved about it. Written in a heightened form of English, it struck me as extremely difficult to grasp with no redeeming qualities at all. 'All right,' said Bill, at the beginning of 2003: 'I've got a slot at Windsor [the Theatre Royal, Windsor, which he ran] and then we could tour it. If it works out all right, we'll bring it in.'

Sheridan had been doing rather better for the previous few weeks, managing to surface before midday and writing some good stuff. He was going to the theatre, usually writing his own reviews, and, although paralysed with unaccustomed stage fright, doing a good job on his radio shows. He was still impossible in the mornings, and very angry when he wasn't suicidally depressed, but he was functional. I thought that a new project, the play he had so much wanted to direct, might be just the fillip he needed to regain his enthusiasm for work and life. Had I not thought he could manage it I wouldn't have let Bill embark on it. Friendship aside, theatre production is Bill's business and I wouldn't have jeopardized him for anything.

He and his general manager, a genial American called Tom Siracusa, asked who Sheridan wanted to cast in the crucial leading roles of the elderly lady, the governess she hires for her grand-daughter and her manservant. This time, there were none of the fun and loony ideas that had so enlivened the casting process for *Song at Twilight*. Instead, most of the actors came through Bill or Tom, and Sheridan displayed none of his accustomed certainty. He wouldn't commit to anyone until he had checked with me and I slowly became part of the process. 'Bill says you can be Assistant Director,' Sheridan told me, generously providing me with a job I didn't want on a play I didn't like, but I realized that it was sensible for me to be at rehearsals to back him up, act as his memory and help him to organize himself.

Tom had planned the rehearsal schedule so that we could be finished each day in time to get to the theatre to do our day jobs and I became fascinated with the opportunity, rarely accorded a theatre writer, of being part of the process. The leading actors in the principal roles would be the very experienced Moira Lister, Belinda Lang and Nickolas Grace, and I was looking forward to watching how good actors go about becoming their roles.

As rehearsals drew nearer, the weather got colder and Sheridan grew more fearful. I was concerned but not worried. He'd be fine once he got started. He knew the play very well, had always wanted to put his stamp on it, had clear ideas about how it should go. He was comfortable with the cast, knew most of them either through his father or from his radio shows. It never occurred to me that he wouldn't be able to complete the job. If I'd had any inkling of what was going to happen, I should have gone immediately to Bill and made him hire another director.

It snowed the night before rehearsals started, making the streets icy and the route to the Maida Vale chapel, where Bill's productions were rehearsed, almost impassable. It was the start of the worst three weeks of my life.

Before the first read-through Sheridan talked to the actors about the play and although what he was saying was cogent and intelligent, I noticed that his eyes were unfocused and he kept looking at me for reassurance. He didn't look comfortable or confident but I hoped that was because he was always terrible in the mornings and it was only 10 a.m. My copy of the script has a note to find the actors something to do in the mornings that didn't involve Sheridan. I think the actors were wondering what I was doing there and, as I heard them read the play, so was I.

That night we went to the Barbican to review a play. Sheridan was panicky when we left Maida Vale, worried that he'd made a bad first impression on the actors and that he hadn't got over what he wanted to say about the play. 'Don't worry, darling,' I said cheerfully, 'you were just fine and, anyway, you've got three whole weeks of rehearsal to make whatever points you feel you didn't make today.' Yeah, right.

In the interval, I stayed in my seat as I usually do but Sheridan said he wanted a drink and would join the other critics in the bar. He returned just as the houselights were dimming for the second act so we didn't have a chance even to exchange a word. At the end, because we were both writing reviews that night, we left as soon as the play finished along with the other critics. I scurried out ahead of Sheridan to pay at the parking machine and there was only one person ahead of me. I was just depositing the ticket when Georgina Brown, the critic for the *Mail on Sunday* and a friend, came running from the theatre. 'Come at once, Sheridan has collapsed in the lobby.'

He was lying on the marble floor where he had landed, no longer unconscious but surrounded by concerned colleagues and Barbican staff. He was bleeding but I couldn't see from where. Concerned for his dignity, he was anxious to stand up, but he was slurring his words and I realized that he had hit his head on the marble when he fell. We went to the theatre's first-aid station where the duty manager patched him up, stopped the bleeding, put on a huge Elastoplast, and with that had come to the end of his medical knowledge.

'Do you want me to call an ambulance?' he asked, anxiously.

'No,' came the agonized response from Sheridan, no longer slurring. 'They'll keep me in and I've got rehearsals in the morning.'

Against my better judgement I took him home and somehow got him upstairs to the bedroom. At some point during the journey the cut started to bleed again. There was so much blood that several towels were saturated as I tried what little I knew to help him. I couldn't believe that one person could have so much blood in him. It was soon clear that he needed more help than I could give him. I dialled 999. By the time the ambulance arrived, only about fifteen minutes later, he had lost so much blood he could no longer stand, much less walk down three floors and the ambulance crew had to carry him.

'We're taking him to St George's, Tooting,' puffed the kind paramedic on the way down the stairs.

Knowing time was of the essence I still pleaded, 'Chelsea and Westminster, please, they have all his records.'

Bless them, they didn't argue and set off for the Fulham Road with me in hot pursuit in our car, my own clothes covered with blood, Sheridan's current medications clutched in my hand.

They admitted him, of course. There was no question of his returning home when he was only semi-conscious and had lost so much blood. He didn't seem to know what was happening although he clung to my hand. I went home about 3 a.m., leaving him fast asleep. Then I wrote and filed his review for the *Daily Express* and mine for the *Wall Street Journal*. As I cleaned up the mess in the bedroom – sleep was out of the question – I tried to think through what would happen now with the play. I realized that, until the hospital told me the results of the tests they had run tonight and would continue in the morning, I had nothing to tell Bill and the cast.

First thing in the morning, I got hold of Tom Siracusa and he was sympathetic. 'I'm on my way,' he said, 'I'll tell Bill. Hold tight.'

I had spoken with the nurse looking after Sheridan and she said there was nothing to tell me until the doctors had seen him on their rounds and the results of the tests they had run overnight were back. Could I talk to him? 'No, sorry, he's asleep.' I told her to call Dr Guiloff, Sheridan's neurologist, whether or not he was on call, and to tell Sheridan I'd be in to see him after rehearsal. I knew he would understand why I wasn't at his bedside when he woke up. He'd want me to hold the fort in Maida Vale.

The snow was now thick on the ground when I got to Maida Vale. I told the cast what I thought I knew, that Sheridan had fallen and hit his head, that the cut was deep enough for him to have been kept in hospital overnight, but that I confidently expected him home later today and to be back at rehearsals by tomorrow. In the meantime, if it was all right with them, we'd just carry on with me in the chair.

As it turned out, although the actors were properly concerned about Sheridan, what was really worrying them was that the chapel was so cold that they could see their breath. The central heating wasn't working and it was impossible to work in that frigid atmosphere. While Tom struggled with this problem, Bill called to ask me to carry on.

'Bill, I'm a cabaret director if I'm a director at all. I don't have the experience for this.'

'Don't worry, my love,' came the cheerful response. 'You'll be fine and Sheridan will be back before you know it.' I didn't like to say that he didn't have the experience for this either.

Belinda Lang saved the day by suggesting that we all repair to her nearby house where the heating *was* working so we got some work done that day although it was all very scrappy. The actors seemed willing (if a bit wary) to continue with me until Sheridan returned which we all assumed would be tomorrow. I left them early enough to get to Chelsea and Westminster where I saw Dr Guiloff, in his black cape, still surrounded by acolytes. 'I can tell you nothing until the MRI gets back,' he said. 'I don't think he's had another stroke but it's possible and he's still not really conscious. Go in and see him.'

I did. He was lying in bed completely uncovered. Last night I had forgotten to bring his own pyjamas and the hospital gown didn't begin to cover him. It was so undignified that I knew that, if he was lying like that, he couldn't be fully conscious. 'We'd better keep him here,' said Guiloff, 'until we know what's happened to him. It could be a simple cut and the sleepiness may be due to loss of blood or it might be something more sinister. We'll have to wait for the test results.'

When I touched Sheridan's hand, which felt cold in that hot room, he opened his eyes. 'How did the rehearsal go?' I almost fainted with relief. He knew me, he knew where I'd been, he was interested, he was worried. I could, I thought, with a clear conscience, tell Bill they were keeping him for another night as a precaution but he'd be back tomorrow. I looked at my watch. 6.15. If I didn't leave now I'd be late for the 7 p.m. curtain to review another show. I explained to Sheridan. He nodded, mouthed 'I love you,' and was instantly asleep.

I called Bill on the way to the theatre and explained.

'Good. Can you cope for another day?'

'Sure I can.'

'That's my girl.'

I went to work.

We had three weeks of rehearsals. For three weeks, between 7 and 9.15 a.m., I answered our emails and mail and dealt with the Leon-Morley family business. Then I went to rehearsals and worked with the actors until 5 p.m. In between, at lunchtime, I discussed doors with the set designer and frocks with the costume designer, mediated rows between various crew members and generally did the job of a drama director. I marvelled at the talent of the actors and the production staff and how, with very little directorial guidance, they managed to extract a playable drama from what still seemed to me a pudding of a play.

At 5.30 p.m. every day I ran to the hospital where all the doctors and nurses kept telling me that Sheridan would be out tomorrow, while saying that they wanted to keep him in for just one more night. Sheridan himself was clearly stronger physically but so depressed the nurses couldn't even get him to walk around the ward and he was losing the use of his legs. Guiloff thought he might have had a series of small strokes or 'events', as he called them, but couldn't see any appreciable brain damage beyond the original stroke. There was no objective reason to keep him in hospital except for the very real fact that Sheridan didn't want to move. Anywhere. Out of bed, home, anywhere. I saw his point, sort of. In hospital, he felt safe. Nobody could telephone him. Nobody wanted anything he couldn't deliver. As long as he stayed in bed, in hospital, he wasn't Sheridan Morley, theatre director; he was a patient, protected from an outside world which was increasingly frightening. If he was willing to go anywhere it would have to be somewhere very far from reality.

When I was there, between 5.30 and 6.30 every day, he would return endlessly to his old desire for us to live in Florida or Hawaii or the south of France or Australia. This riff alternated with one, often on the same evening, about how he would never work again because he had fallen down on the job. After the first week he never even asked how rehearsals were going. At 6.30 I'd head to the theatre then go home, write my review and his, file them both and go to bed, get up the following morning and do the whole thing again.

I didn't know what to tell Bill and Tom other than what the hospital was telling me, every day for three weeks, that they wanted to keep him there for one more night which had now become three weeks. Rehearsals were now effectively over and the company was headed for Windsor at the start of their tour. I'd done everything I knew how to do with the play, the actors had done a great deal more, and they were ready, sort of, to open. I still had no idea what *The Chalk Garden* was about and, although momentarily hurt, I was relieved when the actors asked Bill for another director to get them through the tour.

Sheridan was discharged from the Chelsea and Westminster just in time to come to Windsor with me for the dress rehearsal and made a nice little speech to the cast thanking the new director for 'stepping into the breach' and an apology for 'being so useless' during rehearsals and that was that. I was dismissed.

It had been such an agonizing three weeks that the words *The Chalk Garden* are still seared into that part of my brain where hell resides. Years after Sheridan's death I had to steel myself even to go to the theatre where it was playing in the new production by Michael Grandage. His Olivier Award-winning creation bore no relation to ours in Windsor. He had made sense of the play, decided it wasn't a melodrama at all but a high English comedy, and cast two of our greatest actors – Penelope Wilton and Margaret Tyzack – in the leading roles. It was brilliant. I hated it.

Chapter Twenty-Two

When you decide to marry in your fifties, you have to make a choice. Well, another choice. Either you creep away quietly to a register office, have a few friends round for a glass of champagne and go back to work . . . or you go the whole hog. Sheridan and I were no good at creeping off or, for that matter, doing anything quietly. In the event, we had two enormous wedding parties. And, indeed, two weddings.

In New York, I called my friend Jack Weinstein, Chief Judge of the Brooklyn Supreme Court. He and Evelyn had been good friends of Michael's and mine since we had met them at an Aspen Institute seminar early in our marriage. They had both been upset when we had separated but, along with most of our friends, had stayed in touch with us both.

'I'm getting married again. I wonder if you'd . . . ?'

'Of course, I'll marry you,' said Jack with the endless generosity which characterizes his every personal and judicial determination. 'You'll have to get a licence from NY City first. You can get it from City Hall.'

Horrible experience, most of our New York friends told us. City Hall in Lower Manhattan was always crowded and the queues were endless. What to do? A London colleague, theatre critic for the Sun,

Bill Hagerty, told us that he and his wife had simply taken the ferry to Staten Island, the smallest of New York's five boroughs, and had easily obtained their licence with the benefit of a lovely ferry ride thrown in.

So one gorgeous early June morning in 1995, along with our hostess, the Broadway producer Dasha Epstein, we set off for Staten Island. The photographs show us in summer clothes, prancing about on the deck, ignoring the best view of Manhattan.

At the ferry stop the three of us piled into a taxi and asked to be taken to City Hall. The driver simply pointed at the grey stone building in front of us. We assumed he didn't speak English, not an unusual occurrence for taxi drivers in New York. Sheridan and my mother always assumed that foreigners could, in fact, speak English – they were just deaf. Very slowly and loudly, Sheridan shouted, 'City Hall, please!' and equally slowly and loudly the driver, inches from our ears, yelled back, 'It's right there, dummy!'

Lining up with pregnant teenage Puerto Ricans and their reluctant bridegrooms in a queue that included every possible nationality and gradation of enthusiasm for marriage, we got an uncontrollable fit of the giggles. We behaved far worse than the others in line, most of whom were young enough to be our grandchildren, except for one couple ahead of us, who had given us the giggles in the first place.

This ancient old crone, at least eighty, in a frilly cerise dress and toweringly high platform heels, was propelling what looked to be a twenty-year old drunk in a shiny shirt inexorably towards the licensing window. She was so deaf and her fiancé so inebriated that the thirty-second process took at least ten entertaining minutes, by which time we were reduced to hysterics.

In real disarray, choking with laughter and not paying nearly enough attention to the business at hand, when it was our turn we managed to get our own names wrong on our marriage certificate which is, of course, a legal document. Months later, I was still sorting out the mess we'd made. To the end of his life, the words 'Staten Island' were enough to reduce Sheridan to helpless laughter. At the end of his life, it was one of the few things that could.

We had been together at this point for close to ten years and it was clear that, although we yelled and argued and had very different values in some respects, we would be together forever. I never, not once, doubted Sheridan's commitment to me, not even when, ten years earlier, I had sent him back to his first wife to try to make that marriage work. When he couldn't, and begged me to leave Michael and marry him, I had told him marriage was not in my plans. I didn't feel I'd been much of a wife to Michael and I realize now that, despite my many excuses – my health, my career, my age – I didn't have children because I didn't think I'd have been a very good mother.

As it happened, I had met the only person on earth who could have made me into a carer. Sheridan was so needy after his chilly childhood, his difficult adolescence and his first marriage that I had no choice but to commit to him. He needed looking after emotionally and I found myself uniquely qualified to care for him.

But marriage? In a way, I have always been the polar opposite of the kind of woman who is constructed by nature for nurture. As a teenager, I knew girls who couldn't wait to grow up so they could marry and become mothers. My dreams were made of sterner stuff. I wanted to be a professional, I wanted to be treated the way boys were and allowed to compete equally, I wanted to be the best. And I wanted to get to the top; being some boss's number two or three was never my ambition. Nor was being some man's wife.

But, perversely, I've always been the kind of woman men want to marry. Although I had a modicum of charm, I wasn't particularly pretty, nor quick, nor ingratiating. I wasn't sexy or sexually voracious. In fact, I was the world's oldest virgin. By the time I lost my virginity it was an embarrassment and I would gladly have given it away with Green Stamps. It was, after all, the 1960s and nobody else I knew was a virgin. But before I lost it, before I was even propositioned, I had been proposed to by several lovely young men on a number of occasions. Go figure. I had chosen Michael and never regretted it. We were married for twenty years and, if Sheridan hadn't come into my life with the force of a hurricane in Louisiana, we would have been married forever. But he did.

When I was living in Washington, DC, I had met Dasha Epstein and she had always invited me to stay with her when I was in New York. Above her fireplace is a painting by Degas of his beloved ballet dancers, monochromatic and magnificent, which dominates the room. The first time I saw it, when I was safely married to Michael and the furthest thing from my mind was another wedding for myself, I said, 'This is such a fantastic setting that someone ought to be married under that Degas.'

So when, some fifteen years after this conversation, Sheridan and I returned to New York from our California trip and I called Dasha to tell her we had decided to get married, she said immediately, 'Well, of course you will be married under the Degas.'

Sheridan said to me privately that while it was a wonderful gesture on Dasha's part, we would have to turn it down. We couldn't possibly get married in New York because his parents and mine wouldn't be able to come and he couldn't imagine a wedding without them. 'Fine,' I said, 'we'll have two weddings, one on either side of the Atlantic.' Sheridan, who loved parties, thought this was the best idea ever and started making lists.

Sheridan's New York guest list soon reached 100 and that was just his friends. The main bickering was about who we could leave off the invitation list. Nobody, according to Sheridan. At one point I thought the patient Dasha was going to give up on the whole project and it would have served us right if she had.

The date we picked was around my birthday in April but just as we were finalizing the arrangements in New York, a bombshell dropped in Berkshire. Sheridan's daughter Alexis was pregnant and due to give

*birth at exactly the time we would have been in New York getting mar-
ried. She was engaged but she wanted to be married before the birth
and the baby was due in April. Despite her pregnancy she wanted a
big white Catholic church wedding and the two events would clearly
run into one another. Since I wasn't pregnant, ours clearly had to be
postponed.*

*But not cancelled. Despite our transatlantic life, the complications
of our respective jobs, the disapproval of his family and my own reser-
vations, Sheridan had done it. Ten years earlier he had determined
that we would be married. We had broken up two marriages and
destroyed homes and lives to do it, but it was actually going to happen.*

*To the exasperation of my mother and sister, I had been unable to
find anything to wear for either wedding until the last minute. One
evening, I was running through Selfridges just before it closed, when I
saw The Dress. It was cream silk with a guipure top, neither girly nor
mother-of-the-bride. Rather like a Tom and Jerry cartoon, I screeched
to a halt in front of it. It was perfect.*

*'Tell me you've got that in my size,' I begged the motherly shop
assistant. Realizing she was waiting to go home I promised, 'If you've
got it, I'll take it.'*

*She was scandalized. 'Without trying it on? And it's your wedding
dress? You will not. You'll try it on right now.' So I did, while she kept
the store open after hours for me, and it was as perfect as I knew it
would be.*

*Jack Weinstein married us on 7 June, followed by Dasha's Park
Avenue party. All New York's theatreland came. I solved the music
problem by having my godson play Scott Joplin piano rags instead of
'Here Comes the Bride'. Steve Ross, the cabaret singer, wrote a song for
us as a wedding present; Eli Wallach and Anne Jackson, along with
my sister Adrienne and brother-in-law David were our witnesses; and
the entire event was glamorous as only New York can be. And we then
set off for Hawaii where we had the best ten days of our lives.*

Sheridan knew Hawaii really well, having spent a sort of gap year in Honolulu after finishing university, teaching and directing in the Drama Department at the University. Many of his old friends and teachers were still alive and anxious to see him and entertain us. Before we left in the island-hopper for Lana'i our honeymoon was a blur of lunches, dinners, luaus and beach parties. Sheridan's old drinking buddy was now the gossip columnist of the main newspaper and we were welcomed everywhere. His ex-wife, Sheila Donnelly, a top-flight hotel PR, now married to the writer Paul Theroux, did us proud with accommodation in great hotels and dinners in the restaurants she represented.

On the island of Lana'i, we stayed at the fabulous Lodge at Koele. We became very friendly with the young Japanese-American manager and his beautiful fiancée, so we had the run of the place – the groves of old trees, the wide sweeping views of the Pacific Ocean, the horses and wild animals, the manmade amenities cunningly fitted into the landscape. There were flowers everywhere, hibiscus blooms so large that they were almost vulgar, carpeted every path.

For some odd reason there was a croquet pitch on the lawn in front of the hotel and I remember becoming helpless with laughter as Sheridan, fed up with hearing me go back and forth about the vexed and significant question of whether I wanted to play tennis or swim, only to remain comfortably prone in the garden, removed himself from the decision. He marched purposefully towards the croquet hoops, raised his mallet and played a highly concentrated game against himself. 'It's the only game I was ever any good at, darling,' he beamed, later, while boasting of his phenomenal score.

Sheridan, who didn't know one boat from another, despite having lived near or on the Thames for most of his life, took to messing about on the clear blue Pacific waters, often flopping off the side for a swim or what looked to me suspiciously like a wallow, while I sat or lay prone in the bottom of the boat with a book. Just about every photograph of our honeymoon involves the two of us grinning from ear to ear on a boat or in a restaurant. There was laughter in nearly every moment. Sheridan went out of his way to amuse me and just about all his jokes – about us, about the Hawaiians, about the food, about the appalling theatre we made ourselves sit through – hit their targets.

Every day, Sheridan would ask, 'Why on earth didn't we marry when we first met?' The answer was obvious – when we first met we were different people, younger, more fearful, less sure of who we were and what we wanted. I don't think it ever occurred to either of us that what we wanted was each other because, at the time, and for many years thereafter, it wasn't.

I guess all honeymoons seem in retrospect, or maybe even at the time, to be golden but ours really was: thirty years after we had met, it seemed as though everything we had done had brought us to this beautiful place. We had been friends, lovers, flatmates and colleagues. We had decided definitively not to marry, decided equally definitively not to live together, decided several times that we couldn't make it work and would be better apart, but we had never decided not to be best friends and now, in June of 1995, we were married and that was what, we realized, we had really always been destined to be.

Planning the London wedding had been tougher. Sheridan wanted a big party at a hotel in Chelsea Harbour, near where we lived. We loved its terrace over the marina with a view towards the Thames and it was home. My priority was, oddly you might think, for our marriage to be blessed by a rabbi. A cultural rather than an observant Jew, I have always been clear about my ethnicity and committed to it despite two non-Jewish husbands.

Sheridan had no religion at all. He found religion as ridiculous as politics and so was amenable but uncomprehending when I said I wanted a religious blessing. He had confided his confusion to the intelligent woman sitting next to him at a dinner one evening around the time that we were making our wedding plans. 'It's very odd, I know,' he told her, 'but my Ruth wants a rabbi and I don't know how to find her one.'

'I'm a rabbi,' she responded, 'and I'd be happy to bless your marriage.'

Ecstatic, Sheridan called me to say he, of all people, had located just the right rabbi and she would be available to marry us when we returned from our honeymoon in Hawaii. I didn't know, and he didn't tell me until much later, that this accommodating and friendly cleric was Baroness Julia Neuberger, one of the most distinguished women of her generation. The sheer incongruity of Sheridan Morley touting around London for rabbis was one of the funniest images ever.

So we were all set, arriving back in London in time for our Chelsea Harbour wedding on 25 June. Rabbi Julia performed the blessing in our own sunny garden. Sheridan was particularly pleased that all his children came, and his first grandchild, Barnaby, born in April. For a couple who had known each other for most of our lives and had lived together for ten of those years, we were ridiculously happy.

The party, with 200 of our friends, family and colleagues, was a great success. Even my brother Paul, estranged from my father for years, came, and we were all together on a beautiful sunny June day, enjoying each other and what was both a happy ending and a new beginning.

Chapter Twenty-Three

My New York internist, Dr Edie Langner, is a professor at Columbia University Medical School and one of my closest friends. I had been discussing Sheridan's situation with her as it worsened and it was more often than not she who explained his medical condition to me, based on what his own doctors were saying. She was beginning to think, from Sheridan's behaviour, that there was perhaps some element of dementia in the wildness of his responses and the irrationality of his letters to me. I rejected that tentative diagnosis (perhaps I wasn't ready to take on yet another problem) but could see that something basic had changed in his reactions to me and to the rest of the world, something frightening that threatened his very sanity.

Leaving Peter and Hannah, our housekeeper from Sierra Leone, watching over Sheridan, in 2005 I went to New York to see if Edie could suggest something, anything, that might help him. Over tea, she gently reiterated this terrifying idea and suggested that I should start to prepare for the possibility, she put it no higher than that, that Sheridan might never recover.

I wasn't ready to deal with this. Of course he would get better, I countered, she was just trying to scare me and she was succeeding. He was young, sixty-three, he didn't smoke or drink, he was just suffering from depression as he always had, just this one was lasting a little longer. She didn't try to argue with me; she's a wise woman. She gave me what I most needed – hope – by offering to put me in touch with the head of Columbia Presbyterian Hospital's Psychiatry Department who, when I spoke with him, was kindness itself but sounded an important note of warning. 'Of course I'll look after your husband, he sounds like a most interesting man, but you'll have to bring him here to New York. Nobody can tell you how long the treatment might take. Are you sure he would be able to stay here for what might turn out to be months of therapy?'

Another dead end. There was no way I could afford to keep Sheridan in New York for months on end. I couldn't leave him there by himself and without at least one of us in London to go to the theatre and write about it, there would be no money coming in. And I knew that BUPA health insurance wouldn't pay for it, with the usual issues about pre-existing conditions prevailing. American health care is among the best in the world, if, that is, you are very rich and have a lot of very expensive health insurance. I sighed, and said I would see if I could arrange it, but I knew at once that this potential solution was a non-starter.

But he hadn't finished – he had another idea, an idea that changed our lives. 'The best man in the world for treatment-resistant depression is in Oxford,' he told me. 'Oxford, England. Can you get to Oxford?' I explained that I could drive to it in a little over an hour from our front door. He laughed. 'I don't know why you haven't talked to him before. He's a good guy. In fact, his name is Guy, Guy Goodwin. He's a professor. Super smart. Take your husband to see Guy. I'll write him this afternoon.' I left New York more cheerful than at any time since Sheridan's stroke and flew back to London.

No good deed, as they say, goes unpunished. Despite a letter from one of New York's most distinguished psychiatrists, I couldn't get an appointment with Dr Goodwin. It turned out, in that eccentric

English way, despite being the Ur-specialist in his clinical field, he only saw patients on Thursday afternoons and he never saw private patients. His Thursday afternoons were thus oversubscribed and although his secretary was patient, she was adamant. Professor Goodwin could *not* see my husband.

I talked to Sheridan's psychiatrist. Yes, of course she had heard of Dr Goodwin. He was, she said, the 'shrink's shrink'. He was 'the best'. She hadn't recommended him to Sheridan because she thought he would be too busy to see him and because she knew he only took NHS patients while Sheridan was a private patient, paid for by BUPA. Despite their having cut him off the previous year while he had been in the Priory, it was now a new year and he was covered again by insurance.

The psychiatrist was still Sheridan's doctor of record although it was increasingly difficult to get him to go to his appointments with her. She put up with all his tantrums, kept changing his medication to see if there was something new on the market that might help him, but she agreed with me that something radical had to be done and supported my position when I went to New York looking for further help. She gave him everything she had and I remain very grateful to her.

Eventually, we decided that she would formally transfer Sheridan's care to the local Wandsworth NHS psychiatrist, thus making him eligible for referral to Goodwin. There followed several psychiatric re-evaluations of Sheridan in a dingy local clinic where Sheridan uttered not a word and where I, as usual, talked too much. A key worker was assigned to him and from then on she visited regularly to check on his progress. The office may have been dingy but the community care he received was first-rate, even though the NHS psychiatrist clearly didn't like either of us and couldn't wait to hand us off to Guy Goodwin.

I had been frank with him, as had his doctor, that the reason for the change of doctors was that the specialist we favoured only took

NHS patients but, although this psychiatrist was clearly in awe of Goodwin, I think he was insulted that this was the only reason we had consulted him.

Still, the fact remained that, three months into his referral from the head of psychiatry at one of the most prestigious American teaching hospitals, I still couldn't get an appointment with Guy Goodwin. I returned to New York for more advice and Edie told me to go back to England and stop being a wimp. I was to go and sit in Professor Goodwin's office until he saw me. I was to tell him I thought they'd all got the diagnosis wrong and he was to go back to first principles and find out why nearly three years of twelve different drug regimens had failed to do anything for my husband but make him sicker.

To my amazement, it worked. I spent an entire Thursday sitting in the fairly crummy reception area of the psychiatry department at the Warneford Hospital of the Radcliffe Infirmary until a tall, tweedy and extremely good-looking man emerged, clutching a bicycle helmet. I explained who I was, who Sheridan was, and why I appeared to be stalking him. His reaction was immediate and positive. He listened carefully and, without further comment, made an appointment for Sheridan for the following Thursday.

Rather than repeat everything for this new doctor, I sat down and wrote up what it was currently like to live with Sheridan Morley. The piece is unashamedly written from my point of view. If someone as distinguished as Goodwin was going to have his care he had better know what he was dealing with and what he was taking on wasn't pretty.

Living with Sheridan Morley

Sheridan is a performer. He is dazzling in public and the contrast between his public persona and his private person is, I suspect, unbelievable to anyone who hasn't witnessed it. Trouble is, I'm the only one who has. Well, not quite. The family (his children, my sister, etc.) has seen it too. Sheridan in any public situation can entertain, talk easily, present radio shows, effortlessly dominate a room or a theatre. People, even close friends, who see him in public, congratulate him on how well he is looking and sounding.

Alone or with me, he is usually asleep – left to himself he sleeps until woken, 12 or 24 hours. On one occasion I didn't wake him and he didn't emerge for 4 days. Whenever I checked, which was often, he was actually asleep, not lying awake.

Awake, he is either crying or hectoring, often both at once. He is incredibly angry all the time, usually with me, and his public hail-fellow-well-met attitude means that he can only vent his fury at me. This anger seems to make him incapable of dealing with any of his illnesses. He still confuses diabetes with stroke with depression but his anger seems to block any possibility of his taking responsibility for dealing with any of them.

When awake, Sheridan wants my undivided attention to vent whatever is obsessing him at that moment. These arguments of his are circular and repetitive. They go on for hours, preventing either of us from doing any work. If I try to ignore him he merely becomes angrier. If I say 'no' he hammers at me until he becomes totally hysterical. If I say 'yes' he says he knows I don't mean it (he is right about that). When I give up and go to bed he writes multi-page letters re-stating the same positions again and again, each time ratcheting up his anger with me. Sometimes, it's a determination to give up all work and move to Florida. Sometimes, it's an equally firm determination to tout for any work of any kind, the more public the better. There are about six other obsessions which recur every few days. Our conversations, which are limited to topics which concern him, are identical day by day. He seems incapable of learning anything or gleaning anything useful from talking with anyone else although, if he finds someone who agrees with any aspect of his thinking, he incorporates them into his argument.

I am seen to be standing in the way of everything he wants to do. It is true, I am. His judgement is not flawed but non-existent and I spend much of my time undoing whatever he has done – phone calls, faxes, letters to the newspapers, appointments. He becomes involved in public rows with his colleagues through newspaper columns. He is fixated on himself and how others see him. This is not new except in degree and to the extent that he has no interest in anything outside himself and his own mental illness. He has no interest in his children or his grandchildren, and I have to force him to see them or his 94-year-old mother.

If I don't actually take them away from him he wears the same clothes (and underwear) for weeks. He goes to the theatre (our place of work) looking dishevelled and unkempt and becomes incensed when I try to make him brush his teeth or change his stained clothes, let alone wear braces because his trousers fall down due to his weight loss (he won't wear new clothes nor allow me to alter the old ones).

Sheridan doesn't drink or smoke or gamble. Instead, he spends. Five times in our marriage he has virtually bankrupted us and in each case it has been connected to a bipolar episode. He orders so much that our postman is once again delivering our mail in sacks. Sheridan justifies this by telling me that most of it is videos for which he doesn't have to pay. He goes into bookshops and spends hundreds of pounds on books he already has.

His short-term memory, never very good, is severely affected, whether by the depression, the stroke, or the ECT treatments he had last Autumn, is impossible for a layman to tell. He cannot function without me at his side to remind him of who people are and to stop him from telling them the same story twice.

He is panicked by my absence, tries to stop me going to the ballet (I am a dance and drama critic by trade), but seems actively to dislike me when I am present. Sheridan comes from a family whose first reaction to any form of disaster is 'it's not my fault' but he has extended that into an insistence on finding someone (usually me) to blame for everything that happens. He has always been bad at taking responsibility 'this cup appears to have got itself broken', but he is now incapable of it. There is more, much more, but this should give any doctor some sense of what is currently going on. Should the doctor wish to see some of the letters Sheridan writes me every night I have saved them and can show them to him.

Things moved fast after that. Two appointments were all it took before both an alternative diagnosis and a possible treatment were suggested. Sheridan was completely non-responsive in both meetings, repeating over and over again, no matter what he was asked, that he just wanted to get better. From time to time he would launch into one of his repetitive spiral monologues and Dr Goodwin would skilfully steer him back to his overall feelings, not his desire to move to Florida or his dislike of his employers or whatever it was that was obsessing him that day.

'They've been treating him for depression which is an affective disorder,' he told me, 'and what I think is that the stroke hit him in the emotion centre of the brain and that's an organic illness.' In other words, my poor husband was physically ill but being treated for his previous illness, which was mental. The doctors treating him at the time of his stroke, lulled by his long history of depression, had not looked beyond it to any other possible cause. Neither had I.

I stared at Goodwin, unable to take in what he was saying. Even when Dr Morrish had said that it was possible that the stroke had changed the pathology of the brain it hadn't registered. When Edie had suggested that mild or early dementia might be playing a role in retarding his recovery, it hadn't hit me. Despite the minor differences in his symptoms, it had never occurred to me that Sheridan didn't have the same illness that had dogged him for his entire adult life, only far worse this time because of the stroke. But a *different* illness with the same symptoms? Impossible, surely.

As my own brain began to register what he had said, it all began to make sense. The additional irrationality, the unusual anger, the resistance to hitherto useful drugs, were all explicable if his illness was organic, rather than affective. If he had a different illness, one caused by injury to the brain, no wonder the drugs didn't work. What we had been doing was keeping under control the original bipolar disorder – he hadn't, in fact, had a flare-up of that for some years – but doing nothing for the trauma to his brain.

So, could anything be done for a stroke-damaged brain where the damage was manifesting itself as depression? Professor Goodwin was, for the first time, slightly tentative. 'There is,' he suggested, 'an operation.'

Chapter Twenty-Four

*H*ow we fitted it all in I still don't know. We were incredibly busy.
Besides the books – at any given moment we were writing
at least one book together and working on one each separately –
Sheridan was the drama critic for the Spectator and the International
Herald Tribune, he presented the Radio Two 'Arts Programme', a
thrice-weekly two-hour interview show for the BBC; I was drama
critic for the European edition of the Wall Street Journal and
theatre critic for LBC Radio, and we had more freelance work than
we could handle.

When Andrew Lloyd Webber's Really Useful Company bought
most of London's West End theatres, his wife Madeleine decided that
London theatre programmes were not worth the paper they were
printed on and we should start a new theatre magazine. She was the
publisher and I was the founding editor of Theatregoer. Although it
eventually went the way of most corporate projects and became just
another magazine before it was killed off by its new owners, it was,
for several years, the most exciting theatre publication in London and
everybody wanted to write for us.

Sheridan's father had died in 1992, before we were married, but his
mother and both of my parents lived on into their nineties. Although
my mother-in-law lived quietly in Berkshire with Sheridan's ex-wife

and his elder daughter just down the road, by now my parents were in need of care. My sister and I, alarmed by the ongoing series of crises which involved the usual forgetfulness of old age, spent part of almost every day running up to central London (they lived in the West End) to turn off baths left to overrun while they went shopping, take the heat off pots of soup which had been forgotten during afternoon naps, find lost keys, lost spectacles, lost credit cards and chequebooks, and generally pick up the pieces, literally and otherwise. Eventually, reluctantly, we decided that, no matter what they said, they could no longer live alone in a flat up two flights of stairs with no near neighbours and no help.

They were by now in their early nineties, so we hired several carers to look after them. Each lasted about five minutes. Our parents were strong-minded and feisty: they had run their own business and their own lives, and they made it clear in every way that they neither needed nor wanted help. Except, that is, from us, and they would think nothing of phoning one of us in the middle of a working day to demand that we should immediately drop everything and drive, from Battersea or Teddington, to buy a newspaper or make a soufflé or find their keys or arrange a holiday for them. In the meantime, they were doing all kinds of minor damage to themselves from falls and burns. We knew it was only a matter of time before worse would ensue. We couldn't go on taking the risk, for their sake and for ours.

My sister Adrienne and I, without their knowledge, started the round of visiting sheltered housing options – and there are many within easy reach of central London – with a view to somehow persuading our parents that this was a better idea than continuing to live in their own flat which had by now become a deathtrap. Everybody with elderly parents will recognize the situation in which we found ourselves. We didn't want to interfere in the lives of such fiercely independent people but things couldn't go on as they were. The trouble was, after examining many such facilities, we hated them all. There wasn't one we felt comfortable recommending to our dearly loved, difficult nonagenarians.

It was Sheridan who found Nightingale House. Having never had any money, Sheridan was generous with his time when it came to charity events. He would open a fête, introduce an auction, make a speech, do whatever he could to raise money for deserving causes. One day he came home from just such an event and said, 'You girls are mad. You're driving yourselves crazy looking at homes when just five minutes down the road is a beautiful stately home with a gorgeous garden, full of interesting elderly people your parents would love. I just did a speech there today and it was really fun. It's called Nightingale House. At least go and see it.' We went.

Even while standing outside the glass doors it was obvious that this place was different from the carbolic- and urine-smelling places we'd seen where old people in dressing gowns sat around staring at television sets. Just inside the door was a beautiful flower arrangement next to a desk at which sat a smiling receptionist. There was a whiteboard with activities written on it:

10 a.m.   French conversation in the Long Room;

12 p.m.   Group assembles for the Royal Observatory at Greenwich;

2 p.m.   Book Club in the library with Fay Weldon;

6 p.m.   Group assembles for La Bohème at the Royal Opera House.

This place was busy. Even while we stood outside looking in, well-dressed elderly people bustled in and out of the hall, all going somewhere. Staff helped those who needed help or pushed wheelchairs but for the most part the residents were ambulatory and in a hurry. Some were headed to the conservatory café for morning coffee, others to one of the many activities that go on all day. Just visible beyond the hall, we could see beautifully landscaped gardens with an aviary and a carp pond. We looked at each other. Before we had even entered the house we knew this was it.

Organizing them into it was a nightmare. They were perfectly willing to go for a few days' 'holiday' but there was no question of their actually living anywhere but in their own apartment in Marylebone. They made that very clear. Eventually, after a crisis meeting at our dining table the four of us (Adrienne and her husband, David, Sheridan and I) decided on a desperate plan. Very simply, we would have to lie to them. We told them that they would have to move out of their flat temporarily because their landlord, the businessman to whom my father had sold the building some years earlier on the condition that they could keep their apartment at a peppercorn rent, had found that the staircase leading to the flat was unsafe. Grudgingly, they said they would move into a hotel until the staircase was fixed. We said we had a better solution and it was like a hotel but called Nightingale House, designed especially with people their age in mind.

Fortunately, the day we took them to look at the Nightingale was one of those perfect English summer days. They loved the conservatory café, were impressed with the gardens which were at their best, liked the people they met and found the facilities on a par with many five-star hotels. So far, so good. Within an hour of arriving, they were welcomed by the activities coordinator, a dynamo called Sheila, the nursing director, the catering manager, and several of the residents, many of whom had discovered within seconds that Sheridan Morley was in the house and come to renew acquaintance with him. They were taken to see the art room, the computer room, the library and a flat which, by wonderful chance, had just become available. It had a bedroom, a bathroom, a living room and a quasi-kitchen with a refrigerator and a microwave so that they could get themselves a snack if they felt like eating alone.

There was, of course, a further struggle when it became clear (more lies) that they would not be able to return to their own flat and my father, particularly, found it difficult to settle where he was not in control. Having always had interrupted sleeping patterns, he was accustomed to eating and drinking at unusual hours and there were several skirmishes when he summoned a nurse to make him a smoked salmon sandwich at 3 a.m. Sheridan explained patiently, over and over again, that there were differences between the Nightingale and a hotel and that one of them was that the Nightingale did not offer room service.

There was also the day when Sheila, knowing that my father, Sammy, painted in oils, came to suggest that he might like to attend the classes in the well-equipped art room. 'Well, yes,' said Sammy, grandly, 'I supposed I could teach one or two classes a week. Not more. But then I don't know what you'll do for an art teacher when I return home.' Poor Sheila retreated, never telling him that a professional art teacher was a permanent fixture in the art room.

Between us, we got them settled and one of us, Adrienne or I, often accompanied by Sheridan, was there every day. We had their own furniture installed in their flat in the Nightingale and cleared out their apartment in the West End. It was a lot of work and, although Sheridan's bouts of depression were fairly rare, I always had to be prepared for periods when he couldn't work. Normal life, though, even without my parents and their increasingly frequent illnesses, was full, and Sheridan's reluctance to learn even the most rudimentary elements of computers became something of a burden as all our employers and editors now insisted on having all copy delivered by email.

I had help, though, in dealing with him, at least during the day. We had a part-time secretary who also did our book-keeping, we had Hannah, our wonderful housekeeper who showed up irregularly to bring some order into our domestic arrangements, and we had Peter. Peter almost defies description. He had come to us when we moved *across the river from Chelsea to Battersea. Sheridan, upset that his own improvidence meant that he was going to have to live in a manner more in keeping with the needs and lifestyle of two professional writers instead of the landed gentry, demanded that, if he was going to have to live 'all that way away', (exactly five minutes from the previous house), he needed a driver.*

What he meant was that he wanted someone who, like his father's dresser, John, would do odd jobs around the house and be his chauffeur whenever he didn't want to drive. I said, 'Don't be silly, darling, people like us don't have chauffeurs,' and thought that would be the end of it. I should, of course, have known better. Only a week later, Sheridan was collected by a BBC car as usual for his radio show. The driver was a camp, dapper little man who knew all the back routes, was clearly theatre-mad and who kept up a running conversation with Sheridan all the way to the BBC about what was on in the West End, what he had thought of it, what Sheridan had thought of it and what he was planning to see in the immediate future. Sheridan was enchanted. He told his driver that he was being forced by his wife, me, to move to Battersea and, consequently, needed a full-time driver. Did he know anybody?

Sheridan returned from the BBC that day like a dog with two tails. 'Darling,' he asked, 'do you have any plans during the day tomorrow? There's somebody I'd like you to meet. I think I've found our chauffeur.'

I looked at him as though he'd lost his mind. 'Are you crazy or what?' I demanded, 'We've got the builders in. We're in the process of moving house. We don't need a chauffeur. We can't afford a chauffeur. Let's wait until we're properly installed here, driving ourselves. I think you'll find it's no more difficult than it was at Chelsea Harbour.'

'He's coming for an interview tomorrow at two.'

That was Sheridan. When he wanted something, he wanted it more than anything on earth. And what he wanted was Peter. I was predisposed to hate Peter.

Peter Coller arrived promptly at 2 p.m. the following day, wearing a suit with a white shirt, silk tie and polished shoes. I couldn't help but like him immediately with his ready smile, air of competence and cheeky sense of humour which kept bursting out when you least expected it. He'd had a number of responsible jobs where he had handled money, including that of a cashier in a casino, but most recently he had been a driver for the company with the BBC's account and he was bored. He loved driving and cars, and knew a short cut to everywhere. He was happy to run errands, do our shopping and be available from dawn to whenever we needed him after the theatre. He was gay, he told me, but had a partner he didn't live with, a flat five minutes away from our new house and would work for very little. He wanted this job badly because of his love of show business and desire to be close to it.

The odds were building up in his favour and, desperate to have some reason to reject him, I asked if he did anything besides driving, such as handyman stuff. 'Mrs Morley,' he said, patiently, 'I'm a poofter. I'm frightened of ladders and hammers. I don't do any he-man stuff at all. But I'm very good with window-boxes.' At that moment, I fell in love with Peter. From then on, until the moment he died, he was inextricably part of our lives.

Within a very short time, Peter was running us. He took over the ordering of the theatre tickets so that we never again showed up at the wrong theatre on the wrong night; he drove us to and from wherever we were going so that he practically paid for himself in the money we saved on parking and traffic tickets. He fielded our telephone calls and knew when our deadlines were for articles, reviews and even books. He took care of the cars so we never again ran out of petrol and did our shopping, even for Sheridan's clothes. He and Hannah, our housekeeper, made sure there was always cooked food after the theatre, and remembered everyone's birthday. My sister and cousins adored Peter and he was always invited to family gatherings, not because he was driving us but in his own right. Office supplies miraculously appeared and Peter seemed to have a vast army of friends, all of whom did useful things such as cleaning carpets and mending computers.

He and our then-secretary hated each other and he would occasionally throw queeny tantrums when they had a spat. 'Her or me,' he would snarl. 'Her or me.' But he was so intrinsically good-natured that they always blew over. We never told him (but he probably knew) that if it had really come to a choice between them we would willingly have chopped her up and thrown the pieces out of the window for him. We adored him, and he us, particularly Sheridan to whom he had a limpet-like loyalty. I am still sometimes haunted by the possibility that, after Sheridan's stroke, Peter postponed his own heart surgery so that he could support me over that terrible first Christmas and thereby shortened his own life. But, for the moment, this was our working family and it worked.

Chapter Twenty-Five

'Brain surgery?' I gasped, 'What would that do?'

Professor Goodwin explained to us, for the first time but certainly not the last, the procedure called deep brain stimulation (DBS). This involved the implantation of a device, similar to a pacemaker, which attempts to regulate the activity of certain parts of the brain, just as a pacemaker regulates the heartbeat. He explained that, although this was now being used quite widely for the alleviation of the more distressing symptoms of Parkinson's disease, it was only now being tried out as a possible treatment for the alleviation of otherwise intractable depression. The hope was that with DBS the doctors could adjust Sheridan's moods after the operation with the use of an electronic remote control.

Although a pioneering Canadian neuroscientist, Dr Helen Mayberg, had performed seven of these operations in Canada and in Atlanta, Georgia, it had never before been used in this country or indeed anywhere in Europe for organic depression. Nobody knew whether it worked. Her results had been mixed – one patient had had no reaction at all, four were somewhat better, two were much better – and, of course, nobody knew whether Sheridan was a good candidate for the operation and or even whether there was a chance it might work for him.

Sheridan was still sitting with his head down, taking no part in the conversation. We tried to discuss it with him. All he could say was that if it would make him better he was in favour of it. The problem with that endorsement was that by this point Sheridan was so depressed that if you had told him that we had a solution but that it involved chopping off his head he would have headed for the nearest axe.

Professor Goodwin said it was up to us, which, in effect, meant it was up to me as Sheridan was way past the stage where he could make a rational decision about lunch, never mind whether he would allow someone to enter and operate on his brain. 'What are the risks?' I asked. 'Could he be reduced to a vegetable? What's the worst that can happen?'

The worst, said Goodwin, was nothing. It was possible that he'd have the operation and it wouldn't work. It might work partially. That is, he might feel somewhat better but not much. Or it might be a spectacular success, drive the negative feelings back and regenerate some of the nerve endings or neural pathways that had been destroyed by the stroke, and he might then be restored to something like his pre-stroke self. Nobody knew and nobody could tell. But, he concluded, he won't feel worse than he does now.

Sheridan lifted his head for the first time. 'Not possible,' he said. 'I couldn't feel worse than I do now.'

This was scary stuff. I knew I had to think about it, talk to Edie and my friend Polly, a medical writer, try to find out more via the internet and attempt to read the research papers that existed on DBS. I also needed to consult Sheridan's family and, above all, to try to get through to him. I did all that and not one person I spoke with was against it. It was so new, so experimental, that there were no objective criteria on which a decision could be made. The doctors didn't know, the surgeons didn't know, the friends and the family didn't know. Above all, since it was my decision, I didn't know.

Professor Goodwin didn't push. He said Sheridan should be

seen by the neurosurgeon who would perform the operation to ascertain whether he was a suitable candidate for DBS. He arranged for an MRI and a CT scan and obtained the previous post-stroke results from the tests that had been performed in the Chelsea and Westminster Hospital by Dr Guiloff.

He wrote to Dr Potter, the NHS psychiatrist who had referred Sheridan to him:

10th June 2005

Dear Dr Potter

Re: Sheridan MORLEY, dob: 05.12.41, Patient No 2004005102

Sheridan remains in an extremely puzzling and refractory depressed state. For the first half of the day he prefers to be asleep, exceedingly depressed, unable to co-operate or initiate any sort of activity. The second half of the day he becomes increasingly functional and continues to file copy in his job as a theatre critic. While this is remarkable (unprecedented in my experience) I suppose it has to be seen in the context of his previous history of functional mood disorder and the fact that he has had a sub-cortical brain injury. My assessment is that this is a depressive state which is refractory to treatment and that radical steps are probably necessary to do anything about it.

On the pharmacological side he continues to take moclobemide 900mg, lithium 600mg and risperidone 1mg.

Conclusion:

1. I suggest that we try adding to this modafinil at a dose of 100mg initially taken in the morning in an effort to see if we can reduce the somnolence in the first half of

the day. I have discussed this approach with my colleague Professor Philip Cowen who has expertise in complex poly-pharmacy. The dose can be increased to 400mg depending on his response and how well it is tolerated, and taken either as a single or divided dose. The hope is it will get him going in a way requiring a little less effort from carers.

2. On the more radical side he has had now three years in this condition with a short break of about three months early this year. He has been refractory to all treatments – which have included ECT, augmented venlafaxine treatment and now augmented MAOI treatment. Medical treatment is in any case compromised by his vulnerability to postural hypertension and the unsteadiness that may be a consequence of his previous stroke. I therefore think he should be considered for deep brain stimulation as treatment for his depression. This is an extremely experimental procedure but someone with an essentially neurological component to his depression may be a good candidate. I am taking steps to refer him to my colleague Professor Tipu Aziz who will assess him for surgery and in order to make the necessary financial case to his health authority/ PCT. In addition I will contact Dr Guiloff who is familiar with his presentation with the stroke etc. and whose opinion I would value.

Yours sincerely

Professor Goodwin

cc: Professor Tipu Aziz, Radcliffe Infirmary, Oxford

While the consultation process took its glacially slow course, Sheridan was, against all probability, actually getting worse. Once I had been solidly reassured on all sides that he had nothing to lose if we opted for the surgery, that at the very least the Hippocratic oath would be obeyed ('Above all, do no harm'), I was anxious to get on with it. It was all going too slowly for me and I was getting desperate. I was afraid that Sheridan was now feeling so ill that he would actually find the energy from somewhere to take his own life. The waiting was unbearable for us both. I emailed Guy and my desperation, which I was trying to hide, was bursting out:

Dear Guy,

Thank you so much for the research paper. I understood maybe one word in four but that was sufficient for overall comprehension. Sheridan seems to be crumbling, day by day, without question deteriorating. Pain is overwhelming, concentration non-existent, and I'm losing the battle even to get him to keep his eyes open. What has been vaguely manageable no longer is. This is urgent, Guy, and acute rather than chronic.

I'm attaching the two NY Times articles. Because they don't mention Dr Helen Mayberg and her team, I'm not even sure whether this is the same device but I thought you should have them. Even if the results are as statistically insignificant as these articles suggest, I still think we should try. Any possibility of improvement at this stage is a major incentive. How do we go forward? Is there anything I can do to help?

Dr Guiloff's telephone number is: 020 —. He is Sheridan's neurologist and will, I know, share the MRIs and CT-scans dating from the stroke.

Thank you for your willingness to think beyond conventional treatments. We really have tried and what we know now is that they're not working for whatever ails him.

All best, Ruth

ps Did you talk with Dr Potter or Dr Dix about the stimulant drug? I need a prescription from one of them and they're not the most communicative of souls.

He responded immediately:

Thanks Ruth – this is I think vagal nerve stimulation – we are the next stage on from there.

I attach the letter I have sent to Dr Potter. I have contacted Tipu Aziz and had a polite reply from Guiloff – who had no comment either way about the course of action I was proposing. So next move will come from Tipu. I am in the US this week, but can keep things going from there.

Regards, Guy

As well as to Dr Guiloff, Professor Goodwin wrote to Sheridan's other doctors in case they had comments to make on his suggested course of treatment. None of them did. How could they? They didn't know much about DBS for depression either. Very, very slowly, we moved towards a decision to have the surgery if Professor Aziz thought that there was any chance that Sheridan would be a good candidate for it.

Professor Tipu Aziz turned out to be a small man with glasses. He was very quiet during our first meeting and spent more time examining the MRIs than he did talking to or looking at us. He explained the procedure of DBS more fully than Guy Goodwin had, the clinical ins and outs of the hospital stay, where it would be done (the Radcliffe Infirmary in Oxford), how long Sheridan would be an in-patient (probably two nights) and what the aftercare would consist of (lots of adjustments of the 'pacemaker' and long-term monitoring).

He answered my questions thoughtfully and fully but volunteered nothing. Sheridan said nothing at all throughout the meeting. He didn't even ask if it would hurt.

'When can he have it?' was my question.

'There's a lot of organization on this end,' Professor Aziz said. 'Guy and I will be in touch.'

We were dismissed, not a lot wiser than when we'd arrived. Guy was away in the United States, lecturing, while Tipu was uncommunicative: there was nothing to do but wait.

Not until later did I realize that Sheridan was in the hands of one of the most distinguished neurosurgeons in the world. I had looked him up, of course, but the bare facts of his background, education and work didn't begin to cover the ground-breaking research, the large primate research, the cutting-edge neuroscience for which he was famous in his field.

I had been told that Guy Goodwin was the leader in his area of recalcitrant depression and I accepted that we had the very best psychiatric help. But Aziz was in our lives only because Goodwin had sent us to him. A chance remark on a tennis court that week brought home to me exactly who we had been lucky enough to find. I knew that one of my regular tennis buddies was a neurological research scientist at Imperial College, London, but had never focused on her profession any more than she had focused on mine. We played tennis, that's all.

That Sunday, she and I were partners and as we changed ends she asked after Sheridan. I told her about the putative operation and only when she asked the name of the surgeon did I remember that this was vaguely in her area of expertise. 'A very quiet little man called Tipu Aziz,' I said.

She stopped dead. 'My God, how on earth did you swing that?'

'Dunno, why?'

'You've only got the best neurosurgeon in the world operating on your husband, that's all.' This is a woman not easily impressed and she was looking at me as though I'd nabbed Madonna as the entertainment for my party. 'He is,' she told me, 'the business.'

From that moment on, I never doubted that the operation would be a success.

The half-year it took Guy Goodwin and Tipu Aziz to arrange for the DBS was the longest of my life. Sheridan was in a permanent panic – the doctors didn't know what they were doing, it wouldn't work, he didn't want his head examined, he would die if he didn't have the operation, he would die if he did, it was going to cure him, it was going to kill him, it was like a lobotomy, it was a miracle – and so it went on, inexorably, hour after hour.

He saw Guy a few times but most of the work was going on behind the scenes with the two professors trying to convince their own masters to let them carry out the procedure. I called everybody I could think of. Our own Primary Care Trust in Wandsworth just about laughed me out of the office. Didn't I understand that this was a highly experimental operation? Not to mention a very expensive one? Go away, Mrs Morley. I said that I thought the whole point of the NHS was to provide health care which was free at the point of delivery. If, I begged, this procedure could work for my husband, even partially, wasn't it in the interests of the NHS to remove him from the almost daily workload he was putting on his local surgery? Go away, Mrs Morley.

I called our MP. Go away, Mrs Morley. I asked our GP for help. Go away, Mrs Morley. I spoke to someone at the office of the Secretary of State for Health. Go away, Mrs Morley. I even phoned the Prime Minister's Office at 10 Downing Street. They didn't say, 'Go away, Mrs Morley,' because I never actually spoke to a human being – I just got transferred from office to office until I was cut off. I developed the hide of a rhino, upset by every rejection but determined to continue until I had exhausted every avenue. If there was any way I could get him that operation he was going to have it no matter what I had to endure.

We all know that the NHS is very far from perfect. Our local surgery, almost next door, is a group practice where the doctors are a movable feast. Their appointment system is efficient and waiting time is held to a minimum. But there are so many doctors and locums, all working on their own schedule, that Sheridan never saw the same doctor twice and, when he was with a doctor, they almost never looked at him, being so preoccupied with the time he required and the details on their computer screens.

His depression didn't preclude his catching the usual sequence of illnesses that everybody else gets but it should have alerted one of the many doctors who saw him into agreeing that he should not be shunted from one to another. After one of his many falls, when his face had been patched up in hospital but his dressings needed to be changed and his condition monitored by his own doctor, he was left to sit in a corridor, crying, for an hour before the practice nurse had time to attend to him.

I asked to see the head GP, or the practice manager, or the last doctor who had attended him, or *anyone* in authority but nobody was available. I wrote a letter, pointing out that even the newest locum would only need to look at his notes, so prominent on their computer, to know that Sheridan didn't just have a cold, or a busted nose, or a bruised foot, or a sprained wrist, or a battered face. He was a chronically sick man; he was a diabetic who had already had one stroke and might well have another; he was waiting for a major operation; he was deeply and clinically depressed – but not one of the doctors in the practice had ever even tried to develop a relationship with him. Nobody had even attempted to see him as a whole patient rather than a selection of symptoms; in truth, nobody had even really looked him, preferring to stare at the computer screen and shunt him off with a pill, a dressing, or an ointment.

In response to this letter, the head of the practice telephoned me, said he was sorry I was not happy with the service the practice was giving my husband and, if I would be sure to make Sheridan's appointments on the two days a week when he was there, he would take care of him himself. I think he was genuinely trying to address my concerns but the system, as it is set up, does not allow for personal treatment. When you are ill and feeling rotten, you need that more than anything.

I tried BUPA. Hah! Not a chance. I had continued to pay for private insurance even when Sheridan was transferred to the NHS so that Professor Goodwin would see him. BUPA wouldn't even allow me to send the MRIs to their clinical experts. Didn't I understand that this was an experimental procedure? Didn't I know it would be expensive? Go away, Mrs Morley.

Mrs Morley went away.

Chapter Twenty-Six

*R*adio Four was full of news about Sierra Leone. It was 1999. *There was yet another uprising there and the rebels were getting close to Freetown, wherever that was. I listened with half an ear. Peter materialized in front of my desk, real urgency in his face.*

'You've got to do something for Hannah,' he insisted.

'Hannah? Why? What's wrong with her?'

Until that moment Hannah had been a tall, quiet, dignified presence who appeared some mornings and cleaned the house. I knew nothing about her beyond, 'Good morning, Hannah,' followed by 'Good morning, Mrs Morley. How are you today?' If I'd thought about it I'd have worked out that she came from somewhere in Africa but beyond that, and the occasional request for more Harpic, we had an entirely satisfactory relationship based on a complete lack of communication. I was happy with her and as far as I knew she was happy with me; we had no need for intimacy.

Peter, though, the eyes and ears of my world, knew more. 'She's from Sierra Leone.'

'Oh?'

'Ruth! She's from Sierra Leone!' he yelled. He had my attention. Having a sister-in-law from that part of the world, he had identified her accent and, when that day's news had hit, had asked

Hannah whether she still had family in that war-torn region of the world.

'Peter,' she had told him, sadly, 'I have two children there. The rebels are close to where they're living, and I can't get them out.'

He brought her to me from somewhere else in the house and slowly, with considerable encouragement, her story emerged. The woman who had been cleaning my lavatories had been a respected business-woman before the last Sierra Leone coup. Her father had been chief of police, her husband had been a cabinet minister and she herself had run an import/export business. She had two children, Aminata and Idris, who were doing well in school.

The coup had been sudden and bloody. The rebels had assassinated her father and arrested her husband. Then they went to her house to arrest her. They were just too late. She had taken the children to her sister's house for shelter just before they arrived.

She knew that if she didn't get out of the country immediately, she was next on the assassination list so her sister promised to take care of the children just long enough for her to get to Britain and apply for asylum. She went to the airport, used the last of the money in her pocket to bribe herself on to a flight, and arrived in London some days later in what she stood up in, with no money, no husband, no home, no clothes, no friends, but alive. And pregnant. The rebels had won and she couldn't go to the Sierra Leone representatives in London because they were on the side of the people in Freetown who wanted her dead. She applied for asylum which was granted. She then imme-diately applied for visas for her children. They, at least, were safe in her sister's house in Freetown. She managed to find work cleaning homes and offices for an agency which paid her only a fraction of what the client paid them. That's when I met her.

That had been six years earlier. Ever since, Hannah had been pay-ing weekly visits to the Foreign Office and the Home Office – since she could not return to Sierra Leone for fear of assassination she needed help to pry her children out of Africa so that they could be with her in Britain. On her earnings as a cleaner, she had hired a solicitor and an immigration consultant to help her and they too had been unable to obtain visas for the children.

The Sierra Leone news on the radio was becoming more urgent. 'Do something,' demanded Peter.

But what? It was now lunchtime and Sheridan came home from the BBC or wherever he had been all morning. I briefed him on the problem at hand. 'Whom do we know? We don't know anyone at the Home Office. What shall we do?' It was Friday. If we didn't do something soon everybody in government service would have gone home for the weekend and we wouldn't be able to contact anyone before Monday. I had an important meeting that afternoon at the Really Useful Company with Andrew and Madeleine Lloyd Webber about our then-nascent Theatregoer magazine and I needed to go. This, though, was a matter of life and death. And children. Sheridan was so apolitical that he actively avoided politicians and found dinner parties where they were present a terrible bore unless they were secret theatregoers too. Fortunately, we did know one of those.

I called Penny Gummer. We've known each other a long time and are fellow trustees of my old school, Arts Educational. We have never let the fact that our politics are miles apart interfere with our friendship which is wide and deep and nourishing to us both. Penny is married to John Selwyn Gummer, cabinet minister in John Major's Conservative government and a thoroughly good man.

Penny grasped both the situation and the urgency immediately. 'Don't worry. I'll see what I can do. Go to your meeting, I'll ring you there.'

At about five that afternoon, while I was trying valiantly to concentrate on the Theatregoer meeting, my mobile rang. It displayed a number I didn't recognize but I quickly explained the situation to Maddy and went outside into the Really Useful Company's garden. It was John Gummer.

'Call this number now,' he instructed me. 'This man is expecting your call. They've set up a special desk at the Foreign Office to deal with British subjects who are stranded in Sierra Leone and even though these children aren't British, they can be scooped up with the others because of the emergency situation. But call now.'

My meeting was clearly over. The Lloyd Webbers understood. I called the number and spoke to the man on the newly constituted Sierra Leone desk. A member of the Foreign Office staff, a special envoy, was leaving this evening for Freetown to accompany two children from the British Embassy whose parents felt they'd be safer out of the country. If we could move fast, Idris and Aminata could leave Sierra Leone with him. But there were forms to be filled, passports to be verified, all manner of red tape.

Back home, we had a council of war – Sheridan, Hannah, Peter and me – and divided responsibilities. Peter drove Hannah to her flat to pick up her passport and whatever she had that could support her claim. She had, over the years, sworn a number of statements and obtained many official documents proving the truth of her story. They brought them all back to the house. I took on the red tape, filled out the forms, wrote the narrative claims and guaranteed the airfares. Sheridan negotiated with the Foreign Office.

The Foreign Office man told Sheridan that, if we could get the children to the Paramount Hotel in Freetown by 4 p.m. tomorrow, Saturday, they would be flown out by the Royal Air Force that night. Hannah called her sister and, miraculously, despite being in the middle of a war, reached her brother-in-law and explained what was happening. He baulked at the speed of their removal. Her sister, a nurse, was at work and not coming home until Saturday evening, at the earliest. He couldn't reach her. He pointed out that the children had been living with them for six years and they loved them. It would be so cruel for his wife to return home to find that the children had gone without a word. At least, he pleaded, give us a chance to *prepare them for the journey and to say goodbye to them properly. Hannah said she'd call back when she knew more.*

Emergency or no emergency, it was now Friday evening and by the time Sheridan called, everybody at the Sierra Leone desk had gone home but the duty officer promised they'd be back first thing in the morning. They were. Sheridan had by now become quite chummy with the man who was running the emergency operation. Man to man, he asked him, 'Would twenty-four hours really matter all that much? Couldn't the children leave on Sunday instead?' Radio Four had said on the 7 a.m. news that the rebels were approaching Freetown, not that they were there already.

Sheridan's new best friend said, 'I really think they'd be better off if you could get them to the hotel by four o'clock this afternoon.'

Sheridan, nothing daunted, tried again. 'You see, if they could go tomorrow, they'll be able to say goodbye to their family properly.'

The Foreign Office man sighed, heavily. 'I strongly suggest, in view of the current war situation, that you get them to the hotel by four today.' In his very English understated way, he was telling Sheridan that tomorrow would be too late. By tomorrow the rebels would have overrun Freetown and there would be no possibility of getting any Sierra Leone citizens out of the country.

Sheridan understood. He got off the phone and said to Hannah, 'Call your brother-in-law now. Keep trying 'til you get him. Tell him to get them there today at any cost.' He said to me, 'Once she's reached her brother-in-law, don't use the telephone any more than you have to. The special envoy has the number and will keep us informed.'

Peter went off to deliver the forms to the Foreign Office, Hannah got on the phone and eventually reached her brother-in-law. I remembered that we were giving a dinner party that evening so I repaired to the kitchen. Hannah stayed to help me and to wait for a call from the special envoy.

At 4 p.m. Sierra Leone time, the special envoy called to establish contact and to tell us that he was at the hotel. Idris and Aminata had arrived, their passports were in order and they were set to go. At 6 p.m., the telephone rang again. Hannah and I, two women who until yesterday had barely known one another, held hands and held our breath. The line crackled, 'We're just about to board the RAF Hercules. I'll call you back when we get somewhere.'

Our guests arrived. I don't remember who was there or what we ate, but I remember Hannah's blue blouse and I remember burning my finger on the oven due to inattention. I recall Sheridan explaining what was happening and why we were all so jumpy. By 11 p.m. our time, our guests had sensibly gone home, understanding instinctively that the normally hospitable Morleys were tonight being somewhat less than normally hospitable, and we were a collective basket case. Peter, unable to bear being out of touch because we had warned him not to tie up the phone, came back to the house and the four of us sat around, waiting.

At midnight, the telephone rang again. We were all so nervous by this time that we nearly didn't answer it. I was closest. The special envoy's voice was as calm as though he were in the next room. 'We're in Dacca, Senegal,' he announced, 'and we're safe. I'm standing here watching four tired and very hungry children tuck into eggs and chips.'

'How are they?' I managed. 'Could they talk to their mother?'

'Let them eat,' he advised. 'They're just fine. I'll call you back as soon as they finish their Cokes.'

And so it was. It took another three days for them to reach Paris, then another day to clear all the red tape for entry into the UK. Peter and Hannah went to the airport to meet them and ran into even more bureaucratic nonsense but eventually there they were, a little shy and bewildered but there, after six years of trying. Idris' first question, after he had greeted his mother was, 'Will I be able to go to school here?'

The children wrote beautiful letters of thanks to John and Penny Gummer, to Sheridan and me, and to the man who had brought them out of Africa. I tried to fire Hannah many times over the next few years, as her business grew and it became clear that she really didn't have the time to clean my bathroom any longer, but she wouldn't leave me. Finally, she returned to Africa for a year or so to start another business with her sister. She came back with a new partner and a new baby. We are still intrinsically part of each other's lives.

Whoever said there are no happy endings in real life don't know Hannah. Less than ten years after arriving here as a refugee with nothing, Hannah had bought her council house, was doing three jobs and had started a business importing Chinese fabrics and exporting them to Africa. Idris is now in medical school – he'll qualify as a doctor next year – and Aminata is a paralegal, working towards her law degree. Anne-Marie, the child born here, is a real English teenager, mad about clothes, and, when she has finished her education, plans to go into business with a boutique of her own. So, when anybody tells you about lazy immigrants, think of this family.

And think of the law of unintended consequences. I was, through a friend, able to help a near-stranger back to her children and then, of course, she was no longer a stranger. If I hadn't, I could never have coped with Sheridan during those years of illness. Hannah was there, day by day, as Peter was, with help and support during the worst time of my life and, when the worst had happened, she was still there.

Chapter Twenty-Seven

After Sheridan's stroke in November 2002, Peter was always there to manage our difficult home and office life, and to make me laugh when fear, anger or despair threatened to overwhelm me. He wasn't any more successful at getting Sheridan out of bed than I was but he backed me up when necessary and was always on call to take us to doctors' appointments and hospital visits, no matter how inconveniently they were scheduled.

When I went to the theatre on my own, he drove me if I wanted company or stayed behind with Sheridan to make sure he wasn't alone if I didn't. He was always one step ahead of me, trying to anticipate what I might need or what might make Sheridan a scrap more comfortable. He had finally seen off our secretary, so he and Hannah took care of us.

During a brief manic period earlier in the year Sheridan had agreed to write not one but two books for his old friend, the publisher Jeremy Robson, and had signed contracts for them before I could stop him. As the year drew on it became clear that there was no way he could deliver them without help and I was busy on a single-byline book so he asked his friend Paul Webb to assist him.

By the time Paul had done the research Sheridan wasn't up to writing much at all so I took on both projects and tried to write them myself. Jeremy had been very patient but he had deadlines to meet. Somehow, I wrote the first draft of both of them, assuming that I would be able to get Sheridan at least to look at them and make suggestions for the final manuscripts. Eventually, the books went to Jeremy without Sheridan's even glancing at them. He just couldn't focus.

One Monday in summer 2003 Peter said that he had been walking over Westminster Bridge on Sunday and was surprised to find that he was very short of breath. 'Had to stop in the middle of the bridge for a rest,' he told me indignantly.

'You're not getting enough exercise, you lazy old sod,' I taunted him. 'Can't manage to walk across a bridge without stopping? You're getting old.' Peter was one day younger than me.

It happened again, several times, and Peter's GP referred him to a cardiologist who, after an exhaustive series of tests, referred him to a cardiac surgeon at the Royal Brompton Hospital. He was scared so I went with him to see the surgeon. He had, the surgeon told us, an aortic aneurism, which would, sooner rather than later, require surgery to excise. It was still small, though, and there was plenty of time. But, in the nature of things, these aneurisms tend to grow and become more dangerous until eventually there is a likelihood that they will burst. 'When that happens,' said the specialist, 'there will be no time to get to a hospital. But don't worry, that's not going to happen any time soon. We'll schedule you for surgery as soon as possible. We'll whip it out, you'll be right as rain.'

We left the Royal Brompton somewhat subdued but our mutual sunny natures soon reasserted themselves. We were always able to cheer each other up. 'Be quite fun,' Peter offered. 'You can come and see me twice a day and bring some of that Jewish food from your cousins. And Silvana [my good friend] can come and bring me some Italian goodies. I might not want to go home.' We giggled all the way back to the house, coming up with ever dafter schemes for keeping Peter fed in hospital.

Back home, we became embroiled as usual in everyday problems and solutions, not least that Sheridan was going downhill again. Earlier in the year, Sheridan had decided that we'd hold our annual Christmas party as usual on the Sunday before Christmas. Christmas was Sheridan's favourite time of the year. He loved the trees, the lights, the presents, the parties.

But not this year. Sheridan got sadder and sadder until he was crying all the time and talking about suicide again. There wasn't any choice. I called the Cardinal and took him back to Windsor. I cancelled the party and everything else I could, but the inexorable slog of Christmas pantos and plays still had to be written about and filed. I drove back and forth almost every day to see Sheridan and meet with his doctor. When I couldn't go, Peter went, taking with him whatever Sheridan needed and providing the essential reminder that he had a home and people who loved him outside of the clinic.

A few weeks before Christmas 2003 Peter had a letter from the NHS that his operation was scheduled for the second week in December. Peter was adamant. 'No way. I'm not leaving you here over Christmas with Sheridan in this state. You won't be able to cope without me. They'll have to reschedule.'

I argued with him but, to be truthful, not very hard. He was asymptomatic. He had no pain, no inkling that he was ill at all, except the occasional shortness of breath. The NHS offered him a hospital in Surrey in the first week in January and a surgeon he hadn't met. Peter turned it down. He wanted the Royal Brompton and the surgeon he already knew. He was the best and Peter wanted the best. He held out and got what he wanted. The operation was scheduled for 21 January 2004.

Christmas was pretty awful. Sheridan was still in the Cardinal and I made Christmas dinner for my family and they rallied round me as always but it wasn't much fun. Although he was released immediately after the New Year, Sheridan was still spending most of his time in bed. Peter was an endless tower of strength and humour throughout that grisly 'holiday' and, although he had occasional collywobbles about the coming operation, he was feeling fine.

The hospital wanted him in the night before his operation so, on the afternoon of 20 January, he drove us to the hospital but the car park was full. A block away on Chelsea Square he found a meter. We walked to the Admissions Department and got him checked in. He sat, fully dressed, on the bed in his private room and I stayed chatting with him until he pointed out that the meter was nearly up and I'd better go and rescue the car. I took his watch, wallet and the ring my father had left him, gave him some change for a newspaper and prepared to leave. Just then, a very old, very fat man passed the door of his room, barely able to walk.

'That'll be you soon if you don't get some exercise,' I teased.

'Nah, that'll be you if you don't lose some weight,' came the immediate response.

As I left, I turned in the doorway. 'I won't come tomorrow, you'll be too dopey from the anaesthetic,' I said, 'but I'll be here bright and early on Friday with breakfast.'

He shouted after me, 'You be careful with the car, I don't want to have to take it to the bodyshop.' He managed to make the word 'bodyshop' sound like a gay joke.

I went home, having arranged for the surgical department to call me when Peter's operation ended the following day. Sheridan called him later in the evening to wish him luck. About 10 p.m., Silvana phoned to find out what food he wanted her to bring on Friday.

Thursday was a day like any other except that Peter wasn't around. At lunchtime I thought of phoning the hospital but decided not to. They had promised to call me and maybe they had got him into surgery later than they expected. By 5 p.m. I was worried. I called the hospital but they refused to put me through to the operating theatre floor. I left a message for the surgeon. Ten minutes later my telephone rang and a tired voice asked for me.

'Speaking.'

'This is the assistant surgeon on Mr Coller's operation. You're listed as his next of kin. Can you get here fast?'

'Why? What's happened? Is Peter all right?'

There was a pause. 'There have been . . . complications.'

'What sort of complications?'

'I'd rather not discuss it over the telephone. Please come if you can.'

'I'll be there in fifteen minutes.'

I shouted for Sheridan, 'It's Peter. There's a problem with the operation. I'm going to the hospital.'

'Don't leave me here. I'm coming with you.' He came.

I flew over the Albert Bridge, breaking the land-speed record. I remember nothing about getting there except that when I looked at my watch I'd driven a twenty-minute journey in thirteen minutes. Miraculously, there was a space in the car park. I ran into the hospital, Sheridan following as fast as he could. The reception desk gave us directions to the operating theatre floor. We emerged from the lift into a deserted lobby.

The double doors leading off it opened and the surgeon I had met previously came out in his scrubs, blood staining the front.

'Come with me.' He opened a small waiting room and asked the couple sitting in it to leave. He indicated that we should sit. He sat opposite us. 'We opened Mr Coller's chest this morning just after seven,' he began. 'Everything went fine. We transferred him to a heart/lung machine for the duration of the procedure, removed the aneurism, and began the process of closing. This involves removing him from the heart/lung machine so the heart can restart. But every time we try to get his heart to beat on its own it won't. We've been trying for hours.'

We stared at him stupidly. This was Peter. He was fine last night. He didn't have any symptoms. He wasn't in pain. He couldn't be . . . I couldn't even *think* the word 'dying'.

'What now?' I asked. 'Is there anything else you can try?'

At this point his assistant, the man who had telephoned me, stuck his head round the door and indicated that he was needed. 'We've probably got perhaps two more attempts. Please wait here. One of us will keep you informed.'

Sheridan was sitting with his eyes closed and his chin on his chest. He wasn't asleep. He didn't move for another two hours. In the meantime, I called Alan, Peter's best friend, who lives in Hove, and told him what was happening. 'I'll be there as quickly as the traffic will let me,' he said, and, in a remarkably short time, he was.

Twice during the next few hours, the assistant surgeon came in to say there had been no progress. Finally, at about 8 p.m., both surgeons came in with a tall young woman who I think was their scrub nurse. They were so tired, and so defeated, their announcement was superfluous. 'I'm sorry, we've lost him.'

What? Even at this stage it seemed impossible. Doctors are miracle workers, aren't they? They can do anything, bring the dead back to life, save lives no matter what the illness. But they can't. 'His heart was just too weak. It couldn't take the insult of the operation and the anaesthetic. We did everything we could. I'm sorry.'

I heard my own voice reassuring the surgical team, now seated in the tiny room with us, too exhausted to move, too discouraged to pretend professional detachment. 'I know you did. Thank you for trying.'

There was a voice from the corner. Sheridan had raised his head. 'I want to see him. Say goodbye.' We all looked at him and then at the surgeon.

'Yes, of course. Give us a few minutes to clean him up and we'll come and get you.'

Alan went with Sheridan. I didn't. I wanted to remember the perky Peter, smartly dressed, sitting up on his bed – was it just yesterday afternoon? – making jokes and worrying about his/our beloved car because I was driving it.

We went home, unbelievably without Peter. A few days later, the funeral arranged, Alan asked me to get some clothes to dress him for the cremation. In a way, that was the worst moment, walking into his bright yellow Putney flat, winter sun streaming in, looking around at his treasures, the little car that was really a CD player which I had bought him for his birthday, the painting my father had made for him, his photographs and collections, the things he had loved, all there when he was not. I felt like a burglar, opening his wardrobe and finding his favourite tie that we had bought together in New York when he and his partner had been staying in my apartment. I did what I had come there to do, chose his favourite and smartest clothes, and fled from his flat.

The humanist funeral was just what he wanted ('none of that religious malarkey'). Alan chose the words and the people; I chose the music; Sheridan spoke, without notes, from the heart. His eulogy was elegant and funny, the jokes in all the right places. You would never have known that he was ill. It was perfect. In his final remarks his friend Alan said, 'Sheridan has said that the luck of the Morleys' life was meeting Peter. What he didn't say is equally true, that the luck of Peter's life was meeting the Morleys.'

And it was true, we needed him no less than he needed us. There has not been a day of my life since that moment when I haven't missed him.

Chapter Twenty-Eight

*W*hen *Robert Morley died of a stroke on Derby Day in 1992 ('The only Derby he ever missed,' said Sheridan, proudly), Sheridan decided to write his biography. He called it* Robert, My Father, *a fairly obscure reference to the play which led to what Sheridan considered Robert's greatest performance,* Edward, My Son. *Robert had written the play as a vehicle for himself and had toured it all over the United States and Australia for much of Sheridan's childhood, taking his entire family with him. Later, Sheridan remembered this tour as a golden time, the only part of his childhood he recalled with pleasure.*

In fact, when they left for New York, Robert and Joan fully intended to emigrate. They put their house in Berkshire on the market, took an apartment in New York and enrolled Sheridan in a progressive school on Manhattan's West Side. But when the Broadway run ended and Robert was offered a tour of Australia, they decided that Sydney suited them much better and set off en famille *for the Antipodes which, Sheridan's memoirs recall, involved cruise ships, trains across the prairies, seaplanes which landed on the beach in Hawaii and all manner of exciting modes of transportation which could have been expressly designed to enchant a small boy.*

In the end, though, Robert missed Ascot racecourse and, with the tour over, the family returned to their Wargrave house, still unsold, and Robert resumed the life he had always lived, that of a gentleman actor in a very English setting. However, Robert's blithe assertion that he had really meant to emigrate but, all things considered, had decided not to, did not escape the notice of the British tax authorities who decided that Robert had announced his emigration merely to avoid paying his taxes for the years he had been away. Robert, insisting that his honour was being impugned, sued and won, thus giving rise to an anomaly in the tax law which, until it was closed some years later, became known as 'The Morley Loophole'. The Morleys' love of Australia and Hawaii stayed with them until the end of their lives and it was a rare year that the senior Morleys didn't take themselves to Sydney where both their daughter Annabel and younger son Wilton established homes and families of their own.

Sheridan, though, remained irredeemably English and he never really wanted to live anywhere but in the Thames Valley. All of our homes, except the first one – and that was mine in Regent's Park so didn't really count – overlooked the Thames and, although Sheridan had no interest in boating or sailing as a hobby, proximity to that particular waterway was a priority for him.

He loved Australia, though, and went often, or as often as he could persuade an employer or editor to pay the fares. Once we even got Cunard to send us to Australia on the Queen Elizabeth II, *whose interior decoration resembled an English country hotel circa 1955. We loved it. We had managed to turn our individual after-dinner speeches into a turn we could perform together for the cruise passengers. Usually, on a two-week leg of the world tour Sheridan would give two talks, I would give one, and we'd do two together on the days the passengers were sailing from one port to another. This worked just as well on a five-day transatlantic crossing where the passengers were marooned on the ship with no ports of call between Cork or Cherbourg and New York. Then, they wanted a little more entertainment and we were on hand to provide it with a few theatre stories,*

*some jokes, some well-scripted marital disagreements and consider-
able goodwill on the part of the passengers.*

*These went down so well that we soon graduated from the small
on-board theatre where we started. By the time Cunard had been sold
to a gigantic American conglomerate and the genteel Englishness had
gone, we were drawing huge audiences in the Grand Lounge, the ship's
biggest space where, every evening, showgirls and boys of varying
competence danced up a storm, supporting whichever 'name' singer
we had taken on board at the last port.*

*We were always given the choice between being paid a fee for our
services as guest lecturers and being treated like crew, or not being
paid but being treated as first-class passengers. It was a no-brainer.
Until the Americans took over, at which point we were relegated to a
cupboard under the stairs without a porthole, we opted for a lovely
suite and dinner in the Queen's Grill, the closest thing to real pamper-
ing we'd see in our lifetimes.*

*At lunchtime, the head waiter would come round to enquire what
we would like for dinner. In fact, everything tasted pretty much the
same, whether we ordered Jewish chicken soup or Chinese won-ton,
but I don't expect ever again to be given such choice and to have a staff
of 100 chefs willing to prepare whatever my greedy heart desired. It
was wonderfully old-fashioned. Often I ordered something like steak
Diane or crêpes Suzette, just for the pleasure of having it flambéed at
tableside. Where else can you find that these days? And who cares if it
was upmarket nursery food so long as it was the royal nursery?*

*The old-fashionedness extended to every aspect of the ship's pas-
senger services. Only once did I make the mistake of visiting the
hairdressing establishment on board. I came out looking much like my
old Auntie Lily who never outgrew the 1930s marcel waves hugging
the head in rigorous rows, never moving – perhaps they didn't dare.*

*Best of all was the ballroom which, every evening, before and after
dinner, was the preferred venue for every elderly widow on the ship.*

Dressed in their best – long evening dresses every night we were at sea – the ladies sat at the edge of the dance floor while the orchestra solemnly played strict ballroom tempo tunes for them to dance with the gentlemen hosts, a group of men of a certain age, who were employed by Cunard for that express purpose. They could all dance and were strictly enjoined to partner each lady in rotation, but for never more than one number so as not to risk favouritism and to avoid the ever-present risk of an 'attachment' being formed. The ladies loved it, sure of never being a wallflower, waiting their turn.

For a graphic illustration, with no words, of the inescapable fact that men die before women, leaving them still full of life and enthusiastic about enjoying themselves, you need look no further than the QE2 ballroom during a world cruise. Unfortunately, it is no more, having been retired in favour of the much larger, flashier and less charming Queen Mary II.

I miss it. Sheridan and I made many friends both among the crew and officers and among the regular passengers whom we would see on the world cruise every year, traipsing round the world yet again and complaining all the way: 'Oh no, not going ashore in Fiji, they charge you for the beach, you know'; 'Africa's so hot and, anyway, the bag I bought here last time fell apart the first time I wore it'; and, 'I don't trust the food in India so I've brought a sandwich from the ship.'

Sheridan loved to travel, especially when he could wangle it at someone else's expense, which he usually could. He belonged to the old-fashioned English class of traveller who want to see far-flung places but want to do it in comfort, preferably surrounded by people and food he recognized. In a foreign country I want to see everything, taste the special dishes, meet the people. Sheridan would inevitably want to head for the nearest five-star hotel with a swimming pool where he could lie until lunch when he would take himself, usually still in a wet swimsuit, to their restaurant and order a lovely meal. I soon learned to leave him to soak in whatever pool he'd found and return for lunch to regale him with my morning's adventures in whatever street market or beauty spot I'd found myself. If I absolutely insisted he come sightseeing with me he wanted an air-conditioned bus he didn't have to leave and an English-speaking guide.

He could spend an entire day floating, apparently asleep, in a swimming pool, never emerging until nightfall. On one occasion, in the Maldives, I think, the hotel manager summoned me in a panic: he thought Sheridan had died in the pool, so long had he been floating without moving. 'Shout, "Time for a gin and tonic, Sheridan," in his ear,' I advised. Sure enough, the eyes opened and a very happy and demonstrably un-dead Sheridan clambered out of the pool and lumbered, soaking wet, towards the bar.

This ability to unwind totally, to leave work and cares behind him, to shed worry and to relax completely while on holiday was, I'm sure, what made it possible for Sheridan to get through the enormous amount of work he was able to shift and to withstand the pressures of his high-powered freelance life. And, of course, he would have said that he had me to do the worrying for him.

When Sheridan showed me the manuscript of Robert, My Father, *I was fascinated, not so much by what he had included as by what he had left out. Included was Robert's entire career, a vivid account of his travels, and an affectionate assessment of his films and plays. It was, like all Sheridan's writing, readable, cogent and informative. It held the interest throughout. It gave a fine appraisal of the life of a working and successful actor with a varied career and it left the reader feeling good about Robert and about Sheridan. So what more did I want? Why did I have this nagging sense that there was a hole at the centre of the book which no other book of his had?*

For several days, I cogitated about what I should say. He had given it to me to read because he wanted my comments and I could hardly pretend I hadn't read it. But I wished I could. And then I knew what was wrong and I knew I had to tell him. Missing was any sense of their relationship, of what it had been like to be the son of one of Britain's most famous character actors, of the balance between public and private lives. He had, in fact, written the biography of a man he scarcely knew. It had about as much personal insight as his biography of, say, Katharine Hepburn, a respectful appraisal of an actor he admired but whose real in-depth personality he had almost completely failed to conjure.

I told him, as tactfully as I could, but tact has never been a talent we shared nor was it any part of the way we worked together. Always, we just said what we had to say, straight out, without worrying about hurt feelings. Sometimes we argued about it but usually even fierce professional arguments soon transmuted into practical conversations about how we could fix whatever the other had found objectionable. Not this time; this was personal.

'You're saying I've failed to bring him to life?' asked Sheridan, very hurt.

'No, I'm saying that you've failed to bring you to life or, at least that part of you which is a son and that part of him which is a father. He's there, as an actor, even as a friend, but your relationship is nowhere to be found. Your feelings about him, his about you, are not there at all.'

Sheridan, who never sulked, sulked for about a week. During that time I would hear him bashing away on his old electric typewriter but he never showed me what he was writing. Finally, he went off to have lunch with his publisher, Ion Trewin, carrying a cardboard box which, I realized, contained the finished manuscript of Robert, My Father. *And when the galley proofs of his memoirs came for correcting, I was amazed to discover that the final chapter is titled* 'For Ruth'. *It is his acceptance of my criticism and his valiant attempt to address it. It is a brave and forthright piece of writing and I admire him enormously for making the effort to find out, after his father's death, who they both were.*

Chapter Twenty-Nine

By late spring 2005 I realized that, because of various NHS holdups and the travel commitments of both professors, Guy Goodwin and Tipu Aziz, the operation was not going to happen until autumn.

By this time, we had another assistant to help us organize our lives. I had been so shocked and bruised by Peter's sudden death in January 2004 that it took eight months before I could think about finding someone else to work for us. He was simply unique and I couldn't get my head around anyone taking his place. Exhaustion, and my inability to be in two places at once – working, and available to take Sheridan where he needed to go – finally convinced me to look.

A few people, ex-cab drivers and the like, applied for the job but retreated when told that they would have to work at night driving Sheridan to the theatre and wait until the play was over to bring him home. 'Oh no, I couldn't possibly do that,' said one. 'I have to be home by six to put the children to bed.' Okay, straight men weren't the answer. They had homes and families to go to. Logic suggested that one of the reasons Peter had been perfect for us was that he was a self-described 'show-biz queen'. He had loved the theatre and would often wangle himself a ticket from the show publicist when getting ours. Where he parked the car while in the theatre I never enquired and he certainly never got any parking tickets. So clearly what we needed was another gay man or woman without family ties and with an interest in what we did for a living.

I advertised in the *Pink Paper* and got a number of replies. From this I hired Becca, partly because she was as different from Peter as it was possible to be. She was a tall young woman, half Peter's age, with an engaging grin. A university graduate, she was famil- iar, as Peter had not been, with the peculiarities of computers, and she was currently working as a spotlight operator in a West End theatre.

Unlike Peter, she didn't want to be part of our lives. She did her job and went home. It was a big adjustment for me who was accus- tomed to Peter being there all the time, volunteering for every job and being part of everything we did whether it was his business or not. Becca was much more professional and somewhat detached. She soon mastered the ticketing system, the publicists, the adminis- trative side of the operation and, although she didn't much like the driving, she did it.

She tried to help with Sheridan, getting him out of bed, finding the things he lost and transporting him to where he had to be, but, poor girl, she loathed the regular screaming rows that exploded between us when I wanted him to do something he didn't. Our bickering, always part of our relationship, had transmuted into something else and that something else wasn't pleasant to observe. In fact, it wasn't pleasant to be part of, either. To our surprise, despite her interest in the backstage elements of the theatre, she wasn't all that keen on seeing the plays although she would go with Sheridan when I was reviewing something else and he needed someone with him.

My concerned family and friends had been telling me to take a break. I knew how tired I was, not physically but psychically. I got enough sleep usually but the constant worry gets to you after a while and I'd been living with it for years by then. I desperately wanted to go to my summer getaway in Aspen, Colorado, but couldn't see how to leave Sheridan with someone he hardly knew and he needed someone with him all the time. If left, he would either stay in bed without getting up for months or he would crash around, blood pressure dropping, falling over and occasionally falling down the stairs. He wouldn't take his medication and would eat nothing but sugar, thereby working his way into a diabetic coma. In that state he couldn't reason.

On the other hand, I was becoming an automaton. I lived on a permanent treadmill. I got up, I dealt with the medication, I kept the house and office running, I tried to get Sheridan out of bed, I did the shopping and cooking, I prepared his BBC scripts, I wrote his columns and mine, I went to the theatre, with or without Sheridan, I came home, I made dinner for us, I wrote the overnight reviews, I went to bed.

Whatever kind of joy I had been wringing from any aspect of my life had gone. I spoke to my sister every day and my friends called regularly, from both sides of the Atlantic. I played tennis once a week and I went out for the occasional lunch or weekend dinner. I didn't even enjoy writing anymore. But, desperately though I wanted to, it was becoming clear that I wasn't going to get to Aspen this year.

Then, two things happened to change things. My friend Hilary who lives in Antibes in the south of France was paying a flying visit to London and dropped by for breakfast. Typical of Hilary, she brought with her croissants and her own homemade jam. This is Hilary's idea of a hostess gift. She took one look at me and demanded that I come back with her for a week in France. I couldn't, of course. I couldn't leave Sheridan so she offered to take Sheridan instead. I knew she'd take care of him and he'd be happy to be with her and her husband Roy. At the same time, Sheridan's friend Peter Young, who lives in Spain, suggested that if I put Sheridan on a flight to

Barcelona he would not only look after him for a few days but then drive him to Hilary's house in Antibes. This would get me two weeks in Aspen if I planned it right.

Before I left London I checked with BUPA about the provisions of our travel insurance. If, I asked, I had to return from the United States in a hurry before the date of my scheduled flight ticket, would I be covered? And if my husband became ill while in France or Spain would the insurance cover medical expenses there and would he be covered for repatriation? The answer to both questions was yes.

Why do the best-laid plans always go wrong? Once in Aspen, no sooner had I established that Sheridan was safely in Spain with Peter than my sister phoned to say that our mother, now ninety-four, was unwell again. For the preceding six months she had been in and out of hospital, her carers at Nightingale House preferring to be safe than sorry and taking her to St George's whenever she had one of the many infections to which the very old are prey. She was, said Adrienne, poorly but holding her own. 'Stay where you are,' she said. 'I'll keep you informed.' I agreed gratefully, needing to be away, needing a respite from the constant worry.

All the time I was in Aspen, indeed every moment since his stroke on 21 November 2002, Sheridan was on my mind. There wasn't a second of my life where the 'How's he doing?', 'Is he all right?' and 'Has he done something silly or irrevocable?' questions weren't just beneath the surface. But Aspen, somehow, always has had the ability to calm and refresh and, there, the problems which seem insurmountable in London and New York appear, if not soluble, then addressable from the vantage point of a Colorado mountain top.

Getting up in Aspen is easy because the morning welcomes you with cool, crisp air, the sun making its way over the mountains, the birds wheeling between the peaks, the view of mountains in every direction, the little Victorian houses in bright colours sitting in their flower gardens and the shimmering, shivering, aspen trees that give the town its name.

I played tennis at eight every morning with my friend Karen who is the coach at Aspen Meadows. My tennis gang – a movable feast of a dozen women of a certain age who play well enough but don't allow tennis to get in the way of the laughter that punctuates nearly every point – arrived at nine for our regular doubles-fest. We're not all that serious about it. 'Does anyone have any idea of the score?' is a frequent cry. 'Gossip with racquets in our hands,' is how the beautiful Maureen describes our morning activity. 'The tennis hasn't improved this year,' Hermine emailed me in her usual clear-sighted style before I arrived, 'but the recipes are great.'

Catching up is always fun. Someone had got married during the year, someone had written a new book, someone had moved house, someone was planning her first trip to Africa – over the first few mornings each told of her year with that astonishing intimacy that women are able to establish with one another in an instant. Each of them wanted to know about Sheridan and they were all genuinely disappointed that all their hopes and prayers hadn't had much effect. He wasn't better, was the bottom line, and I sensed their concern for me, manifested in lots of jokes and an unwillingness to talk about their own husbands unless they too were ill. Maureen and Hermine are in regular touch throughout the year from, respectively, Colorado and New York, but the others remind me that they care too, with terrible online jokes, occasional tactful enquiries and funny cards which seem to arrive exactly when I need picking up.

Aspen, for me, has several sets of such friends, rarely interlocking but each of long duration and all so close and easy that there is no distance caused by a year apart, just joy at being together again. There are the locals, those who live in Aspen year-round. The best houses are hidden away and don't advertise either their architectural excellence or the priceless art collections they house. Their views of the mountains are nonpareil. I may be all agog to see what Antonio Banderas and Melanie Griffith's house is like, or to catch a glance of tennis star Martina Navratilova's home, but the real locals just giggle at the incoming stars and occasionally invite them to one of their endless charity events.

There are the thinking friends who come in the summer for a brain MOT. The Aspen Institute, where you go when your brain is turning to scrambled eggs from too much hiking or biking, is walking distance from where I play tennis at Aspen Meadows. The Institute is the summer retreat of choice for heavyweight intellectuals. In twenty years, although I've heard many speakers with whom I disagreed, I've never heard a boring or intellectually lazy lecture.

Then there are my music friends, my main reason for being in Aspen. The views, the outdoor sports, the great food, the intellectual stimulation and the hospitality are wonderful but, after twenty-odd years, if it weren't for the Aspen Music Festival and School, I might go somewhere else occasionally. But the music and the young musicians change every year and they are an addiction. Six hundred and fifty instrumentalists, trainee conductors and singers from all over the world, roughly fifteen to twenty-five years old, audition (often many times before they are successful) to come here and be taught by some of the world's leading musicians and musical pedagogues. This group of friends are international conductors, soloists and chamber musicians who travel constantly throughout the world; I see them rarely except in Aspen. Here, not only do they play and teach, but also hike, eat, gossip, laugh, entertain one another (and me) and generally let their hair down, because this is their vacation, too.

That year I went to at least one concert a day. Some days I attended two. On a couple of occasions I took in three. The festival is generous to me and I always write an article or two, or do an interview for the BBC or American radio, just to sing for my supper. It was a glorious week, full of friends and laughter and good music, marred only by Sheridan's illness and the sinking feeling that I should be home with him, not out here in the mountains, enjoying myself. At least my holiday had loosened my hold on resentment and fury.

But it couldn't last. A week into my Aspen idyll, when Sheridan was just preparing to be driven from Spain to Hilary's house in France, my mother died. It was a beautiful clear morning and Karen and I were playing tennis surrounded by wild flowers and the occasional inquisitive deer. It was so quiet that I heard the ringing of the mobile phone between the thwacks of the tennis ball. It was Adrienne, who had been with Rosie that morning when she had died, quite peacefully.

It was time. Until the last six months she had been amazingly bright, still ruling everybody's roost, fussing over what she wore and how she looked. Unlike me, she was wonderful with Sheridan, knowing what to say that would calm him. She told fanciful stories and because she often fell asleep in the middle of a thought, when she woke up she would continue telling the story but with the contents of her dream included. She had the paranoia common to many old people, sure that we and others were stealing from her or hiding things, and she wouldn't eat anything that wasn't sweets or biscuits. The last six months had been difficult for her and for us. Despite our sadness at her death, just one year after our father, both Adrienne and I were somewhat relieved that the constant alarms and infections, the running to and from hospitals and the emergencies were now over.

I flew back to London by which time Adrienne had heroically organized the funeral and done most of the boring tasks associated with death. On the flight over I tried to decide whether I should tell Sheridan or not. By now he would be in France with Hilary and Roy, lying in their pool and, hopefully, feeling a bit better. He would, I thought, be something of a liability at a funeral, depressed as he was. He adored my mother and I could imagine how upset he would be on learning of her death. I decided not to call him and take the flak later when he found out. Having made the decision I promptly changed my mind and as soon as I got home I called him in Antibes.

'Darling, there's no need for you to come for the funeral,' I told him. 'You're not well and she knew that. She wouldn't expect you to be there.'

'Nonsense,' he said in a voice very close to his own, 'I always promised her that I'd speak at her funeral and I shall. Nobody, not even you, can stop me from doing that.'

It was true. She had always said she didn't care what kind of a funeral she had as long as Sheridan spoke for her. It was the only preference she expressed but their relationship was so warm and deep that if she had known how much it cost him to be there she would not have asked it of him.

I spoke to Hilary who arranged to accompany Sheridan and make sure he got on the right flight, etc. and, just like that, we were back in London. We had been a family of five, two parents and three children; now Adrienne and I were the only two left. The funeral was on a hot August day and even our rabbi was on holiday. The substitute had not known Rosie but we sat in my cousin Mildred's little garden and talked about her until it was dark. At the funeral itself, Sheridan had sat in his usual pose, completely still with his chin on his chest, until it was his turn to speak. Then, just as he had at Peter's funeral, he pulled it together, stood tall at the lectern and delivered a beautiful eulogy, full of love and warmth, telling what kind of person she had been and how blessed he had felt to have had her for a mother-in-law. He had returned her love for him in full measure.

Chapter Thirty

*W*hen Sheridan and I got together it was with a sense of recognition. He encouraged me to develop my passion for the songs and their authors, to direct whenever there was time, to write about the Great American Songbook and to enjoy the singers. Through Don Smith, who runs the Cabaret Convention in New York every year, we met everybody who matters in cabaret as well as the up-and-comers who were just beginning to make a career as singers.

Very frequently, when friends had a new show to try out, they would ask me to come and hear it in case I had suggestions for staging or emphasis. Two of these – K.T. Sullivan and Mark Nadler, both highly successful cabaret artists and good friends – were just starting to put a new show together, a collection of the songs of George Gershwin. They were going to preview it way out on Long Island so we trekked out there and I heard what Mark, who is a pianist and dancer as well as a singer, had done with the arrangements and how K.T. was singing them. They were marvellous and I knew immediately that they had an enormous success on their hands if they could build a whole show on what they had already got. The three of us talked way into the night and the upshot was that they asked me to direct and co-write a show that would change all our lives.

We called it Gershwin's American Rhapsody: A New Musical

Revue. *We never meant it to be more than a cabaret, albeit a very classy one. Mark had the idea that it should be a kind of biography of George Gershwin in song, with him as George and K.T. as the embodiment of his songs. I co-wrote and directed, giving it a gloss that the songs themselves already had. It soon had a producer on board and turned into an Off-Broadway revue.*

While the show was being written I had contacted a wonderful man called Edward Jablonski who had written the best biography of Gershwin. I had no sooner walked into his rambling West Side apartment full of Gershwiniana than he asked me, 'Do you drink beer?'

'I sure do,' I replied, and found myself pushed out the door en route to his favourite bar. Until the end of his life I spent a lot of time in that bar, learning about my favourite composers and lyricists, swapping stories, hearing the folklore and the truth about the men who wrote the Great American Songbook.

One afternoon in his apartment, a few days after we met, I showed Ed the script Mark and I had written for American Rhapsody *and asked him to look it over for mistakes. Ed was not given to praise but he read the papers I gave him, nodded once and left the room. He returned with a songsheet. 'How'd you like to include a "new" Gershwin song in your show?'*

'My Little Ducky', a cheeky comic duet, had been cut from a Gershwin musical in 1927 and never sung in public since. Ed was offering it to me on behalf of George Gershwin for a show he hadn't even seen yet. It was a mark of trust I never forgot. K.T. and Mark learned it that night and it went into the show immediately.

Spending time with those gorgeous Gershwin songs, beautifully sung, was reward in itself, which was a good thing because I never managed to get our sainted producer to pay me what she owed and neither did anybody else. But 'Embraceable You', 'Fascinatin' Rhythm', 'Our Love is Here to Stay', 'Rhapsody in Blue', 'Summertime' and the rest of those glorious tunes were more than their own reward. Working with this material and two singers who loved and understood it, and a crew determined to make this show the best it could possibly be, made every day a joy.

Opening night was a real kick. It opened at the Triad Theater, off Broadway, in November 2000 to the kind of reviews first-time directors dream about. By this time, everybody knew we had a stonking great hit and, thrillingly, we had a post-show party at Sardi's, the famous theatrical restaurant. It was noisy and fun. Everybody sang, everybody made speeches – all the work had been worth it. Mark, K.T., and I enjoyed every minute. When the reviews came in, we were made.

Sheridan, who was marooned in England making a television series, wasn't able to be at our opening night but he was as supportive and encouraging as only he could be. He called me several times a day, listened to my joys and despairs, and never went to bed without phoning to tell me how much he loved me. He came over a week later to see it and everybody on the crew fell in love with him at once. He was as proud as if he had written it himself and he talked about American Rhapsody to everybody he met. There couldn't have been a Wandsworth postman or a West End theatre usher who didn't know that his wife had directed a show in New York and that it was, in his words, 'a triumph!' For months afterwards strangers who had talked to Sheridan would come up and congratulate me on a show taking place 2,000 miles away.

I left New York soon after our opening night but my love affair with the show, and with George Gershwin, continued. I came back once a month as the run proceeded to see how it was going, but K.T. and Mark really only ever needed two recurring notes: Mark would over-act when he got excited and K.T., whose phrasing was perfect when singing, had a tendency to gabble when she was speaking. So, before I left, I would leave two notes on the dressing-room noticeboard. One said: 'K.T. – SLOWER'. The other said, 'MARK – LESS'.

When Barbara Schwepcke of Haus Publishing said she was releasing a series of short but essential biographies of the great composers and asked me which one I'd like to write about, I didn't hesitate. This was the year after American Rhapsody *had finally closed and I was missing George. But, before I accepted the contract, I went back to New York and Ed Jablonski.*

'This is your guy,' I said to him, 'you're the Gershwin maven. If you want to do this, I'll ask Barbara to issue the contract to you instead.'

I thought he might relish, as I did, the opportunity to write a serious biography for the general public about the man he revered as one of the greatest composers who ever lived, a book not for the aficionado willing to toil through 700 pages of arcana and facts, but for people who loved 'Embraceable You' and wanted to know a little more about the man who wrote it.

'No,' said Ed, with typical generosity. 'I've said what I wanted to say about him, it's your turn. You're ready. You write it. I'll help.'

And help he did. I sent him the pages as I wrote them and he marked them up with a thick red pencil. Sometimes, not often, the red scrawl was complimentary: 'I didn't know about this but you're right. Good for you.' More often the red pencil would seem to yell at me, 'You know better than this,' underlined twice, and I'd have to try harder. One thing I know for sure, there are no factual mistakes anywhere in that manuscript; Ed wouldn't allow it. He went over every single word of that book and by the time I delivered it to Barbara it was ready for the printer.

Ed used to say that I did all the work and he just got to drink beer with the author. This was far from the truth. Barbara wanted to augment the text with photographs, preferably pictures that hadn't been seen before, and Ed produced these from out of his dozens of drawers. Whenever I went to see him for a beer, I'd always learn something that was not in his book but could be used in mine.

Over several years I met Ed's family and we became close enough to have Thanksgiving together. Ed's wife had died some years earlier and I still regret not having met her. Their daughter, Carla, an actor and performance artist, and I became friends and it was to her that I confided, when I was halfway through the book, that I didn't think Ed was looking well.

'He's not,' she sighed, 'but he won't see a doctor and he's a stubborn old man.'

From her apartment in Brooklyn she tried to look after a father who didn't want any interference and did her best to get him to eat properly, drink less beer and take it easy. She failed, but not through lack of trying. Having tried myself to take care of cantankerous and independent parents I could sympathize but, unfortunately, because of Ed's resistance I had nothing to offer except support and a sympathetic ear.

Writing Gershwin was a privilege. To live with this happy man as he lived his tragically short life (George died before he was thirty-nine), to accompany him as he composed his songs, his shows, his concert music and his movies, was sheer pleasure. The book wrote itself quickly and I had access to the manuscripts, the scores, the letters and the papers that documented a life well lived. I lived through his many love affairs, his passion for his brother and the rest of his noisy family, through his burgeoning interest in art, his fascination with interior design, and his gift for friendship with everyone, from princes to ordinary people he met on the street. Somebody, I told myself smugly, somebody is paying me to do this.

As always, I drifted back and forth across the Atlantic, writing my book, and each time I came back to New York, Ed, never robust-looking, was thinner and greyer. It emerged that he had cancer and that his chances of recovery were slim. Still, he persisted in editing the book, demanding pages even when he was in hospital. I told Carla I wasn't going to send him any more, it wasn't fair to put so much pressure on a man who was clearly dying. But Carla was adamant.

'You're keeping him alive,' she said. 'He lives for that book. If it were up to me you'd never finish it.'

Four days before he died he lay, grey and wasted, in a hospital bed in his apartment, but he was still sending Carla and me from one drawer to another to find another perfect illustration for the book. He could barely speak but he managed to tell us how stupid we were when we couldn't find something and through our tears we laughed at each insult, glad he could still find the energy to tell us off.

The family asked me to speak at his memorial. What I said found its way into the dedication for our book, Gershwin, *published that autumn.*

This book is for Edward Jablonski who taught me everything I know about George Gershwin, everything, that is, that George didn't teach me himself through his music and his life.

Ed's friendship and dedication to 'getting it right' have been an inspiration and, Ed, whatever I've missed, or mistaken, or overlooked, or overemphasized, is my fault and not yours. You've been the best mentor and one-man cheering section any writer could possibly have. You have allowed, even encouraged, me to plunder your books and corrected me when I've gone off the rails. Thank you.

When you wrote your great biography you thanked your friend and editor and said, 'I only hope it is worthy of the subject and of you.' I had the same hope, Ed, wanted to put the first published copy of this book into your hands. But then, on 10 February, early this year, you went and died on me. What kind of comment is that? But this book is still for Edward Jablonski who will live as long as anyone writes about George Gershwin.

Chapter Thirty-One

Our summer over, brought to an exclamation mark by Rosie's death, we lived in a kind of suspended animation, waiting for Guy or Tipu to tell us when Sheridan's operation would take place or even whether it would happen at all. I have a flurry of emails between the two of them discussing scans and dates for MRIs, when they will be available, who will arrange them and a lot of medical minutiae that reassured me of their continuing interest in Sheridan's case. However, I realized that, between the lines, they were both concerned that the NHS and the Radcliffe were not as enthusiastic as they were about the procedure and that the funding might not be forthcoming.

Finally, I said, 'OK, I'll find the money. I'll pay for it. Tell me what order of magnitude are we talking about here? Am I selling my mother's jewellery or am I selling the house?' By this time, I'd have taken a long-term loan, anything I had to do, to get this operation done. I knew it was experimental, God knows, enough people had told me that, but I had great faith, some might say blind faith, that it would work. No, no, they soothed me, we'll work it out. Don't worry about the money.

And, out of the blue, we had a date – 19 October 2005. Suddenly, it was real. After three years of abject misery, something was finally being done to try to alleviate Sheridan's pain. I realized that I hadn't asked enough practical questions of either Guy or Tipu, having been so focused on just getting this far, so I asked to see them. The week before the operation, I went to Oxford without Sheridan; these two exceedingly busy men, top of their respective fields, had cleared their afternoon to speak with me.

It was a beautiful autumn day, Oxford was dressed in all her leafy finery and the three of us sat in a conference room at the Warneford Hospital looking out over a meadow. It was all very bucolic, worlds away from the space-age technique we were there to discuss. Knowing that they might be called away at any moment had concentrated my scattered mind. I had made a list with three columns of questions: before the operation; during the operation; following the operation. I got a chance to ask them all and I got answers to everything I asked. At this distance I remember none of the details. What I do remember is that they treated me like a colleague, only rephrasing when one used a medical or surgical term I didn't understand.

To my surprise, Tipu asked if I'd be willing to be in the operating theatre during the procedure. The surgery involved a vast team and would take some hours. Sheridan would have to be conscious until nearly the end and they wanted me to be there to keep him calm if he panicked, to be the familiar face he could see. That they were willing to take the risk that I'd be able to take the tension of the atmosphere in the theatre and cope with the unfamiliar process was a compliment as well as a warning. Tipu told me who would be with us in there and approximately how long it would take. Guy explained the psychological tests he and his team would perform throughout the operation. Neither knew what to expect of Sheridan, the patient and principal player.

As I drove back to London in my little open-topped car, an enormous prickly horse-chestnut dropped out of an overhanging tree and hit me squarely on the bridge of my nose. Instead of cursing it, I accounted myself lucky beyond belief. It had fallen only a fraction of an inch away from my eye; another centimetre and I'd have been blinded. An omen, I thought – I, who don't believe in them. Although my face swelled up and I got a ferocious black eye from the impact, I was happy. This was a lucky endeavour and it was all going to work out fine.

I wrote to the closest of our friends and to Sheridan's family:

Hi y'all

Hope you don't mind, but you all emailed on the same day to ask how we're doing and you're all close enough mates that I'm sure you'll understand if I respond collectively.

As those of you who are in regular touch already know, Sheridan is to have an operation called Deep Brain Stimulation to try to relieve the constant and severe depression from which he has now been suffering for nearly three years. This procedure is to implant what has been described as a pacemaker for the brain, to regulate his emotional thermostat which was damaged by his stroke. The diabetes which caused the stroke is now under control and he no longer needs insulin.

He is not, in fact, suffering from severe bipolar disorder (manic depression) which is what they've been treating him for (with twelve different drug regimens over two and a half years) but an organic illness directly resulting from the stroke. This apparently hit the emotional and mood centre of his brain, resulting in the symptoms of depressive illness but making him untreatable with drugs. He is, in other words, on this occasion, physically, not mentally ill.

The professors at Oxford University and the Radcliffe Royal Infirmary who now have his care are convinced that the operation will work for him and that it will do so fast if not instantly. It has not been done in this country before for the relief of depressive symptoms but is regularly used for the relief of other brain-related illnesses, such as Parkinson's, and has been used for his illness in Canada with very good results.

The neurosurgeon who is performing the operation is the head of neurosurgery at the Radcliffe, and the psychiatrist who is in charge is head of the psychiatry dept. at Oxford University. They both check out as among the top men in the world in their fields and the surgeon tells me that he has performed 1000 of these operations for Parkinson's, etc. with spectacularly good results. The operation does not hurt and cannot harm him. Other than the obvious risks of any surgery, it cannot leave him worse than he is now. The worst outcome therefore is that it might not work.

Sheridan's condition is pretty dire and has been deteriorating ever since the stroke. He is able to do only a minimal amount of work necessary to keep his jobs and he finds even that almost impossible. His quality of life is almost non-existent. He needs constant care and cannot be left alone for more than a few minutes because his behaviour is unpredictable. There was a brief remission between Christmas and Easter but that proved to be ephemeral and the doctors cannot even explain why it happened.

We have no choice but to go ahead with the procedure, despite its experimental nature, which we have just been told will be done at the Radcliffe on October 19th.

Sheridan is in favour of the operation although naturally nervous and apprehensive. He has repeatedly said that he doesn't want to live the way he is living now and I agree with him that he is existing, not living at all.

So that's how we are. Desperate though I am to get to NY (my bloody landlord is trying to evict me again!) there's no question of my leaving London until we find out how he weathers the operation and what its effects might be. As for me, I'm doing my famous Little Mary Sunshine imitation and continuing to tap-dance madly in the form of writing two books for S (both on subjects about which I know nothing) and reviewing theatre and dance for as many different employers as continue, thank God, to pay us. In between, I eat. Isn't it good that, being Jewish, I don't drink?

I WILL get around to emailing you all individually but I know you'll understand the current time constraints.

Much love to each of you, Ruth

PS Those of you who pray, you know what to do. Those who don't, spare us a thought on Oct. 19

Two days before the operation, plans went badly askew. These are the events as they unfolded.

Monday, 17 October 2005

In my diary, Becca has helpfully written, 'Call Bed Manager' and left an official-looking letter on my desk. This is a reference, one of the few, to the fact that the operation is to be done on the National Health. It suggests the possibility, albeit remote, that they may not be able to find a bed for Sheridan. I'm not really worried about this, and tell myself that Tipu is a star, he's going to be performing groundbreaking surgery, he's assembled a huge team for Wednesday and he's not going to take 'no' for an answer. This confidence is about to take several hard knocks.

I look at the letter that instructs me to 'Call Bed Manager'. There is an address for the hospital, to be sure, a telephone number for the ward, a telephone number for the nurses' station on the ward, but no telephone number – or name, for that matter – for the Bed Manager who is clearly a Very Important Personage.

I call the ward – they have no record of Sheridan's imminent admission and no number for the Bed Manager. They give me the main Radcliffe Infirmary number. I call it and ask for the Bed Manager. There is no answer, no machine, no secretary, and the call doesn't kick back to the switchboard. I call back. May I please leave a message for the Bed Manager? 'I'll connect you with her voice mail,' but there was no voice mail, no answer. It takes three hours but eventually I reach her. Her name is Jan. She is crisp, not rude but not helpful either, and her message is unequivocal, 'I don't have a bed for him right now. You'll have to phone me tomorrow, after ward rounds, at ten a.m. I won't know until then.'

I splutter, 'You mean there's a real chance my husband *won't* be admitted tomorrow? But, but, my husband is supposed to have blood tests, scans, pre-operative *stuff* tomorrow. He's having *brain surgery* on Wednesday. We're in London. It's Monday today. If I don't know until the end of Tuesday morning whether you even have a bed for him it'll be impossible to get him there in time for the tests, etc.' Her response was, basically, tough luck, lady, call me tomorrow.

I called Tipu's NHS secretary, Jo, in Oxford. No reply, no machine. I call Tipu's private practice secretary, Jocelyn, on her mobile, the only number I have for her. No reply, but I left a message – 'Call me. Quickly. Please.' In desperation I call Lucy, Guy's PA. No reply, but at least she calls me back within the hour. 'Can't find Tipu,' she reports, 'Guy's not here either.' She's much more gentle than Jan but her message is the same: if there are no beds, he can't be admitted. She calls back to say she's left messages for Jo but, like me, hasn't been able to reach her. I hear my voice responding to hers and it's at least two octaves higher than usual. I'm beginning to panic.

What I didn't say was, I've cleared his schedule and mine for these two weeks which took the most enormous effort and I don't know if I can go back to his editor and mine, his BBC producer, my editor at the *Lady*, my Bloomberg editor and all the others to reschedule. It's not the same if you have a single job and a boss: 'Sorry, he's having an operation; here's a note from the doctor, back in two weeks,' bunch of flowers, card signed by the whole staff, Bob's your uncle. We have, between us, more than fifteen employers, each of whom has their own agenda, a constant need for our copy and their own problems.

Right now, the *Daily Express* Arts Editor is happy for me to cover for Sheridan, to write his 'Backstage' column, and to use his taxi account to and from theatres. My editor in New York has agreed to the arrangements I've made for a colleague to cover for me. Things change in our business with such rapidity that I'm afraid if he can't get this operation done this week I'll never be able to unscramble the arrangements I've made and remake them at a later date. Editors change, policies change, studio time is unavailable, crews can't be found, Humpty Dumpty can't be put together again.

And worse, having brought Sheridan to the psychological boil at exactly this time, having kept his fear at bay just enough for him to agree to go ahead with the operation, I don't think I can do it again. The whole damn edifice could crash down around my head. At this moment, the weight of the responsibility of the decision to go ahead without what could be construed as informed consent from Sheridan is just crushing and, for a fleeting moment, I can't breathe.

The phone rings. It is Dr O'Reilly from the GP's surgery next door. She is kind but thinks we should know that they have received an email from the Battersea Primary Care Trust, addressed to Professor Tipu Aziz, saying that they won't pay for an operation which has already taken place (as Sheridan's will have by the time the funding comes through). She is telling me that there is no local funding for Sheridan's operation.

Although Tipu and Guy have categorically assured me that they will arrange funding through the NHS and that I am not to worry, of course I worry that this is the money they were counting on and that I'll have to find £30,000 to £40,000 by tomorrow or the operation will be off. I try Tipu's office again. Same result – no answer, no machine. Tipu has several times given me his mobile number. I'm panicky enough to use it but efficient old me can't find it.

Francesca, the therapist assigned to Sheridan by the local council, calls from Dr Potter's office. Potter is the local NHS psychiatrist whose detachment is absolute. He has met Sheridan only once, when he referred him to Professor Guy Goodwin, and has displayed not the slightest interest in following his illness or seeing its progress for himself. He thinks Goodwin walks on water and is scared to do anything that might be construed as countermanding a Goodwin directive. He stays firmly away.

Francesca has the same bad news as Dr O'Reilly. Turns out, Potter has seen the self-same email from Battersea Primary Care Trust to Tipu and wants Francesca to let me know that there is, as far as they know, no funding for the operation.

So far, it's been an awful day. Sheridan hasn't uttered a single word all day except to tell me how frightened he is. I eat an enormous meal, always my harbinger of severe stress; I can't sleep. Finally, having watched television until about 3 a.m. and listened to BBC7 radio after that, I finally fall asleep about six on Tuesday morning, the day Sheridan should be admitted to the Radcliffe Infirmary for radical brain surgery: I still don't know whether he's going to have the operation or not and who is going to pay for it.

Chapter Thirty-Two

*W*hile I was in New York with American Rhapsody *and Sheridan was in London with* Song at Twilight, *we tried to maintain our usual pace without dropping any balls. No matter what he had to do during the day, Sheridan went to the theatre every night because he had a weekly review column to deliver to the* Spectator *and another to the* International Herald Tribune. *When I returned from the States I had to hit the ground running as the theatre season was in full swing, I had two cabarets back to back to write and/or direct, I was overnighting theatre reviews for the* Wall Street Journal's *European edition and I was back on LBC, having been fired for the second – or was it the third? – time. Every time the programme direc- tor changed, and that seemed to be every other week, the new boy or girl decided that theatre wasn't important to London and promptly sacked the theatre critic: me. Then the listeners or the presenters com- plained and the critic got rehired – me again – until I decided they weren't paying me enough to put me through all this.*

Sheridan hosted the two-hour 'Radio Two Arts Programme' every Friday. For many broadcasters it would have been a killer but Sheridan loved it. In each of the eight quarter-hour segments he would interview someone different in the arts and then play a record. Sometimes the music would be related to the guest, at other times it would just be something he or his producers liked. But he had to keep eight interviewees straight in his head, along with all the content, intros and outros, music IDs and station bumpers. Unless he was unwell, he did all of it without a script, straight off the running order.

It never occurred to anyone, in particular those he interviewed, that his 'homework' amounted to an hour or two before the studio recording, browsing through the books and reading crib sheets his producers prepared for him. Quite by accident, one evening at dinner I was sitting next to a world-famous cellist who had been interviewed by Sheridan only that morning about his autobiography. He told me that of all the shows he had ever appeared on, only Sheridan really understood his work, had really listened to his music, had really read his book. What he didn't know was that, on the way out of the door that morning, Sheridan had said to me, 'Darling, this bloke who's written this book. He plays the piano, right?'

People in our business get hired and fired all the time. Usually it's a change of editor or a sudden money crisis or a directional shift, and nothing to do with the person being sacked who is usually blameless. I got Sheridan fired from the Tribune *because I was dumb enough, in the early days of emails, to send the same story to both the* Wall Street Journal *and the* Tribune. *It was, of course, an accident, but the* Tribune's *deputy editor saw the same piece in the rival paper under my byline and chucked him out. Sheridan was annoyed, both with me and with the* Tribune, *but not heartbroken. In our business, it happens. You lose one job, you find another. You can't take it personally, but sometimes you do.*

Sheridan particularly loved working for the Spectator. *Tory magazine though it was, and owned by Conrad Black though it was, the writing was good and he was proud to be in the company of that particular gang of hacks whose work he respected. In any case, Sheridan had about as much awareness of party politics as a banana and cared even less. He had been snapped up by the* Spectator *the minute that the late, lamented* Punch, *where Sheridan had been arts editor as well as drama critic, had been bought by Mohamed Al-Fayed. As the drama critic of the* Spectator *Sheridan was the dean of London theatre critics. His opinion was sought and followed all over our admittedly narrow arts world and when the 'Today' show or 'Newsnight' wanted an informed opinion on a theatrical subject Sheridan was the one-stop shop to whom they went.*

One day, the new editor of the Spectator, *Boris Johnson, yes, that Boris Johnson, had his secretary call to invite Sheridan to join him for a drink at the Savoy. Sheridan speculated that Boris was just being polite and getting to know all the magazine's columnists, having just taken over the editorship. As I was getting ready to leave the house to meet Sheridan at the Vaudeville Theatre, just opposite the Savoy, the telephone rang.*

'Are you on your way, darling?' asked Sheridan's voice, sounding very shaky.

'Going out the door now,' I said. 'Why? What's happened? Are you all right?'

'Yes, I'm okay, but hurry. Something very odd has happened. If you leave now we'll have time for a drink before the play. Meet me in the American Bar at the Savoy.'

He saw me come in and his smile wasn't quite as broad as usual. 'You won't believe it, darling, I hardly believe it myself, but the bugger sacked me.'

'Who did?'

'That new boy, what's-his-name, Boris Johnson.'

'Why?'

As close as I could piece together Sheridan's version of the encounter, Boris had ordered champagne for the two of them and then announced that an old friend of his, Toby Young, son of a peer, having blotted his copybook with a series of appalling gaffes while the Evening Standard's *correspondent in New York, was returning*

to Britain and that Boris wanted to give him a job. 'And,' concluded
Boris, 'I'm afraid the job that he wants is yours. Don't know how good
he'll be at it but there it is. Sorry about that, old chap.'

Sheridan was knocked sideways by this cavalier and insensitive
firing, which was not for drunkenness or having his hand in the till or
his snout in the trough, but for old-school-tie nepotism, and by Boris'
bare-faced brass in admitting that he was getting rid of London's best
and most respected theatre critic in favour of someone who had never
done the job and knew nothing about it.

But, being Sheridan, he was graciousness itself. He invited Toby
Young to lunch and gave him what he described as a three-hour
seminar on the London theatre. He discovered that not only had the
Spectator's new drama critic never been to the National Theatre, he
didn't even know where it was or how to get to it. And, just to make it
perfect, he didn't even offer to pay for lunch. Sheridan came home in
despair and practically in tears of humiliation.

He was immediately snapped up by the New Statesman, but he
never really got over being fired from the Spectator. Toby Young, sad
to report, couldn't be bothered with the job at all. He took to going to
the first half of plays and fairly soon afterwards gave up completely.
Sheridan had lost his favourite job on the whim of a pair of spoilt
schoolboys, one of whom is now the Mayor of London.

In an act of similar spiteful symmetry, several years later, when
Boris Johnson's sister Rachel became the editor of the Lady, where I
had been theatre critic for more than ten years, she didn't even have
the courtesy to fire me. She disposed of me cruelly but efficiently by
the simple expedient of waiting until I was out of the country and
then appointing one of my colleagues as her new critic, thus leaving
me – and my replacement who happened to be a friend of mine – in
a hell of an embarrassing situation.

Soon after the Spectator debacle, a mysterious stranger called
Peter Hill telephoned, announced himself as the editor of the Daily

Express *and invited Sheridan to lunch. He came back looking some-*
what bewildered: he had been offered the job of principal drama critic
of the Express, *complete with overnight reviews and a weekly Friday*
column in which he could write whatever he wanted about show
business.

The Express *already had a critic, a good one, and Sheridan asked*
whether he would be replacing him. It is considered very naff for a
member of the theatre reviewer's trade association, the Critics' Circle,
to lobby for or even accept the job of another member. No, said
the editor, it had been agreed that he would continue to write for
the paper but since he lived out of London and had a family which
required a good deal of attention, he had asked to be relieved of the
job of overnight frontline critic. It was all arranged.

Well, of course, it was not. When Sheridan was announced, with
great fanfare, by the Express *as its new critic and columnist, Robert*
Gore-Langton, the incumbent, was hurt and outraged. He insisted
that he had known nothing about the change and complained to the
Critics' Circle that Sheridan had, in effect, hijacked his job. Sheridan
immediately called Peter Hill, who was equally vehement in his
assertion that Gore-Langton had resigned. Stuck between the Critics'
Circle and his new employer, with whom he now had a signed con-
tract, he kept telling everyone that he was not to blame for the mess
that ensued.

It was a disaster. Nobody believed him. Colleagues he had known
for his entire professional life ignored him or shouted at him in theatre
lobbies. Critics he had supported and defended in other skirmishes
literally turned their backs on him. The Daily Mail's *critic, with whom*
Sheridan had always tried to be friendly despite his animosity, called
him a 'c**t' across the bar of the Barbican. Sheridan, who never refused
an appeal for help, who was always available when anybody in the pro-
fession needed him, when a charity event needed opening or a benefit
needed a compère, was now without professional friends himself.

Nobody defended him. They all believed that poor Robert Gore-Langton had been elbowed out of his job by a bigger and more famous name. Indeed, he had been royally shafted by the editor at the Express, *but not by Sheridan who was truly blameless in all this. That didn't stop it from being open season on Sheridan Morley and all the critics who hadn't achieved his level of celebrity had their day throwing rotten tomatoes at him in the stocks.*

Sheridan was bereft. All the people he had sat next to in the theatre for forty years weren't, in fact, the friends he had thought they were. He had always seen himself as a working critic, happy among his peers, part of a loose fraternity of brothers (it was nearly all men then) who lived their lives in the dark, clutching a programme and scribbling their notes. Now, he found himself alone and was devastated. Without any information except rumour, he had been ostracized by those he had counted as friends, who had been instantly willing to believe the worst of him.

Sheridan called Robert Gore-Langton and explained what had happened. Robert, gentleman that he is, accepted Sheridan's explanation and the air between them was cleared. But the damage was already done to Sheridan's relationship with his colleagues and to Sheridan's sense of himself as part of the circle of critics. I have often wondered whether it was guilt over that rush to judgement that made the other critics protect him later, after his stroke, when it was obvious to all that I was writing his reviews, a transgression that was unquestionably a firing offence if anyone had blown the whistle.

Chapter Thirty-Three

Tuesday, 18 October 2005

About 8 a.m., Jo calls me. I'm so dozy I don't catch her name and all through the call I'm playing catch-up because I don't know who's talking to me and the moment has passed where I can gracefully ask. Her news is not good. There's nothing she can do to magic a bed if there isn't one. Jan is a good Bed Manager and Jo will talk to her and see how the land lies. She'll have Tipu call me about the funding crisis.

Tipu calls me back from Edinburgh airport. 'I'll have a word with the Bed Manager,' he says. 'I'm sure she'll do her best but if there's no bed, I can't make them find one. Oh, and don't worry about the funding. Guy and I have it under control.' I heave half a sigh of relief.

On the dot of 10 a.m. I call Jan. She's not there. I leave a message. She calls back to say that she has nothing to tell me. Rounds are running late. She'll call back in fifteen minutes. At 11.15 I call her. I'm fearful of antagonizing her, but equally fearful that, if there is a bed, she'll assign it to someone else. 'I'll have to call you back,' she says again. Next time, she bends slightly. 'OK, bring him in. I don't have a bed but maybe he can have the scans and go to a hotel overnight and then tomorrow, if I have a bed, he could still have the operation.'

This sounds completely crazy to me but I'm not about to argue. I say thank you politely and go to get Sheridan out of bed, washed, dressed, breakfasted, medicated and into the car. During this long process, made even slower by Sheridan's fear and my hamfistedness from having had so little sleep, Jan calls again. 'I've got a bed,' she tells me crisply. 'Take him to Admissions and then to Osler Ward. They'll be expecting him.' By the time I've got him ready, packed his bag – one pair of silk pyjamas, one pair of cotton pyjamas, sponge bag, silk robe, towelling robe, Alan Bennett's new book, this week's *Time* magazine and Sheridan's least disreputable pair of Boots reading glasses – it's one o'clock.

We drive to Oxford, with Sheridan sunk in gloom and me not far behind him. By now, I am so spooked by the events of yesterday that I'm having trouble believing that anything good will come out of any of this, especially when we get to the ward and they seem not to know anything about him. They sit us in the Day Room, a singularly depressing area, and I look around and announce that we need a cake (a fine thing to say to a depressive diabetic awaiting surgery), so let's get some tea until they're ready for you.

As we make our way out of the ward, a compact, good-looking man with cropped grey hair is standing at the nurses' station and I realize that he has been there since we arrived. It takes a while for it to dawn on me that he is in fact waiting for us. He wears the anonymous blue pyjamas of the operating room and a large tag identifying him as Dr D. Schlugman. He first tells us about a marvellous French café almost next door where we can find great cakes, and then gently suggests that, before we go in search of our tea, he will find us a quiet place to talk.

David Schlugman is the consultant anaesthetist and he works regularly with Professor Aziz. This gentle soul, with whom I fall deeply in love over the following two days, is the Big Beast responsible for the extraordinarily complex anaesthesiology for the operation. Think about it. He is going to have to do three quite separate and, to a layperson, conflicting things: he has to 'freeze' Sheridan's scalp so that he won't feel Tipu boring into his head with a drill, making holes as large as 5p pieces on both sides of his forehead; he must sedate him because by now Sheridan's fear is achieving the status of another character in the drama; and, just as importantly, he has to keep him awake enough to be able to answer Guy's questions as to his state of mind.

His eyes are kind but focused during our short, pre-tea conversation. I can see him weighing Sheridan's mental condition – his panic, his depression – with his size and physical condition. All these (and, I'm sure, many other factors) go into what seems a fairly inconsequential chat and he recognizes, indeed specifically says, that he will need to give Sheridan more sedative than he would normally use in order to allay his fear.

Tipu appears towards the end of this chat – whether summoned by the nurses, by chance or by magic I never discover – dressed entirely in black leather and looking super-cool. I was so pleased to see a familiar face that I hugged him. He looked slightly startled but not displeased.

With him was Dr Alex Green, his number two, young and very tall, good-looking in an academic way – glasses, a slight stoop, and a proper shirt and tie. I like him immediately, although he doesn't say much at this first encounter and scribbles diligently on a clipboard which turns out to be a consent form. We discuss videotaping the operation. I can see how that would be extremely useful as a teaching aid but I insist, wary television producer that I am, that the tape may not be used for any commercial purpose.

Green, it turns out, is a neurosurgeon with a particular interest in the electronics associated with DBS and it will be he who will lead the subsequent explorations of the frequency modulations and the currents, he who will wield the all-important remote control which will govern the juice going through the stimulator after the operation.

Tipu patiently goes through the procedure again with Sheridan who says yes, he understands what is going to happen, but doesn't really want to know. Poor Sheridan. He looks so lost, so agitated, so lonely, despite all of us surrounding him and willing him to succeed in this risky venture. He sits quietly enough with his huge head resting on his chest. I don't know how he can do that without terrible pain in his upper spine but this is now his accustomed posture. He never once looks at any of the doctors, not even Tipu, but makes an enormous effort to find his own speaking voice on the rare occasions he is asked a direct question.

Everybody has a part to play but only he is actually going to endure the operation and everything depends on him. With some part of his damaged brain he knows this and doesn't want to fail; with some part of his damaged ego he is enjoying the attention; but with every part of his damaged sense of himself he is terrified, and nothing any of us can say will assuage that for him.

'Is there anything else you want to know, Sheridan?' asks Tipu. 'Any part of the procedure you'd like me to explain again?' Sheridan looks as though the only explanation he wants is how to get to the nearest taxi rank. I make several stupid jokes to lighten the weight of his anxiety. He doesn't react to any of them, although the doctors pretend they're funny for his sake.

David Schlugman slips out soon after Tipu arrives, having found out what he needs to know for tomorrow and, when he leaves, I miss him. South African by birth, he exudes an aura of calm and confidence that is much needed on this day of unaccustomed panics and unfamiliar environments, and which he will maintain throughout the next two days.

He and I will have several short chats on Wednesday, about his family, about mine, about South Africa and Israel, being a doctor, being a theatre critic and, somehow, it is often he who is at my elbow to guide me through the sometimes bewildering series of events. Whether Tipu or Guy have asked him to take care of me, I don't know, but he does and I'm grateful.

The cakes at Maison Blanc are as advertised and by the time we get back to the ward they've found Sheridan a bed so I unpack the little case, get him tucked in and flee in the direction of the M40, promising to call him as soon as I get home. He isn't usually worried about my driving, just my sense of direction. Tonight he seems worried. I have a play to see and a *Daily Express* review to file for him and, *pace* Robert Frost, miles to go before I sleep.

I haven't left myself enough time to drive those miles home, drop off the car, pile into my taxi and get to the Albery for a 7 p.m. curtain. As traffic gets heavier at Ruislip I realize I'm not going to make it. It's raining, there's an accident somewhere ahead, and I'm in a panic for the third time today. Not a panicker by nature, I force myself to think instead of reacting.

My mobile rings. Shall I answer it? My little sports car has gears so I can't drive and talk, it's illegal, and I'm in the middle lane. On the other hand, it could be the hospital. It's some minicab driver who speaks no known language and is lost in Battersea on the way to my house to pick me up. I make him call Becca for directions. With the mobile still in my hand and the traffic at a dead stop I remember to phone Sheridan. I call Osler Ward. The staff nurse is busy, would I hold?

'Well . . .' I begin, but they've put me on hold.

After what seems like hours, the same voice returns with the same message. The staff nurse is busy.

'Could you possibly give my husband, Sheridan Morley in bed fourteen, a message for me?'

'Oh yes, of course.'

'Would you tell him his wife called to say she's home and safe?' I lie from a rainswept traffic jam on the A40.

'Oh yes, of course', says the cheerful voice. Sheridan never gets the message and tomorrow the first thing he will say to me is that I failed to call and he couldn't sleep from the worry of it.

At 6.15 p.m. and stuck in darkest Acton, I call Becca. My voice is steady, I'm in 'don't argue, just do it' mode.

'Is the taxi there yet?'

'Yes, just arrived.'

'OK, here's what we're going to do. You get into the taxi and come to the theatre. I'll go straight there instead of coming home first. I'll meet you there and you can take the car home. That way, I won't have to park, the taxi's going where he's supposed to be, and you have a way of getting home in the rain.'

Against all the odds, it worked perfectly. I arrived at 6.50. Five minutes later, Becca got there and took the car off my hands in Cranbourn Street. I was in the theatre foyer before the last bell sounded.

Penny Gummer was already there, waiting, unfussed and unworried. Many years of marriage to an MP have taught her not to be fazed by last-minute arrivals. She had offered to be my date for the theatre on what she knew promised to be a fraught evening. The minute I saw her in that crowded lobby her calm presence and ever-ready sense of humour calmed me. Penny and I have spent many years giggling together in very unseemly fashion but I have never been so glad of her undemanding company as tonight.

Years of experience, and the sight of the ubiquitous notebook and programme on my lap, the usual fumble to turn off the mobile and the dimming of the lights complete the transition from worried wife to working critic. The play, *Heroes*, is flimsy but the fine translation by Tom Stoppard and the marvellous acting of Ken Stott, Richard Griffiths and John Hurt, are enough to carry the production to success. Penny and I hit the street at a dead run, scream at the taxi-driver because he's late, and I drop her off at the House of Commons on the way home to the waiting computer.

The review writes itself, the *Express* duty editor acknowledges it quickly and it's 11 p.m. For the first time today, I'm not supposed to be somewhere I'm not. The house seems so peaceful that even the cat's mini-tantrum at not having been fed yet is soothing. There is nobody to worry about, Sheridan is in safe hands but, for the first time in years, they are someone else's, not mine. I'm not hungry, just tired, and I fall into bed, setting the alarm for 5.30 a.m.

Wednesday, 19 October 2005

Getting into Oxford was a nightmare I should have anticipated. Got up at 6 a.m., fed the cat, decided against making sandwiches with the smoked salmon Adrienne had given me for Christmas, now defrosted, because I couldn't imagine when Sheridan would eat them. I dressed and left Battersea about 6.20 a.m. By 7.30 I was at the Oxford end of the M40. Plenty of time to get into the city centre, find a place to park and be at Sheridan's bedside when they came to take him down to the operating theatre at 8 a.m. Except it wasn't. What with the fog, the roadworks and the diversion at the entrance to the ring road, I crawled for the next half an hour, becoming first panicky, then tearful, until at 8.12 (I remember the exact time) I called Tipu on his mobile and explained that I was in a traffic jam in Summertown and had no idea how to get out of it. He was typically reassuring: 'Don't worry, we'll wait for you. I'll tell David [Schlugman, the consultant anaesthetist] to slow everything down till you get here.'

I arrived at a dead run at 8.35 a.m., having failed in my first goal of the day which was to be at Sheridan's bedside when he woke up and to keep him calm in the run-up to the operation. Guy Goodwin was already there, sitting on his bed, talking quietly to him, trying to allay his panic.

Within moments, a porter appeared (they clearly *had* been

waiting for me) and an assorted assembly of porter, Goodwin, two of his neuroscience team (Rachel and Ursula), a nurse whose name I didn't catch, the most junior of Tipu's team of doctors and I escorted Sheridan's bed down two floors, through many corridors, up a floor, through many sets of double doors to the little anaesthesia room off Operating Theatre No.1.

Sheridan was almost comatose with fear and kept losing consciousness, even through the bumpy ride to the operating theatre. He knew I was there and asked at one point about the play I saw last night, but otherwise displayed no interest in anything except how scared he was. I felt equally frightened now the moment had actually arrived but tried desperately to look and sound positive.

Polly Davis, an anaesthetist on Dr Schlugman's team, did the preliminaries. A jolly young woman, she commiserated about the traffic. 'I live ten miles north,' she said, 'and I have this nightmare every day.'

Dr Schlugman arrived, just as pleasant as he had been yesterday. I warned him again about Sheridan's low pain threshold. 'I'll give him a bit more sedation than usual,' he assured me. By the time he and Polly were finished, Sheridan was barely conscious, although he complained when Tipu injected more local anaesthetic in the area where he was going to set the crown.

The little room was beginning to fill up – doctors, nurses, specialists of one kind and another. A smashing specialist anaesthesia nurse, Mike, a big bruiser, was clearly in charge at this time. He and Polly inserted little tubes in the back of Sheridan's hand for the various fluids which would be needed, attached a line for anaesthesia and another for blood. They were warm, friendly, professional and, although they were trying hard not to show it, slightly excited.

'Have you ever been in an operating theatre before?' Mike asked me.

'No.'

'Well, if you feel light-headed, sit on the floor.'

'On the floor? Why?'

'That way you won't do much damage to yourself if you faint, and you won't fall into the instruments that we need to do our job.'

Christine, one of Tipu's seemingly endless supply of specialist nurses, introduced herself and took Rachel and me off to the women's changing room to divest us of our street clothes and dress us in the shapeless blue pyjamas so familiar from a thousand episodes of 'ER'. Mine were at least a foot too long and, as the white clogs were also enormous, the overall effect was of a baby clown wearing his father's clothes. There was no mirror in the changing room; when I caught sight of myself later in the day I knew why.

Tipu materialized like a diminutive version of the White Rabbit – one moment he wasn't there, the next he was – and, in his calm professional way, bustled about with hollow frames that looked like Sputniks with additional spikes sticking out of them. He tried one of them on Sheridan. 'Bigger,' he muttered. I thought he was saying 'Bugger,' but, no, the Sputnik crown wouldn't fit on Sheridan's large head. He used a screwdriver to change the circumference and tried it on him again. 'Bigger,' he muttered again. More screwing, larger circle, another try-on, but again it got stuck. The screwdriver activity became more intense and this time it went over the patient's head, leaving his nose poking out of a hole in the middle.

'Whew,' Tipu said to a totally inert and inattentive Sheridan who had not been mentally present throughout the circus of the hollow crown. 'One more turn and the frame would have been too small for your head.' This would, it was clear, have been an unprecedented catastrophe and one for which Tipu was not prepared. Once the frame fitted it was screwed on to the head with a succession of rubber bolts ('Ouch,' said Sheridan, the only sign of pain he was to manifest all day, 'that hurts.') and the first stage – and, Dr Schlugman assured him, the worst – was complete.

Next stop, the CT scan room. More corridors and lifts. There was a small room where I had to wear a lead pinny, and the others disappeared inside what looked like a television control gallery to stare intently at a series of screens. The team made sure that I stayed so close to Sheridan that I could have been Velcroed to the side of his bed. He mustn't, each of them told me in turn, lose sight of you. Nobody told me what might happen if he did so there I was in the CT scan room, clutching on to his hand. The machine was a sort of archway of coloured lights into which Sheridan's head, still in its frame, was inserted. The MRI is more accurate than the CT scan but they couldn't use MRI at this stage because the Sputnik crown is metal and, just as you can't put a spoon into a microwave oven without destroying both the spoon and the oven, you can't put the crown into an MRI without destroying the machine and, I suspect, the patient.

Back in the anaesthesia room the atmosphere (and the temperature) was hotting up. Tipu went off to change into his pyjamas and, David Schlugman told me, to do some sums where he compared the latest CT scan with the previous MRIs to come up with one picture from which he could work in the operating theatre. David, Polly and Mike the nurse did a lot of complicated things with injections and intravenous lines to ensure that Sheridan would be awake enough to answer questions but sedated enough to be calm, and anaesthetized enough to feel no pain. I worried privately that he was too doped up to know or care where he was and would be no use to Tipu or Guy when they needed him to react.

Going through the double doors into the operating theatre was like the curtain rising on an eagerly anticipated play. Sheridan's bed was placed at centre stage. The room was full of people – seventeen at the only time I tried to count them – and they were all busy. Each had a specific job and I never quite identified all of them. Directly behind Sheridan's head there was Tipu on a box to raise him above the action and Alex Green, his registrar and lieutenant, who was tall enough not to need a box, and a junior surgeon, Ronald, who would struggle with the stitches. There was a nurse to Tipu's left who handled the electronics and one to his right who handed him the instruments. There was Guy off to the far left with his team, Ursula and Rachel, and a videotape gang in the far right corner. At the foot of the bed was the anaesthesia team – David, Polly and Mike – with their dials and screens. The arrangement was clearly deliberately designed so that the patient could see none of them. Except me. I stood next to the bed in Sheridan's direct line of vision. When he opened his eyes he could see only me. All the others were hidden from him by their positioning in the operating theatre. Throughout the operation I held on to his hand or knee.

My view was perfect – I could see his face but the gory bits were masked from my vision by the Sputnik crown around his head. At one point, after some hours, Tipu asked if I wanted to see what he was doing and I explained carefully to Sheridan that I was going to drop his hand but I wasn't leaving. There was a sort of sound which could have been anything from 'Don't go' to 'Bugger off', so I carefully put his hand on the bed and walked behind him to see these two open flaps in his scalp with the metal contact points already fixed in place. If I was going to faint, this would have been the moment. But keeling over was the last thing on my mind. I knew I was privileged to be allowed to see this miracle.

The atmosphere was full of wonder. Every person in the operating theatre, except possibly Sheridan, was alive to the extraordinary event they were witnessing. The focus was intense. Conversation was minimal and quiet. Occasionally, Tipu talked with Guy or with one of his team but mostly there was a collegial, almost reverential, quiet. Each team, each individual, was watching to see if there was anything they could do to help, to be sure to hear if Tipu needed anything or if Sheridan said anything.

I had experienced this atmosphere before, very occasionally, in a crowded theatre when a great play by a great playwright turns into stage magic and the audience knows that they are in the presence of something very special indeed. Then the audience leans forward and listens so intently that their reaction actually becomes part of the play. This is what happened during this procedure.

Before they started, Rachel asked Sheridan a long list of questions from her clipboard. 'Tell me, on a scale of one to five, one being not at all and five being extremely, what you feel about each of these. Angry, scared, relaxed . . .' and so it went. Then Guy asked how he felt.

'Suicidal,' came the predictable response. 'There's no future. I know Ruth is going to leave me, all my editors will fire me, I've got no pension and no money, my children hate me, I've made such a mess of everything.' No change, there, then.

Working quietly, Tipu and his surgical henchmen made their incisions, peeled back the flaps of skin and adjusted a scary-looking hand drill with a crank handle. 'This won't hurt,' Carol the nurse said to Sheridan, who was beyond caring, 'but it is noisy. So don't worry.' Actually, it isn't even as loud as a dentist's drill, but it was nice of her to try to reassure him just in case he heard an unaccustomed noise and became scared. Tipu wielded the drill with the aplomb of a masterchef with a whisk.

His face was entirely obscured by his mask and a pair of big round glasses. He and the other surgeons wore long dressing gown-type robes over their pyjamas and rubber boots. The rest of the team, including me, wore blue pyjamas and white clogs with our dreadful paper hats. Because my only job was to be the face that Sheridan recognized when he opened his eyes, I was allowed to be in the theatre without a mask. In truth, he rarely opened his eyes but did respond when I spoke to him. He knew I was there, at least intermittently.

Suddenly, Tipu inserted a long probe like a meat skewer and asked Sheridan to tell him what he was feeling. Cautiously, not wanting to overstate, Sheridan said, quietly and haltingly but in his normal voice rather than the awful whine that had replaced it for nearly three years, 'Well, I don't feel suicidal anymore.' Then he corrected himself, 'The suicidal despair has lessened. It's still there but it's less.'

Tipu indicated to his nurse with the remote control to raise the current level. 'And now?'

'Now I can see some rays of hope. I think maybe the future isn't so bad. Maybe there's a future after all.'

It was the best moment of my life. Guy looked at me over his mask and I could feel the warmth of his grin from across the room even though I could only see his eyes. It was working. As far as I could tell, behind the mask and glasses, Tipu's expression didn't change. 'Let's do the other side,' he said.

The right side wasn't quite as dramatic. Sheridan reported that his mood was lighter now but not very. I was jubilant. Tipu explained later that this was because Sheridan's stroke had occurred on the right side and less could therefore be expected immediately. But this was where they were hoping that the stimulator would encourage the regeneration of brain cells destroyed by the stroke.

Guy had warned me that there might be a placebo effect where Sheridan would be so caught up in the drama of the moment that he would feel improvement where none existed but, we agreed, whatever made him feel better was worth having, placebo or not. In the event, when they tried fooling him by turning the current down or off, Sheridan was clearly not having any. 'It's gone again,' he said. 'I feel just as bad as I did before.' No placebo effect, then, the improvement he had experienced was due to the stimulator and it worked.

Only in the evening, when I was alone with Sheridan after he had been returned to the ward, did I realize the fullness of the privilege that had been accorded me. I noticed almost subliminally that no other patient was allowed to have a relative in the recovery room. There were no other relatives in any other area I had been in all day: none in the ward in the morning, none in the anaesthesia room, none in the operating theatre, none in the CT scan room. I had amazing access, thanks to Tipu and Guy. In the event, Sheridan's calm acceptance of what was happening to him had more to do with David and Polly's skilful manipulation of his sedation than anything I did or said.

As soon as the probing was over, they were ready to put him under so they could implant the stimulator. Once he was asleep they didn't need me so Tipu suggested this would be a good time for me to grab a coffee. Before that, though, there was a brief conference in the ante-room with Guy and his staff about whether or not to turn on the stimulator.

I argued for it, hoping that when Sheridan woke up the astounding improvement we had just seen in the operating theatre would have returned. The medical staff said that the trauma of the operation would be such that it would block any effect from the device. This was the first time I heard that, in the case of Parkinson's and pain management stimulators, they often don't turn on the machines for six weeks to allow the swelling to go down. Apparently, there is swelling in all operations around all incisions and until the body returns to normal – and in the head it takes longer than in the body – the current can't be regulated properly.

I was expecting an immediate improvement, however slight, and then a slow adjustment over the following weeks and months. I didn't know it wouldn't even start for about six weeks. I'm not even sure whether Guy Goodwin knew that but I wish they'd warned me. All my energy had been building to the date of the operation. I realized that I had little left over for the aftermath.

The general anaesthetic and implantation must have been done amazingly fast because I barely had time to call my sister before the nurse called me to the recovery room. Sheridan was coming round and they wanted me there when he did.

In the event, it took ages for him to wake up. The recovery room nurse was tiny and gentle. 'Sheridan, Sheridan, open your eyes. Can you wiggle your toes? Can you grip my hand?' she whispered. 'Come on, open your eyes, please.' The toe-wiggling and the hand-gripping were acceptable, it seemed, but eye-opening was not on Sheridan's agenda and the little nurse was no match for Sheridan in full denial.

The anaesthesia nurse, Mike, my new best friend, was sent for and not as easily put off. He told me in a loud voice about two inches from Sheridan's ear that if he didn't wake up soon he was going to have to reverse the anaesthetic with an antidote which, he said, 'is unpleasant for the patient but may be necessary if he doesn't open his eyes'. Sheridan opened his eyes. Mike grinned. He had clearly used that tactic before. 'He can go back to the ward now,' he told the relieved nurse.

Back in the ward, Sheridan slept on. My sister Adrienne arrived and we watched him sleep for an hour or so. The nurses came and went, taking vital signs and blood sugar levels, making sure nothing bad was happening. It was now about 3 p.m. Over the course of the next few hours, just about everybody who had been in the operating theatre came into the ward to see how he was doing before they went home. This included Tipu and Guy, of course, the latter carrying his bicycle helmet, but the nurses came, too, and David Schlugman, Polly Davis, Alex Green and Ronald Bauer. They cared, and it showed.

Sheridan slept through most of it. Adrienne and I received his visitors, these amazing people who had looked inside his brain, no longer dressed in the garments of their trade but looking like regular folk who had done something very difficult very well. They were, one and all, demonstrably tired. And clearly exhilarated.

Adrienne left. I sat with Sheridan for another couple of hours. By the time I left he was awake, sort of, and quite chatty for the few seconds his eyes were open every half-hour or so. Guy said to me, 'Go home. If you don't go soon you'll be too tired to drive.' We arranged to meet the following morning at ten for the post-operative tests.

I don't know exactly how long the operation lasted because there was something to look at, something to absorb at every moment. Every time I looked at the big clock on the wall behind the surgeons' heads another hour had passed; I never knew where the time went. But watching Tipu and his team perform this surgery from close quarters was one of the most exciting experiences of my life.

The fact that it might save Sheridan and, incidentally, me from a life bounded and limited by his depressive illness was, on that day at least, merely one more miracle

Chapter Thirty-Four

Sheridan stood next to the lamp looking puzzled. 'You want me to do what?' he asked. 'I want you,' I said, with exaggerated patience, 'to change the light bulb.' He looked without comprehension from me to the paper package in his hand. 'In that square box,' I continued, 'is a glass thing called a light bulb. You remove the packaging and take it out, being careful not to drop it, and then you insert it into the little holes at the base of the light under the lampshade. You push it into the slots and then you twist it slightly until it fits snugly.' 'Oh, darling,' he expostulated, 'don't you know any electricians?' 'Are you really telling me you've never changed a light bulb and genuinely don't know how to do it?' 'Of course not,' came the immediate and baffled response, 'I don't ask electricians to write reviews for me and they don't expect me to change light bulbs. It's a perfect arrangement.'

I burst out laughing. What else could I do? Sheridan and I had just moved into our first flat together and here was proof positive that the man with whom I had chosen to share my life not only couldn't do the simplest domestic task but, worse, could see no reason why he should. This man who could effortlessly voice-over an hour-long documentary without a single note, who could write a brilliant article in half an hour, quite literally couldn't change a light bulb.

I cursed his mother. What woman would allow her son to grow up without a single domestic skill? A woman with staff, of course. As the daughter of a star, my mother-in-law had never seen a man do a job around the house unless he was a gardener or chauffeur and so when something needed to be done she simply hired people to do it. It wouldn't have occurred to her to ask Robert Morley to take out the rubbish or to teach her sons to make their own beds.

When he moved in with me, Sheridan was in for a big surprise. Working daughter of a working mother, and straight from a marriage to an American who believed in sharing the load, I had no intention of reverting to Edwardian domestic servitude. While he never exactly qualified as a domestic god, under my less than gentle tutelage Sheridan learned to use an electric kettle, a toaster, and even, eventually, a microwave oven although we had to replace that most weeks when he forgot that spoons are made of metal. Nothing except the vacuum cleaner actually exploded under his tender ministrations, and he was an avid indoor gardener, watering and re-watering even the most pathetic houseplants, giving them so much love that most of them died.

He believed with all his heart that the world had been expressly arranged for his comfort and, when it didn't conform to his expectations, he just smiled beatifically and waited until whatever the problem was was solved by someone else, preferably me. His solutions were always too grand to be taken seriously. When the car got a puncture on the way to a speaking engagement in Plymouth, Sheridan had to be forcibly restrained from entering the car showroom outside which the misfortune had occurred, and buying a replacement. Car, not tyre. When I would make the ritual apology that dinner might be five minutes late, he was reassuring, 'Oh darling, we'll go to Le Caprice instead; I'm sure they'll find us a table.'

On one particularly cold day when I had left my gloves in my other coat, I asked him to pick up a pair of warm gloves for me at Marks and Spencer. Sheridan bought them in every colour in stock. Then, unsure of the size, he played safe by buying all the sizes. He met me at the theatre with an enormous bag containing seventeen pairs of gloves, and was rather surprised when I indicated that I'd take the other sixteen pairs back tomorrow. 'Oh keep them, darling, you never know when they might come in handy.'

I knew that he cared nothing for money for its own sake; he just wanted it so he could buy presents or things that caught his eye. He came home one afternoon when I was struggling to decide whether to pay the electricity bill or buy him a new dress shirt. With eyes full of excitement and a smile broad enough to split his face in half, he put his hand into his jacket pocket and pulled out a diamond ring. 'I thought this was so pretty that you just had to have it,' he said with such sweetness that my initial inclination to box his ears vanished. What do you say to a man who thinks a present is more important than paying the electricity bill?

On another occasion, when I was in New York, he took my mother, Rosie, as his date to the awards ceremony for the BP Arts Journalist of the Year. He won, and was given a beautiful crystal decanter. He thanked the judges profusely and returned to his seat. After a few minutes, Rosie asked what the piece of paper in the bottom of the decanter could be. 'Oh,' said Sheridan airily, 'it's bound to be a nice scroll with my name on it commemorating the prize.' Rosie looked at it for a few more minutes, then, taking a long fork, fished the paper out of the decanter. It was a cheque for £1,000 and, without hesitation, Sheridan cashed it that afternoon and, taking Rosie along, bought me a bracelet with the entire proceeds.

The generosity and eccentricity were both qualities central to Sheridan's nature. No matter how many people we ran into when we were out for dinner, Sheridan picked up the bill. This wasn't showing-off – half the time they never knew he had paid for their dinner – but a deep-seated desire to make other people happy. He never bought one of anything but when queried as to why he needed four identical ashtrays or six salt cellars or eight sets of stationery he would say, 'For presents, of course.' He very rarely found the opportunity to give away the mugs and trivets and other tourist tat he bought when we were abroad, but it made him feel good to know that, if the need arose, the treasure trove behind his desk would yield gifts for dozens.

Maddening though his indiscriminate generosity was, especially when we were broke, I loved it. It displayed his open, loving personality, a rage to please, and an insouciance about tomorrow that were the opposite of my more closed, more cautious nature. Sheridan would talk to anyone. I would wonder why the plumber wasn't getting on with fixing the boiler, only to find him deep in discussion with Sheridan. Bleakly uninterested in sport of any kind, Sheridan would sit for hours talking with a stranger about Formula One. With no interest in furniture or art, 'a mystery to me, darling,' he had a large collection of books about interior design and another of catalogues from art auction houses. Why?

Never known to read a book which wasn't about the theatre or, for some odd reason, the Royal Family, he'd pick up a book about football or electronics or wine-making and read it avidly for an hour or so before putting it aside forever. The only books I never knew him to buy were novels, which he thought, loudly, with great good humour and without giving offence, were a waste of time; an opinion he never scrupled to express just when we were having dinner with friends who were novelists, just as he was rude about classical music to musicians. It was just Sheridan, they concluded, unique and irreplaceable.

In many ways, Sheridan was unforgivably naive, even childlike, but he was so much fun that everybody tended to accept his more outrageous statements as well-constructed jokes and skated over the very real possibility that he actually believed the things he said. He had always been able to express himself in complete thoughts

*and sentences, no matter how strange the content. I came across
an old school report from his headmaster at Sizewell in 1954 when
Sheridan was thirteen:*

> 'His conversation and sense of humour are, at times, alarm-
> ingly adult and I have to remind myself sometimes not to
> ask him to come along after school hours for a drink and a
> cigarette.'

*His conversation and sense of humour became even more sparkling
as he grew up. No, he never grew up. He just got older. We laughed
all the time. Unlike me, Sheridan could find something funny in just
about everything and a fraught day could be lightened by just one
droll line delivered on his way to the kitchen for yet another 'cup of
filthy instant coffee'. I never found him 'larger than life' as so many
people did. For me, he was life – big, funny, smart, sweet, gifted –
and I couldn't imagine living without any of his gifts, although
he never understood that the gifts I valued most weren't the ones he
paid for.*

*He positively sought out the company of actors and writers who
were as eccentric or perhaps just as theatrico-centric as he was. One
of his favourites was Sir John Gielgud whose biography would be one
of his big successes. What he loved best about Johnny G., as he called
him, were the gaffes which Sir John made whenever he stepped outside
his own world. 'If I go through a stage door I know absolutely everything and everyone, but if I walk back into the street, I know nothing
about anything.' I was there when he said this to Sheridan, who was
much the same: his knowledge of the theatre was deep and true, his
unworldliness outside it profound. And, while I heard a melancholy
regret in Sir John's tone that he didn't know more about life, Sheridan
heard a triumphant trumpet of satisfaction with the life which had
chosen him.*

One day when they were on their way to the Garrick, they bumped into Mrs Thatcher, buying Christmas presents in Hatchards bookshop. Sir John, recognizing her only vaguely, thought to identify her with some well-placed questions, 'Tell me, my dear, where are you now living?' She looked somewhat surprised. 'Ten Downing Street,' she replied, convinced that instead of Sir John she had encountered his lunatic twin brother. 'Oh, you women,' he rejoined, 'are always so clever at buying the right sort of property. I never seem to meet a good estate agent.'

'She's the Prime Minister,' hissed Sheridan as they beat a hasty retreat from Hatchards, 'you're supposed to recognize her.' 'That's nothing,' said Sir John, sliding into his favourite corner of the Garrick bar, 'I was once accosted by a rather pretty woman whom I didn't recognize so I asked after her family. "Very well, thank you, Sir John." Well, that wasn't very useful so I took a chance and asked what her sister was doing these days. "Still being the Queen," she said.'

It never mattered to Sheridan or to me whether the stories he told were true. None was malicious, all were funny, and they were so perfectly constructed and delivered that even the people he told them about took to telling them about themselves. Around the time West End theatres were changing hands and being renamed for theatrical luminaries such as Noël Coward, Sheridan was telling a story, undoubtedly apocryphal, about Tom Stoppard meeting Harold Pinter outside the Comedy Theatre. 'You know,' said Pinter to Stoppard, 'they're thinking about naming this theatre after me. Would you mind?' 'Not at all,' replied Stoppard, 'but wouldn't it be easier to change your name to Comedy?' His own grandmother, Gladys Cooper, used to tell Sheridan's story of being so exasperated by her tendency to drive the wrong way down one-way streets, bump into bollards, and generally raise the blood pressure of her passengers, that, watching her drive into yet another No Entry, he banged his hand on the dashboard and exclaimed: 'Stop, G, I can no longer stand your driving.' To which she responded, 'Am I, dear, I rather thought you were?' The eccentricities of grandmother and grandson matched perfectly as did their politics.

Sheridan had some distinctly odd political ideas. One was that Parliament should be shut down except for ceremonial occasions and no new laws made for twenty years. 'At the end of that time,' he said, apparently seriously, 'we can see whether we need any new laws and, if not, shut it down for another twenty.' Politics, he said, only cause trouble. Once, when he actually drove me to the polling station for a general election he refused to come in with me to vote. 'Voting only encourages them,' he said. The first time he said all this I thought he was joking. The longer I lived with him, the surer I was that he actually believed everything he said, no matter how bizarre.

Other than murder, which he agreed ought to be against the law, he wasn't against anything. I was scandalized the first time he said this, 'What about rape? What about child abuse?' 'Don't be silly, darling, everybody knows that's wrong and if there wasn't a law against it, nobody would do it.' He believed that actors and writers, anybody who entertained the public, were a distinct species and deserved to be taken care of by the rest of the population, forgiven taxes and unpaid mortgages. 'What about nurses?' I bleated. 'Firemen? Teachers?' 'Oh no, darling, they're not nearly as amusing as we are.'

It was eccentricity that Sheridan most loved, secure in his belief that the theatre was all that really mattered and everything outside it – the mortgage, the children, the vagaries of everyday life – were unreal, insubstantial, and didn't actually exist at all.

No wonder he couldn't change a light bulb.

Chapter Thirty-Five

I was alarmed, when I got to bed fourteen, Osler Ward, at 9.45 a.m., that Sheridan wasn't in it.

'He's having a shower,' said the helpful old bloke across the way so I sat down in the only chair and waited. And waited. Guy's team, Rachel and Ursula, arrived for the 10 a.m. meeting but Sheridan didn't. I was beginning to worry. I found the ward clerk.

'Er, my husband has gone for a shower,' I began apologetically as wards are frantically busy places in the mornings, 'and I'm worried that he may have got into difficulties. He had surgery yesterday and perhaps the shower is too much for him and I don't know if there's a nurse with him.'

She disappeared, returning almost instantly. 'He'll be ages,' she beamed, 'because he's in the shower with a very pretty nurse.'

By the time he returned he was bright pink and unsteady on his feet but, at least, walking. Sort of. Alex and the rest of the surgical team, minus Tipu and Guy who both had previous commitments, had arrived to take Sheridan to the lab to test his post-operative reactions and to begin to turn on the stimulator. Sheridan was too shaky to walk anywhere so they decided to do the tests at his bedside, which made it pretty crowded. Sheridan's blood pressure was far too low and his blood sugar level far too high. They had been fluctuating wildly since the operation and he wasn't making much sense. He didn't seem unhappy or frightened or more than usually depressed but he was waving in and out of consciousness and he couldn't answer basic questions except intermittently. Rachel and Ursula asked their usual litany of questions about his mood and feelings but it was clear that he was still light-headed from the surgery and nothing he said was helping them much.

They all crowded round the bed, with Alex wielding a machine that looked like a big television remote control. He changed the frequencies and, each time, Ursula asked more questions. They had to wait several minutes for each change of frequency to take effect and the conversation flagged. Finally, Sheridan grudgingly agreed that he felt 'a little bit better', I think more to please Alex and Ursula and to make them go away than because he really felt a lightening of mood.

During a lull, young Ronald, the stitches surgeon, peered closely at Sheridan and, more to fill the increasingly long silence than because he wanted to tell us anything, he remarked that Sheridan's black eye hadn't set in yet.

'Black eye? What black eye?' I asked.

'Oh, well,' he shrugged, routine for him, 'usually the coagulated blood above the eye from the operation drops and gives the patient a terrible black eye.' At that moment, a porter arrived to take Sheridan for an MRI and the meeting broke up.

Tipu had ordered the scan to make sure the stimulator and all the wires were in the right place. For some reason, the X-ray Department of the old Radcliffe Infirmary is decorated with fanciful murals of Oxford gardens and animals, the only part of the hospital that is not strictly nineteenth-century utilitarian. They are pretty rather than gorgeous but they made a great change for my weary eyes while I sat in a dressing room, reading the latest Frances Fyfield novel and waiting.

As I sat there, it occurred to me once again that as I had got Sheridan geared up to the operation at the right time I had done the same for myself, focusing my energy to be ready on Wednesday. Now it was Thursday, and I realized that I had not kept any juice in reserve. I was tired, and could only get more tired.

Alexis, Sheridan's daughter, had left me a message that she and her sister, Juliet, would go to see him that afternoon so, having fed him the sandwiches I had brought, I drove back to London to look at my computer for the first time since the weekend, knowing Sheridan would not be alone.

My first order of business was an email to all the friends and family who were waiting for news. The phone rang incessantly with well-wishers and co-workers enquiring how the operation had gone. I told Becca to take all calls until I'd finished the email. Nonetheless, after one, she came over to my desk, looking ashen.

'It was Shirley Rilla,' she said, meaning my friend Shirley who has run my favourite hotel, Le Moulin de la Camandoule, near Fayence in Provence, for many years. 'When I told her it wasn't a good time for you because your husband just had brain surgery, she said it wasn't a good time for her either because her husband had just died. Of a heart attack. Yesterday.' Disgracefully, I burst out laughing and immediately called Shirley back.

When she came to the phone I told her how sorry I was. Wolf Rilla, who directed the cult movie *Village of the Damned*, had been a lovely man, given to sudden inexplicable rages, endless generosity and wicked laughter. I would miss him. I pointed out to Shirley that there was a scale of family traumas. It went like this: my husband has a cold; my husband broke his leg; my husband had a heart attack; my husband (here's where it gets interesting) has had brain surgery; my husband (and this trumps the lot) is dead. Shirley wins!

Shirley, as I knew she would, shrieked with laughter and the two of us got the giggles on the trans-Channel telephone for ten minutes. Inappropriate laughter is best of all for trauma, mark my words. I promised I would come to France, with Sheridan, to visit her as soon as Sheridan was well enough, a promise I never kept.

After the call, I had to complete the note to everybody – dozens of people, all over the world – who knew Sheridan was having his operation this week. Email was the best medium for that.

Sheridan – Day One

Hello dear everybody, our friends and family who have stuck with us through this whole frightening time.

Here's the story so far. Sheridan had Deep Brain Stimulation yesterday and they implanted a machine, similar to a pacemaker, and connected it to his brain. He was conscious throughout, though sedated, and was able to respond to the doctors' questions. On the left side, it was little short of miraculous. As they turned up the current, he felt better and was able to describe the improvements. Results on the right side, where the stroke hit, were not so dramatic but he certainly responded to the probe. They then turned it off to allow his body to repair itself following the trauma of the operation. Now there will be weeks and months, starting today, of experiments in how best to use the stimulator, what level of juice will bring the best results, etc. and whether there are any limits to his recovery.

Physically, although there were huge swings in blood pressure and blood sugar levels yesterday and today, Sheridan came through brilliantly. Although warned that he would be sore, he claims to have no pain less than twenty-four hours after the surgery. There is a possibility that he will be allowed to come home tomorrow if he remains stable. I'll email you all again over the weekend with an update.

In the meantime, you can't know how much your cards and calls and emails have meant to us. Thank you.

With love, Ruth

'It didn't work,' he wailed. 'I went through all that and it didn't work.' It was Friday morning. I had got to Oxford early to take Sheridan home. Becca came with me to help and do the driving. He said he was not in pain, but that it was obvious to him that the operation had failed. Nothing any of us could say would make him believe that the swelling from the incisions was blocking the operation of the stimulator. He put up with the tests that Alex Green, for Tipu, and Ursula, for Guy, put him through and, finally, satisfied that he was in as good shape as they could possibly have hoped, they agreed that nothing would be gained by his staying in hospital and he could go home. In sharp contrast to his mood, both Dr Green and Ursula were delighted with his condition and both reported that he had come through the operation brilliantly.

Swathed in gloom, Sheridan slumped in a chair in the hospital hallway while I went back to the ward to collect his ring that the nurses had removed for safe keeping. After the usual farting around to find the right person, then the keys and then a second person to open the cupboard, which lasted about half an hour, I returned to find him sitting in exactly the same position with his eyes shut. A treat, I thought – he needs a cake to cheer him up. Off we went to Maison Blanc, normally his idea of heaven: a little French café with wonderful patisseries, nice young French waitresses and a pile of newspapers in both French and English.

Becca and I chatted amiably through our salads and cakes; Sheridan uttered not a word. He was silent all the way home, and then went straight to bed. Anaesthetic, I thought – he needs rest. I woke him for dinner. Since we'd arrived home at about 3 p.m., I'd sent 120 emails, talked to about forty people who'd called about Sheridan, sorted out the reviews for next week, got the schedule arranged and made a three-course dinner of some of his favourite foods. Somehow, through a fog of fatigue, I got it to the table hot and delicious. When we sat down to eat I was so exhausted I could barely find the chair.

The phone rang yet again; 'I'm not speaking to one more person tonight,' I said to Sheridan. 'Let the machine pick it up.'

He got up, went to the phone and answered it. I heard him say, 'Hello, Mildred darling. Yes, I'm fine, thank you. Why not talk to Ruth? She's right here, I'll get her for you.' Not only had he answered the phone when I'd told him not to, he'd made it impossible for me not to talk. I rudely told my cousin I couldn't talk to her because dinner was cooling on the table and she understood. But it was ruined for me. I was furious with him.

Only later did I realize that this was the first sign of the behavioural changes that Guy had told me to expect. Instead of sitting, waiting for me to make the decision, Sheridan had acted on his own volition, done what he would always have done before the stroke – whatever he wanted to do, no matter what I thought or said. A week ago, he wouldn't have done that. It was starting.

On Sunday, I sent this email:

Sheridan – Day Four

Dear Family and Friends

It's been quite a week. Sheridan is home, allowed to leave the Radcliffe Infirmary on Friday after many tests and manipulation of the stimulator's frequencies. It's turned on but, because of the swelling from the incisions (he has four – two in his forehead where the probes were inserted, one behind his ear where the wires go, and one in his chest for the machine itself), he won't feel any benefit from it for a while. The docs say that head swellings take much longer than body swellings to go down and that usually they don't even switch the machine on (with Parkinson's patients, for example) until six weeks have passed. But, in Sheridan's case, in the event the swellings go down faster than expected, the stimulator is turned on and he will feel better as soon as they do. In the meantime, he's furious that he isn't entirely cured already and can't understand why he won't be ready to tackle King Lear by Tuesday. He's in a filthy mood and has to be prised out of bed. This is apparently par for the course, only I wish they'd warned me before the operation that he'd be even harder to deal with after it than he was before – then I could have left for the moon or at least the South of France. Prof. Goodwin tells me to watch him closely, not for mood changes which he's not expecting soon, but for the behavioural changes which have already started. Sheridan's voice is much stronger than it has been for a long time. His daughters, Alexis and Juliet, visited him on Thursday, a scant 24 hours after the operation and both separately reported that he was much chattier than he has been. Lexi says that, for the first time in years, he was talking about things and people outside himself, as she put it, 'outside the box'. I notice that he is more definite than he has been since the stroke, more sure of himself and more determined to have his way. He wakes up more easily, even if he won't get out of bed, and is clearer about what he wants and intends to do, firmer in his refusal to do anything that's good for him such as get up, take his medication, eat something, go for a walk, whatever. To improve his mood still further, he's got a massive black eye from the coagulated blood and is vain enough to be cross about that too. And it's only Sunday.

Love, Ruth

The behavioural changes that Guy had told me to watch for, while visible perhaps only to me, were manifesting themselves daily. Sheridan got up, he washed and dressed himself, he returned to the newspapers and to the news on television. His mood was black. He was angrier than ever, mostly with me, and convinced that the operation had given him nothing but scars on his face. 'They'll go, darling, they're already fading.' But nothing helped. There were changes happening, to be sure, but they weren't in areas he recognized. Nothing would do for him but a complete instantaneous return to the status quo ante and that was never on the cards. Anything less seemed to him abject failure. On one occasion he became so agitated that he accused me of wanting it to fail so that I could maintain control over him: 'I only did this because you wanted it. Now you've got what you wanted.'

Nothing could have been further from the truth. The last thing I wanted was control. What I wanted more than anything else was for someone to take care of *me*. I wanted someone else to make the decisions, someone to make me a cup of tea, someone to write for me, someone to worry for me, someone to make it all go away. The responsibility crushed me. I knew that what I decided every day could change Sheridan's life forever and he wasn't in any shape to make decisions for himself. Becca helped, of course, and kept the office worries to a minimum but I was so afraid that I was too tired and beaten down to make the right choices for him or for us. My friends were supportive and generous but they couldn't be expected to make life decisions for us. That was my job.

Being brave is hell. 'Fine,' I heard a voice approximating mine say on the telephone fifty times a day, 'he's just fine. He came through the operation with flying colours and he's going to be right as rain just as soon as the swelling goes down. Thank you so much for asking. Thanks for calling. Yes, thank you, of course I'll tell him you called.'

I just wanted them to go away. I was grateful that they cared about him but the constant emailing and telephoning was in itself getting me down. Sheridan, of course, didn't talk to anyone, didn't return a call, respond to a message or thank anyone for the flowers or chocolates or grapes. He left all that to me.

Delighted as I was with the operation and the promise of better times to come, I wasn't sure I could hold out until they arrived.

Chapter Thirty-Six

*H*aving grown up in the country, Sheridan didn't 'get' public transport. Even when he moved to London he never took a train or a bus, preferring to jump into his car, terrify pedestrians with the worst driving this side of an anger management course and park wherever he happened to end up. One Christmas Eve he was outraged when his car was towed away while he was shopping.

'Where did you park it, darling?'

'Outside Harrods.'

'Exactly where outside Harrods?'

'Oh darling, don't be dense. It's Christmas Eve – there wasn't anywhere to park on the street, traffic's terrible, so I parked on the pavement outside the main entrance, of course.'

I sighed. Only for Sheridan would this be normal behaviour.

So the car got towed away and Sheridan, far from being ashamed of blocking the whole length of the Knightsbridge pavement the day before Christmas, was beside himself with fury. His position was nutty but consistent and the harrumphing lasted well into the New Year – the traffic warden was a Nazi; he should have known that the car belonged to Sheridan and that he had to do his Christmas shopping before Christmas; and he should have left it alone or, better yet, helped him carry his packages to the car. 'Doesn't he understand that

I had to go all the way to God knows where to retrieve the car? And they charged me £200 to get it back. Bloody Nazis.'

Peter always said that Robert, Sheridan's father, must have bribed a local Berkshire driving inspector to close his eyes and pray during Sheridan's test because, he contended, if he'd ever actually seen him drive, Sheridan would have been refused a licence forever. However he got it, somehow Sheridan had a driving licence and a car almost before he could walk and so he almost never did. Walk, that is.

Because he drove everywhere, he couldn't understand why I didn't. For years after we got together I didn't have a car. It would be a liability, I told him. In the evenings we were always together in his car (with me driving whenever I could persuade him to let me), while during the day I could take the tube or the bus. I could get heavy groceries delivered or borrow his car. If I was wearing high heels or it was raining I'd take a taxi. I told him that I simply didn't need a car.

To Sheridan, this was a bit like saying that I didn't need a nose or an elbow. It just didn't compute. To him, everybody *needed* a car. I was just being perverse or modest, or I did really want a car but I didn't want him to spend his money on me, or I was just being difficult. His explanations for my intransigence were many and various. The one thing that never occurred to him was that, just possibly, I didn't *need* a car.

So, for Christmas one year he bought me a vanity registration plate (B2 RLM for Ruth Leon Morley). 'Thank you so much. How lovely!' I squealed, quite untruthfully. 'But, darling, if you look closely, it's rather an odd present for someone who doesn't have a car.'

The reason for this eccentric gift soon became obvious. It turned out that Sheridan wanted a personalized plate for his own car, not because of vanity but because he couldn't remember his own registration number. When he was towed away once too often and the man at the car-pound asked him to prove the car was his, Sheridan couldn't remember the number plate. Consequently, the man wouldn't release *the car. He had to phone me to come and rescue him. His solution to such problems was to buy a personalized plate, A1 SRM (for Sheridan Robert Morley). He knew I would object to his reasoning, so he hit on the wizard ruse of buying one for me, too. What did he think? That I wouldn't notice that I was now the proud possessor of an accessory for a nonexistent primary object? B2 RLM sat quietly in our utility room for three years.*

When we once again got into serious financial difficulties we were still living in the enormous house, on which we had taken a mortgage, in Chelsea Harbour. There was a part of Sheridan's brain that knew that he had got us into trouble again but these kind of problems, so 'boring', were simply relegated to the status of stuff he couldn't be bothered to deal with. If he ignored it, it would sort itself out, he believed. He used to quote Gertrude Lawrence, about whom he wrote an enchanting biography, who, on coming out of bankruptcy court and having been stripped of all her jewellery, cars, furs and homes, laughed and said, 'Well, someone will simply have to do something.'

But because he never talked to me about money troubles – indeed, he did everything possible to keep them from me – I wasn't the someone who was expected to do something. So I didn't know that Sheridan hadn't been paying the mortgage on the house until I received a very unpleasant call from his bank manager (we always had separate bank accounts) stating in no uncertain terms that if we didn't put the house on the market, he would.

I was horrified and humiliated. Sheridan was totally unconcerned. 'Oh, darling, don't take it so seriously. He's not going to do it. He's just trying to frighten us into paying.'

'He's succeeded,' I mumbled, through tears of anger and humiliation. 'We're going to lose our home because you just had to buy another hundred books or CDs? Or another bloody gadget?'

And, of course, it wasn't a bluff. The bank manager, so oleaginous when persuading Sheridan that all that stood between him and the house of his dreams was a small mortgage, was now implacable that the loan had to be repaid. Now.

Because Sheridan had loved it so, I had put all the money I had ever earned and saved into that damn house and he had chucked it away by adopting a lordly manner to the repayments. Convinced that nobody would ever dare threaten his home, he had, I discovered, not paid the mortgage for most of the time we had lived there, although we could have afforded to do so. Now it had mounted up to a level we couldn't possibly repay.

Typically, Sheridan wasn't contrite: he was furious. He refused to accept that the bank might just possibly have a point – they had lent him money; he had promised to repay it; he hadn't – and ranted about the iniquity to which he was being subjected. He wouldn't accept that we would have to move and threw every possible difficulty into the arrangements to market the house and to find another. He wouldn't sign the necessary papers, made every excuse not to come with me to look at houses and, when he did, would reject them on the most spurious of grounds. I found a perfect house in Regent's Park that even after paying off the bank we could have afforded, but he wouldn't even enter it because, he said, he didn't like the colour the current owners had painted the hall.

My neighbours in our garden square in Chelsea Harbour had become friends. Sally Burton, Richard's widow, lived directly opposite while, next door, was Samantha Brantley. We had met on a tennis court shortly after we moved to the Harbour and liked each other immediately. Although Sally Burton was of our world, with similar interests and mutual friends, Samantha was as different as it was possible to be. Had we not been neighbours I think our friendship would never have happened and I would be much the poorer. She was a teacher at the American School in London and married to John, a partner in a huge international accounting firm. Samantha had no showbiz pretensions and came from a different universe.

Once we had established, following our first meeting, that we lived next door to one another we immediately began to use each other's houses as extensions of our own.

'Do you know where I've put the soup ladle?'

'Yes, it's in my dishwasher. Couldn't find mine, took yours.'

Variations on this conversation took place every day. We adopted a cat together, whom we named Byline, and he wandered happily between houses, flying scarily between our balconies in death-defying leaps. We did all the boring errands together, with one of us driving and the other running in and out of the dry cleaners and the chemists, shared our grocery shopping for both houses ('I'm off to Sainsbury's, where's your list?') and played a lot of tennis.

I thought I'd live near Sally and Samantha forever and it had never occurred to me that any of us would be forced to move, much less that it would be me. Typically, though, they threw themselves into the project of finding us somewhere nice to live that was not too far away.

But it was really difficult. Not only did Sheridan not want to move at all, but our requirements were hard to fulfil. Our house was packed with thousands of books, videos, cassettes and paintings. We worked at home so we had to have a study each and one to share, but we only needed two bedrooms – ours and a spare. I looked at dozens of houses and I was at my wits' end when Sally found an advertisement in a magazine for a most peculiar and interesting property, so close to Chelsea Harbour that we could actually see it from our windows. The only flaw was that it was on the other side of the Thames.

'I don't see myself as a Battersea kind of chap,' said Sheridan, when shown the advertisement.

'Get over it,' was Samantha's forthright response.

Sally, Samantha and I ignored him and went to see Plantation Wharf, a mixed-use development carved out of the old wharves that used to house the entrepôts and shipping of the last century. There were offices, retail units, flats in various configurations and three rows of what were pretentiously called 'ateliers' – spaces designed for living and working. It was an atelier, really a house with a large office space attached, that we were interested in. It had four bedrooms, three parking spaces, a balcony overlooking the river, a working fireplace, a conservatory; a tiny, paved, walled garden and twenty-four-hour security. There was a beautiful river walk, and the entire estate was landscaped with flowers and trees. It was on the market for less than half what we expected to get for the house in Chelsea Harbour. In principal, it was perfect.

In actuality, the atelier was pretty nasty. There were lots of rooms but most of them were small and dark, the ceilings seemed low, the bathrooms were cheap and the kitchen was in a narrow corridor with fake wood cabinets. When I took my mother to see it she burst into tears. She said this was exactly what our family had escaped from and that she had hoped never to see the like again. In vain, I dried her tears and said that there was magic in the house. Just give me time, I said, I can make it beautiful. She was not convinced.

Sally and Samantha put a brave face on it but I could see they were dismayed at the prospect of my moving out of Chelsea Harbour into . . . this. To my surprise, Sheridan was much less daunted by the house than either my mother or my friends. He saw Plantation Wharf first on a sunny August Bank Holiday. It was quiet, birds were singing, the river flowed quickly past the house and there was nobody around. He could see how the large office space would make a fine home for his extensive library and that we would be only fifteen minutes from the National Theatre. He barely glanced at the living space. 'It's better than anything else we've seen.' At this point he'd actually seen and rejected a total of three houses while I had seen dozens. 'Let's buy it.'

Once he had decided, Sheridan wanted to move in then and there, but there was the small matter of having to sell the Chelsea Harbour house first. This wasn't proving as easy as we'd thought and I barely managed to stop him from taking a ruinously expensive bridging loan in order to buy the Wharf house before we had sold the Harbour one.

After months of fighting with Sheridan, the bank manager, the estate agents, the surveyors, the buyers of our old house and the solicitors, it was done. We had sold Sheridan's dream house in Chelsea and bought a dump in Battersea. Of course, I was the villain. By now, Sheridan was very sad and I watched him carefully for signs of another depressive episode, which didn't happen. He went manic for a while but never tipped over into depression.

Nobody believed the Battersea house could be transformed into Tara except me. I hired a structural engineer, showed him all the dark little rooms, and asked which walls were holding up the house.

'That one, that one, and that one,' he pointed.

'Fine. Take down all the others.'

'But, Mrs Morley, you can't.'

'Why can't I?'

'That would turn it into an American-style open plan, like a loft.'

'Good. That's what I want.'

He didn't see it. I fired him and hired a young architect who 'got' it. Karenna was fabulous. She turned my ideas into workable plans that a builder could actually build. Even after paying off the bank and all Sheridan's debts, there was enough left over to buy the house for cash and treat it like a very expensive house, which it wasn't. We took down nearly all of the walls and made ourselves a glass-enclosed dining room, a state-of-the-art black kitchen and, with its two staircases, a living room large enough to give parties for 400 guests. There was light everywhere, from garden to riverside.

We removed all the partitions in the workspace and designed bookcases two deep on runners around the walls. There were specially made drawers for Sheridan's collection of videos and custom-designed CD shelves. I got the best study – a lovely room up a spiral staircase leading to the patio garden – but Sheridan's, by the front door, was soon jammed with his favourite stuff and he hung the covers of all our books in frames all down the staircase that led to it. With Karenna's help, and a first-rate builder, we did all this in just ten weeks.

And all this time Sheridan was working against me. He hated the house, he told me twenty times a day, he'd never be happy there. He couldn't bear the changes, he couldn't bear the main road off which the development was built, he couldn't bear the disruption, he'd never work again. I deliberately planned the work on the house to save him inconvenience by doing the ground-floor working space, the library, first, and only then did we tackle the living space. However, he got it into his head that he couldn't possibly work with builders in the house. So he went to the head builder every day and offered him money to leave.

'How much would you take just to down tools and get out?' he'd ask Simon every morning. He was a nightmare.

The conversation usually foundered on Simon's first question, 'Have you discussed this with Ruth?'

Simon, not just a good builder but a man possessed of a sense of humour, simply bashed on, attacking room after room, wall after wall, until it was done. He took no notice of Sheridan's wheedling, coaxing and threats, and enjoyed the cut and thrust of the battle. I finally got so fed up with Sheridan that one day I turned on him. 'All right. I've had it. I'm going to finish this bloody house if it's the last thing I ever do. Then, I'm going to Aspen and New York and I'm NEVER coming back.'

Simon, Karenna and I, with a lot of encouragement from my friends, grudging applause from my still-worried mother and an absolute determination to prove everybody wrong, finished the house. It was far better for us than the Chelsea Harbour house had been. All the rooms were in the right place, we had space where we needed it, the library was a triumph and the living room/dining room/ kitchen *complex was a joy. There was light everywhere. By now, we had hired Peter and he had already become indispensable.*

I was exhausted. I went to Aspen. But as I left to drive to the airport I looked back at the house and wondered if my determination to make this house as good as, and finally better than, the one we had just left, had in fact destroyed my marriage.

When I got back, four weeks later, with my resolution never to return forgotten, Sheridan greeted me with his usual enormous smile and a heartfelt, 'Oh, darling, I missed you terribly.' And, as though I were an honoured guest invited for the first time to the lord's manor, he said, 'It's wonderful here, come and look.' But before I got inside the door I noticed an addition to the landscape. There was a tiny but sexy bright blue sports car in the driveway. At both ends it bore the legend B2 RLM.

Chapter Thirty-Seven

There was nothing to do but wait. Sooner or later the swelling would go down and the stimulator would kick in. Only then would we know the extent to which it might work to improve Sheridan's mood. Guy and Tipu had warned me that the technology was so new that we really had no idea what to expect. Improvement could be dramatic or it could take some time. Or it could not happen at all.

My memories of that time are coloured by the conversations I was having with the doctors who themselves weren't sure what exactly we were waiting for. We had a number of visits to the GP at the local surgery where the nurse who removed his stitches was in a hurry and far from gentle. Sheridan was better enough to be deliberately making my life miserable on the principle that misery loves company. He was awful to everybody, not just me, whining and complaining.

'It didn't work . . . You made me have this operation and now I've got cross-stitches all over my face . . . Make them take it out . . . I've got a black eye . . . I'm hungry . . . I'm not hungry, take it away . . . I hate this house . . . I want to die . . . I want to move back to the country . . . I hate walking . . . I'm sicker now than I was before the operation . . . I want to run away and never work again . . . Why can't I go and live in the South of France? . . . It's never going to get better and you put me through all this for nothing.' And on and on.

I stopped listening almost as soon as he started. He would ask one of us to do something for him and by the time she'd done it he'd have changed his mind. He'd tell Becca to change her schedule to take him somewhere he didn't want to go. Only Hannah was exempt. At this time it was virtually impossible to remember the lovely jovial man he had been for most of my life and all of his. My state of mind can best be judged from the bulletin I sent to family and friends on Day Eleven after the operation.

Day Eleven – Sunday, 30 October

Dear Family and Friends

Well, I suppose I'm meant to be brave about all this and bear it all with patience, and remember that the docs warned me that it would be at least six weeks, but the fact is that Sheridan is not doing as well as I'd hoped. He's feeling very low and has decided that the operation hasn't worked because he can't yet feel the benefit of the stimulator-thing. Nothing I say can convince him that he *will* feel better soon, just not instantly. In his misery, he knows better. He just *knows* he's condemned to be this miserable for life and that anything I say is just me trying to cushion him against his fate. He thinks I'm humouring him while I decide on fresh tortures such as refusing him a diet consisting in its entirety of chocolate digestives and Crunchie bars. For instance, Prof. Goodwin says exercise is an important treatment for depression. We aren't talking three hours a day in the gym here, or a brisk run round Battersea Park. No, I'm *making* him take a walk around the block with me every day (Sheridan, not Goodwin. Goodwin rides a bike. Sheridan's never even seen a bike. Maybe that's the problem). This 'walk' requires hours of begging, resisting, cajoling, complaining, and, finally, a fifteen-minute outing by the river outside our house so slow as to be below measurable speed. And for my next trick . . .

I can't decide how much is sheer bloody-mindedness because he's not instantly cured, how much is trauma from the operation, and how much is residual depression. The docs are caring and watchful but they don't know what to look for and are really relying on me to observe rather than telling me what is going to happen. They are as clueless as me, which is scary. The differences between the way he was and the way he is are small and have to do with slight changes in patterns. Trouble is, after a while, you wonder whether you're imagining them or making them happen. Physically, though, he's doing well. He had the stitches out on Thursday and the Frankenstein effect of the cross-stitching on his forehead is already diminishing. I can't, though, see him working this week, although that was the plan. Fortunately, his editors and producers are sympa-thetic and, thank God, so are mine, and we're up to date with the columns, etc. We're in uncharted territory here and the invisible ink on the roadmap does not seem to respond to a hot iron as it did when I was seven.

Love to all, Ruth

And then, things did get better. Just as I thought I couldn't take it another day, Sheridan began to show definite signs of improve-ment. It wasn't all about him. He didn't feel any better but he was definitely more functional.

Here is an email from our dear Oxford friend, Jo Durden-Smith, who had written a book about the brain, after a further update:

11 November

Thanks for the update. Fascinating. Seems like a big improvement in 'will to do' or whatever, but still affective disconnection – all of which is a fancy way of saying exactly what you did: Does things, but doesn't see them as victories. Still, why should he? They were, after all, exactly what he used to do as a matter of course. So 'the matter of course' is returning, c'est tout. And he must of course see them as victories somewhere inside, though all that's happened really is that he's back. The natural reaction is to take it for granted with no whoop-de-doo.

Whoop-de-doo is a slow builder – definitely second stage. How are you in all this?

Love, Jo

So the friends were encouraging even if Sheridan was not. But ordinary domestic crises don't stop happening even during times of greatest stress. In the interim period between Sheridan's operation and his stimulator kicking in, there was suddenly a huge great hole in our household. Hannah needed to return to Sierra Leone. I was heartbroken. But her elderly mother was ill, her sister needed help, the older children could continue their education without her and her youngest, Anne-Marie, needed to connect with her African heritage. Hannah had been there for me at times of critical need and it was clear, even through my fog of fatigue and selfishness, that she had to go. I wished her Godspeed and cried.

My neighbour, Rosemary, suggested that a woman who worked for her might be able to give me a few hours a week to help out temporarily while Hannah was in Africa. And that's how I met Anne Bond who started as a stopgap and who eventually became my indispensable friend and secretary. For a few weeks, to ease me through the transition, Hannah, Becca and Anne were working side by side so there weren't seams to sew up in the work itself, it was more the loss of Hannah's smile around the house that made me so sad. Her calm acceptance of whatever life threw at her was a lesson I try, and frequently fail, to learn.

One morning, five weeks after the operation, Sheridan actually got himself up, came downstairs and said a pleasant 'Hello' to Anne and Becca. It was now thirty days after the operation. I wrote another bulletin to family and friends, sitting at my own desk opposite his, covertly observing him.

Day Thirty

Dear all

He's sitting opposite me writing postcards. Not so odd, you might think, for a man who doesn't do email and doesn't have a typewriter on this desk. No, the oddity lies in his writing anything at all of his own volition. 'Doing the desk' is what he used to call this activity, which involves going through the invitations, scripts, CDs, catalogues, emails and letters which have collected there. I can't remember the last time he 'did' the desk. Not that there's anything on it that could upset or frighten him; Becca and I have already answered the important enquiries and letters, made the appointments, arranged the tickets, and gone through everything before deciding what he might be able to see. But still, he's 'doing the desk' and nobody has asked him to or is helping him.

He has just picked up the telephone to make a call and dialled the number for himself. I'm listening while pretending to write. It's not an important call but a routine answer to a routine enquiry. It is the first call he has made himself in nearly three years. He doesn't realize this and I'm not going to tell him.

Yesterday, he had an early check-up appt. at Chelsea and Westminster Diabetes Unit. I woke him, then disappeared to my own bathroom and when I returned, instead of the usual sleeping Sheridan, found him showered and dressed, and, of course, swearing. I can't say he was cheerful but he was up. I can't remember the last time he didn't need to be woken again and again.

We saw a very nice new twelve-year-old doctor who was so enchanted with the idea of using DBS for depression that she called in the entire staff of the Unit to hear about it, including the boss, Dr McIntosh, who was the original endocrinologist when Sheridan had his stroke and probably, with Dr Guiloff, saved his life. No other diabetic in Chelsea or Westminster got much medical attention or service while I told the story yet again. Sheridan became the centre of attention and, for the first time in at least two years, was, I think, enjoying it, as much as he can enjoy anything. Anyway, his diabetes is under control, so is his weight and blood pressure (and, yes, dammit, I *will* take credit for that) and the twelve-year-old offered him her virginity or her first-born child or somesuch if he'll keep up the good work.

Today, we had lunch with Penny, who runs the Jermyn St Theatre. Sheridan was quiet but engaged, occasionally told a story and, imagine, actually laughed once. All right, it was more of a chuckle, but it was audible and it was, I promise, Sheridan making the sound. Penny says the three-handed show we're doing with Michael Law on Dec. fourth is sold out and Sheridan suggested – not me, not Penny – that we go into the theatre for a longer run.

The other good news is that this week he's not only done his radio programme, he's also written all three of this week's reviews himself. When complimented, he mutters about how difficult it is but that he's determined not to let down his editors who have been so sympathetic to us both but he's writing exceptionally well, better than before the operation.

Look, folks, this is not Oz and we're not living in the

Emerald City. It's not even Kansas and Auntie Em is not going to show up and make him instantly better. Within every day, every hour almost, there are advances and retreats and the picture changes to colour and then, just as quickly, back to black and white. Sheridan still doesn't believe the operation has worked and he's still deeply depressed. He has never been one for believing evidence that is in front of his eyes and it is hardly credible to me that he can't see the strides he has made in the past week. But he can't.

He still finds interaction hard and getting out of bed well-nigh impossible. He's still a gigantic baby who won't go out alone or carry keys or make any independent decision that doesn't involve biscuits. He still has to be persuaded to do just about everything and he still repeats endlessly his various depressive mantras about running away. Ask him how he is, he'll say, 'Bad.' Ask him how his radio programme went, he'll say, 'Badly.' Tell him how much better he looks, he'll say, 'Well, I don't feel better.' Tell him how good his copy is, he'll say, 'You're very kind but I know I couldn't do it alone.' Sometimes, I want to hug him, sometimes I want to hit him over his scalloped head.

It's been four weeks now since the surgery. The incisions on his head have healed nicely and the resemblance to Frankenstein's monster has faded. I'm now as impatient as he is to start on the fine adjustments that the two Profs – Aziz and Goodwin – must make to the frequencies, etc. of the stimulator to lessen the pain of the depression and get his brain back in gear. Six weeks, they told us, then we can begin. It still seems a long hill to climb. But not a mountain any more. Not a mountain.

Lots of love to you all, Ruth

Friends and family began to respond with heartening and

encouraging messages which somehow seemed to arrive about the time I was ready to take the rolling pin to Sheridan's much abused head and managed to raise my battered compassion quotient a tad.

My friend Maureen, a retired but still highly regarded psycho-therapist, emailed from Aspen to say:

> It sounds like you're not in Kansas anymore!! There are now at least two Sheridans rattling around in there. There is the remains of the 'old' depressed, lethargic, negative Sheridan and then there is the 'new' functioning, creative, self-moti-vating Sheridan that is the result of the doctor's tinkering. The old Sheridan must feel a bit like he's on automatic pilot being ferried around by the new Sheridan and not being able to figure out what's going on or why. I guess the 12-year-old and company are giving him antidepressants. It would be nice if they could diminish the old Sheridan and let the new one kind of continue to expand and take over. I feel as anxious as you for the two weeks to pass so that they can begin more refining and tinkering. You are the best, and this time I send you a zillion hugs.
>
> xxxx Maureen

Exactly!

Somebody, possibly our local GP, suggested that I contact Social Services to see if there was anything they could do that would give me a break. Although Sheridan's Aunt Sally and my sister Adrienne were wonderful, they had their own lives and the help they could provide, while essential, was necessarily limited.

The Wandsworth branch of Social Services assigned a social worker who helped me fill in the forms to make me an official 'carer' and recommended an agency that could provide some practical help. This is how Elaine came into our lives. A huge Jamaican lady with a voice that shattered glass, she hove into view every weekday morning bearing a capacious plastic handbag and a collection of horror stories about her own daughter and her various 'clients' that made Sheridan's case seem like a piece of cake to her.

When I had to get Sheridan out of bed I couldn't leave him for a moment or he would slide back under the sheets. Even if I got him as far as the shower, one moment's inattention, a single query from Becca, a telephone call that distracted me momentarily, and Sheridan, sopping wet, would be asleep again. Then, of course, the sheets had to be changed, his clothes and towels replaced, and another hour was lost. There had been days when it had taken five hours to get him ready to go out. I've read of mothers of disabled children who spend much of the day preparing them for ordinary events such as a bath. I know what it's like, only my baby weighed sixteen stones and was articulate about what he didn't want. Which was anything I was trying to get him to do.

Elaine changed all that. While he wouldn't get up for me at all, he would occasionally get up for Hannah because he loved her or for Peter because he made him laugh, but he got up every day for Elaine because she terrified him. She used to cook his breakfast, encompassing foods he didn't like or of which he'd never heard. 'What's a plantain?' he'd enquire, plaintively. 'Thought it was a banana. Doesn't taste like a banana . . . Why's she putting tinned pineapple in my eggs? Sweet eggs. Revolting.'

She didn't take any nonsense. She even made him go for a short walk by the river every day. Sheridan hated exercise of any kind and he hated her. I, on the other hand, regarded her as a saint sent from heaven, or at least the agency, expressly to stop me from losing what was left of my mind. For my part, as long as someone else was doing the cooking and making him eat it I wouldn't have cared if she'd fed him the soles of his slippers on toast seasoned with stewed toenails. He was up, he was eating and I was free to work, so Elaine was queen of my heart.

When, eventually, he was feeling better, Sheridan begged me to fire 'that bitch from hell'. He promised that he would actually get out of bed without her. I half believed him – I wanted so badly to believe him – so I told Elaine we didn't need her any more. She didn't believe me. She was right not to, but that's another story.

In the meantime, Sheridan was turning back into himself, despite his own belief that nothing had changed. The characteristics that were returning weren't the ones I married him for. Gone – but not forever, I prayed – was his sense of humour, his warmth, his curiosity about everybody, his sudden laughter and the sideways brilliance of his verbal dexterity. The irascibility and irritation were returning. The cavalier assumption that the world revolved around him ('Why is that woman parking where you want to park? Doesn't she realize I'm in a hurry?') and the maddening habit of blurting out other people's secrets to strangers also reappeared. Worst of all, he now once again regarded me as someone he had to lie to. He was a terrible liar, in both senses of the phrase – he was bad at it and he did it all the time. ('Oh no, of course I didn't finish the trifle' – this with whipped cream still on his chin.)

I recognized that something had changed or, at least, reverted. For much of the previous three years, Sheridan had been sufficiently docile and dependent that his passion for drawing attention to himself by saying something shocking had been in abeyance. Now, when he got a good bit of gossip, he couldn't resist sharing it. That was the old Sheridan; infuriating as ever, and, in a way, I celebrated being exasperated again.

We were, I think, becoming an awful couple. Friends who didn't witness my impatience with Sheridan, and had no idea of how awful I could be to him, thought that I had the Mother Teresa gene. They would write wonderful emails about what an amazing woman I was and how he should kiss my feet. God help me, I blushed becomingly and begged for more. I was becoming a praise junkie and that's seriously unattractive. I hoped it was my guilty little secret and I was quite subtle about it, indicating by a well-dropped phrase that he was extremely difficult but I was rising above it.

Well, I wasn't. I couldn't seem to stop myself from criticizing him: he doesn't lay the table, the clothes he's put on are dirty, he's said or done the wrong thing, won't go for a walk, doesn't get up fast enough. I belittled what he did try to do and I was, I think, the wife from hell.

Everything he did at that time irritated me. When I wasn't with him I beat myself up mentally – how could I be such a bitch when I knew he was sick and couldn't help it? – and, when I was with him, he simply made me crazy. I would tell him endlessly how much I was doing for him: how I drove, cooked, took care of his medical needs, arranged his pills, made his appointments, lied to his bosses, wrote his reviews, organized the house, the office, the staff, the family, the friends and the money – Oh God, the money – and did all the worrying for us both. He would look at me with wounded eyes and say, 'Don't be angry. Please, don't be angry.' And I hated myself.

For some extraordinary reason, those who loved us still loved us even at our most unlovable. I still can't believe how each of our friends was helpful in a different way and was somehow able to find an individual route to telling me how much they cared, without getting soppy about it. Over and over again through those years, there were constant, supportive emails, phone calls, visits and cards.

I can't imagine how I managed to acquire such a wonderful bunch and I'm aware, every day, how blessed I am to have them. When I most needed them they carried me through so many terrible times and I know I couldn't do without a single one of them.

The unique gifts they gave us in time, in energy, in innovation, in ideas and in love kept me going. It's so sad that they weren't able to do the same for Sheridan. One of the many things that the disease of depression robs from its victims is the ability to appreciate others. It narrows the world of the sufferer until there is only one person in it. I've seen it before – both my parents' worlds narrowed to self-absorption before they died – but never on such an industrial and comprehensive scale as happened to Sheridan.

Never a naturally empathetic man, as his doctor pointed out more than once, Sheridan could no longer feel anything for anybody but himself. He said he loved his children and grandchildren but that was not so much emotion as sense memory, a belief that he, as their father and grandfather, should love them and so he believed he did. He didn't, however, really want a relationship with any of them – it was always me who made arrangements to see them, always me who had to persuade him to go.

My sixtieth birthday passed without comment from him. Although I was treated to many celebratory lunches and dinners by my friends, Sheridan took no part in it. Before his stroke he would have planned an elaborate party somewhere extravagant, like the dinner party at the Ivy he gave for my fiftieth. Now Sheridan, who had been obsessed with giving presents and planning parties, seemed not to notice. Becca sent me a birthday card which purported to be from him; Adrienne had a beautiful pair of earrings made for me which she gave me as a 'joint' present from her, David and Sheridan. I doubt whether he even knew she'd done it. We had made a reservation at the Ivy for just the four of us that evening. Sheridan wouldn't get out of bed so I cancelled it.

He would tell me many times every day that he loved me. I knew it was not love but fear. For him, I no longer had any reality outside fulfilling his own needs. If I left him, he worried constantly, who would take care of him? Like a small child who cries when his mother leaves the room, fearful that she has ceased to exist, Sheridan was afraid when I wasn't with him but he had no interest, on my return, in where I'd been or with whom. That I might have needs, desires, interests or problems separate from his own was of no importance to him.

I write about music but since his stroke my hearing had begun to deteriorate. In other times, he would have understood how terrified I was of short-changing musicians and of not being able to hear the music I love. He would have worried with me and we could have discussed whether I needed to stop or whether there was a doctor on either side of the Atlantic who might be able to help me. Now, every problem I encountered had to be dealt with alone. The tsunami, the Pakistani earthquake and the London bombings passed him by. My outrage at the second election of George W. Bush was incomprehensible to him.

I missed him, the 'him' he used to be. I missed the jokes and the one-liners that nailed whatever was going on in a single glancing blow. I missed the 'bigness' of him, his huge jovial presence in our small world, the beautiful voice telling me whatever I had, as usual, failed to glean from today's newspaper. I missed his schoolboy idea of gossip and his glee at telling me something I didn't know. I missed his blocking the aisles in the theatre and telling everybody he met the same titbit. I missed being able to rely on him.

I missed his standing in front of my desk literally hopping up and down with frustration because I was on the telephone or on deadline and he couldn't wait to tell me something he had just discovered or been told.

I missed his encyclopaedic knowledge of theatre, film and books, and his prodigious memory. When the reference books disagreed, Sheridan's answer would always be the one I wrote down because Sheridan was never wrong. He carried all this around in his head and was able to retrieve it as a moment's notice when he needed a fact or an idea for an article or book.

I missed his excitement at birthdays and Christmases and his delight at making me laugh. Above all, I missed the sound of his laughter.

Maybe, I hoped, it was still there and somehow sealed in. Maybe one day I'd find a way to unlock it again.

Chapter Thirty-Eight

Sheridan and I loved being together. From the beginning, we fash-ioned a life where we mirrored each other throughout our day. Work was at the centre of everything we thought and did although we didn't think of it as 'work' – it was not what we did for a living but what we were. Everything else – family, friends, dinner, travel – came in second. People never understood that we actually preferred to take holidays where we had to lecture or teach rather than decide where we wanted to travel, book a hotel and go on our own. It was more random somehow and therefore more interesting to wait and see who would invite us where.

Although we had different tastes and, in some ways, different values, we each understood how the other operated. We often talked about how extraordinarily lucky we were to have found each other because nobody else would have put up with either of us. We knew this, having both had long first marriages that each of us had sacri-ficed to our own needs. It is not so much that we were unselfish with one another, more that we were selfish in the same ways.

Although the theatre and the remorseless necessity to be sitting in the dark every evening at 7 p.m. with a notebook on our laps was at its centre, the glue in our marriage was laughter. Sheridan's sense of humour knocked me out every time and I could never understand why others sometimes found him boring or pompous. Private Eye *would refer to him as 'Sheridan Borely', which I thought was wounding but he thought was funny. To me he was always fresh and his voice was incorrigibly loud so that his sideways swipes for my ears only often found themselves being passed around as that week's bon mots.*

He wrote both faster and with greater facility than I did. Some mornings, the ones when he had an 11 a.m. deadline, he'd wander about the house all morning in his towelling robe, watering already over-watered plants, making endless cups of disgusting instant coffee, reading me bits of the newspapers and generally not *working. At about 10.30, he'd sit himself down at the desk and, like a concert pianist preparing to play, would sit still for maybe fifteen seconds. Then his big hands would fly, typing faster than I could read, until, perhaps ten minutes later, he would hold them up in front of him like a surgeon who, having already scrubbed, is sterile and can't touch anything, and say, 'Finished, darling. Could you please send this for me?'*

I never managed to teach him to send an email, open an attachment or format a document, but he could write and type faster on a typewriter or computer than anyone I knew and he almost never missed a deadline. More maddeningly, having written his article or review, he never changed so much as a comma so, even on a typewriter, his manuscripts were clean and unblemished, as though a professional typist had copied his work. Whilst every other writer I know, including me, adapted with relief to computers so as to be able to move paragraphs, change punctuation, format documents and do all the other labour-saving things the damn machines can do, Sheridan never saw the point as his manuscripts were already printer-perfect.

In Plantation Wharf we had a study each, a private place to work, as our working styles were different. Sheridan loved 'doing the desk', answering invitations, ordering stuff from catalogues, chatting with people on the telephone and clearing all the detritus of a writer's life off his desk, and seemed to be able to do it at the same time as writing. He never minded being interrupted, could write an article, read a magazine, talk on the telephone, handwrite a thank-you note, listen to the radio and even watch the television all at the same time. His working life was noisy, with show music playing constantly and not always in the background.

I hated all that. I'd answer letters and pay bills if pushed by our secretary but all I really wanted was a clear desktop, a keyboard and whatever I needed for what I was writing that day. I would re-shelve the reference books as soon as I'd finished with them. I worked in a tomb-like silence and could be distracted by anything – a child playing in the street outside, a telephone ringing, a sudden worry that I hadn't turned off a tap or shut the refrigerator door, or the cheerful thought of what I could make us for lunch.

When we started writing books together it was a big adjustment for me. I write quickly but it takes me so long to get rid of all the jobs that have to be done first that I appear to be dawdling. Then, everything has to be read over and corrected. Sheridan not only wrote like the wind but he could work through anything. That's what made it so infuriating when we had builders in and he claimed he couldn't work with them in the house. I'm sure he could have worked in the Chicago stockyards at dawn, if he'd wanted to.

That was the amazing thing about him; he could do anything in his field and all of it equally well. He could stand on the stage of the London Palladium and have an enormous audience in stitches over a story about his grandmother. No nerves, no stage fright, he could have been standing in our living room. He could write and present a two-hour radio programme as though it were a two-minute commercial. He could do voiceovers in precise timings: 'We need seventeen seconds here, Sherry,' – he wouldn't give them sixteen or eighteen but seventeen exactly.

His interviews, whether radio, television, live or written, were little masterpieces and nobody refused to talk to him (except Charlton Heston after Sheridan had written that the most moving thing about his performance was his toupee). He made after-dinner speeches called 'My Life and Other Disasters' in which he talked mainly about his family and about the small catastrophes that make up life in the theatre. He told anecdotes about those who peopled his books and about those he had met on his travels. Whether or not they were true was entirely beside the point. They were funny and he told them brilliantly. When he was sick, he lost his confidence and would insist on my being with him onstage in case he needed prompting.

He – we – always had too much on the boil at once. Nothing was ever on the back burner. Sheridan always said 'yes' to everything. I was more cautious. I needed to be, as he had to have back-up when things went pear-shaped, as they often did. Whenever he'd agree to write two articles on the same subject with the same deadline or he had several things due at once I always had to take on one. I liked the frantic heightened tempo of our lives and the danger of living on the edge. It was risky, we could always get caught, but we never did. Sheridan loved the idea that we lived better than two journalists had any right to expect and that we did it solely with our pens. We weren't playwrights or screenwriters, just arts writers who worked all the time just for the fun of it.

Chapter Thirty-Nine

By now it was April 2006. Since that Eureka moment in the operating theatre Sheridan had been getting daily more despondent. There was now not a single moment when his depression lightened although he was, when he wanted to be, much more functional than he had been before the operation. In the evening he was able to read the paper, sit in the theatre, and write a review faster and better than I could. But the negativity was overwhelming and he now couldn't even pretend to be interested in anything but his illness.

I had another birthday, my sixty-first. Everybody tried to create the birthday spirit for me – once again Becca bought me a card and gift, ostensibly from Sheridan – but it was another miserable Saturday watching Sheridan sleep and, when he finally woke up in the late afternoon, listening to him complain. As usual, I was not sufficiently sympathetic. I wonder if there is enough sympathy in the world for someone this sorry for themselves. I wanted to shout, 'It's my birthday, you selfish sod. Say something that isn't about YOU.' But I didn't.

The day wasn't a dead loss, though. Borough Market in the morning, a couple of hours looking at my nephew Lance's stunning photographs in his new loft and, in the evening, Eric Sklar's eightieth birthday at Prince's Club in Ruislip. I envied him and Sylvia their partnership, their closeness. Somewhere along the line Sheridan and I seemed to have lost ours.

The drive was a horror. Indeed, every drive was a horror. As we set off Sheridan would say, 'I'm so sick.' Then, 'What would happen if I resigned from the *Express* and the BBC?' ('You'd be out of work and even more broke than you already are.') 'Let's sell the house and live on the money.' ('But it wouldn't last more than ten years at most.') 'Why don't we have the money to retire?' ('Because you bought that ridiculous house in Chelsea Harbour and used up all the money either of us had ever earned.') By this time, I would have lost my temper and be screaming again, exactly what I promised myself I wouldn't do.

After the party, the drive home produced largely the same litany but with a variation. When we had lived in Nottingham Terrace, Regent's Park, we had become very friendly with our neighbours, Maurice and Valerie Halperin, whom we saw at Eric Sklar's birthday party. On the way back Sheridan decided that we should sell the house, move back to Regent's Park and retire on the money from the house sale. No matter how I explained it, he could not or would not grasp that if we sold the house we'd have to spend the same amount on a flat in Nottingham Terrace. He could either have the house or the money, not both. He didn't get it. By the time we got home I was screaming with frustration and furious with myself for being drawn into it yet again. I simply never learned.

The following day, I talked to Guy.

'It's not working, Guy.'

'I know, I've been thinking the same thing. Let's do an MEG,' he said. This is a magnetoencephalograph, which maps activity in the brain.

There followed an email exchange about an appointment in Birmingham on 11 April, which happened to coincide with one of the big theatre openings of the season, *Phaedra* at the Donmar Warehouse in London.

'Can you make it?' emailed Guy.

'Not easily,' I responded.

'Try,' he emailed back. 'It's the only day I can get there.'

'OK, but it's not easy.' I should have known better.

The evening before the MEG was the press nights for both *Movin' Out* at the Apollo Victoria and *Mack and Mabel* at the Criterion, two big musicals, both of which had to be covered for the *Express*, for Bloomberg and for the *Lady*. Our *Daily Express* arts editor and I agreed that I would overnight *Movin' Out* for the *Express* while Sheridan would review *Mack and Mabel*, and she would run it instead of his Backstage column on Friday. Somewhat fortunately, the press night for *Phaedra* was delayed by a week, but Sheridan was still complicating matters, first insisting on seeing both musicals and then claiming that he couldn't go to *Mack and Mabel* without me. Eventually, though, after standing by the door for twenty minutes, thus making both of us late, he decided by default to go.

In the meantime, Bloomberg had also asked me for an overnight on *Movin' Out* and I knew it had to be completely different from the *Express* review. We left for our respective theatres at the same time, with Sheridan still begging me to go with him. I couldn't make him understand that I couldn't be in two places at once. So, Becca went with Sheridan and brought him home within seconds of my own arrival. By 11.45 p.m. I'd written and filed two entirely different reviews of *Movin' Out* and filed Sheridan's *Mack and Mabel* review – I was too tired to eat. I was energized by *Movin' Out*, though, and thrilled to be sitting next to Carlos Acosta, my favourite ballet dancer.

Elaine came in early the following morning because we had to take an 8.40 a.m. train to Birmingham for the MEG, which would tell us whether the stimulator was working. We knew that at that time in the morning it would take both of us to get him up. I was up before 7 a.m., more dead than alive, and couldn't get Sheridan out of bed. Fortunately Elaine succeeded and we made it to Euston with ten minutes to spare. Sheridan kept getting lost, wandering away when I was buying tickets or looking at the timetable, and I had to keep looking for him and retrieving him. Birmingham was, as usual, grey and miserable, drizzling but not pouring, and our directions were on foot so we arrived at Aston University wet and both depressed.

The contrasts in the scanner department were so extreme as to be funny – three scientists (Ian, Ned and the boss, Morten) guarded a space-age scanner, several million pounds' worth, in a kind of bank vault off a derelict room with government issue NHS furniture consisting of two rickety chairs, one stool, a few computers and a lot of cables. Poor Sheridan was docile as they taped little sensors on cables to his head, measured it, drew electronic pens across his nose and then discovered that the machines weren't working. There followed a miserable hour in which the technicians tried to get their equipment to work and the doctors tried to mask their understandable irritation at the delay. Sheridan was shown into another room with a glass wall in which a machine, which resembled a gigantic hairdryer, was waiting to receive him.

Alex Green and another doctor from Tipu's team were there to adjust the stimulator and Guy, predictably, left a message on my mobile that he was too busy to make it. I was bitterly disappointed that he hadn't arrived. I wanted to talk to him about Sheridan, to review whatever options we might now have, and to tell him about the improvements in behaviour and the deterioration in mood. (I wanted to yell at him, 'If I can bloody make it to Birmingham in the rain with a sick husband on an opening night, so can you,' but of course I didn't because he wasn't there.) I needed some kind of support from Guy as I was feeling pretty bleak.

The scientists eventually got the machines and the computer to work, and Sheridan sat in this enormous hairdryer without moving for two hours. At the end of it, they still couldn't tell us whether the stimulator was in the right place and, perhaps most importantly, whether the stroke had in fact destroyed the neural pathways they were trying to stimulate. In fact, they couldn't tell us anything. The data, said Morten, would be analysed in Oxford, which would take about two weeks.

I took the entire team out to lunch. Sheridan had still barely uttered a word all day. Suddenly, in the restaurant, with an audience of strangers, he started to tell stories and interact with the doctors. Back on the train, he reverted to abject misery. Not fair. On him or on me.

Even when the results came in, we were none the wiser. I hope the information gleaned from the MEG was useful to somebody, but they certainly didn't share any revelations with us. We'd gone all the way to Birmingham in the rain, had a thoroughly uncomfortable day and neither Guy nor Tipu had shown up. I was feeling more than usually mutinous.

Somehow, I got through the next few months but, as spring turned to summer, I thought wistfully of Aspen.

Then help arrived from a most unexpected source. Sheridan's brother in Florida offered to take care of him for a fortnight, which was exactly the time I needed for my own break in Aspen. I don't know whether Wilton actually meant to invite Sheridan to stay but I took a fairly offhand email as a definite invitation and fired back a response saying, how kind and here are details of the flights I've booked for him.

Alexis, Sheridan's older daughter, was pregnant, this time with a girl. I thought it would be lovely if Sheridan could meet the baby, his first granddaughter, before he went away to Florida, a kind of beacon of hope to come home to. So that's what happened; Evie was born on 2 August, so Becca took Sheridan to see her in the hospital on their way to Stratford-upon-Avon for a production of *King John*. A week later, with mother and baby both well and home, Becca and Sheridan went off to Gatwick for his flight to Tampa. The previous day, I had set off for Heathrow for my flight to Aspen.

How could I possibly have known when I booked his flights that this was the Thursday when the British police would uncover a plot to blow up twenty-one transatlantic airliners travelling from London to the United States? Long-haul passengers like Sheridan littered the halls and corridors of Heathrow and Gatwick, and stood in queues forever. Sheridan and Becca were in the check-in line for four hours and were then transferred to another queue for a security check so draconian that he wasn't allowed any hand luggage. Becca forced its contents into his main suitcase and he was finally allowed on to the flight carrying only a transparent plastic bag, courtesy of British Airways, containing his glasses, his wallet and his travel documents. No book, no newspaper, no diary – nothing to do on a journey which lasted eleven hours, including two hours sitting on the ground before take-off.

Becca said he was almost catatonic by the time they got to the front of the line, standing with his eyes closed and not uttering a word for the four hours they stood there. Clearly, had she not been with him, he would never have made it through check-in. Equally clearly, if I hadn't already left for Aspen she would have let me know what was happening and we'd have called off both holidays. By the time she had to leave Sheridan at the security gate, she thought I had made a thoroughly selfish decision to go to Aspen and she was right. Sheridan was clearly not well enough to go anywhere on his own and she worried that he'd get lost at the other end and become even more disoriented.

He did, of course. I never really got to the bottom of the story but, piecing it together afterwards, Becca had conveyed to Sheridan the information about where to meet Wilton, but of course he didn't take it in. She had also written the details on a piece of paper, but this was now in his main luggage. I think Sheridan was expecting his brother to pick him up at the gate.

The upshot was that Sheridan was wandering around the inside of Tampa airport while Wil was driving around the outside. A local reporter came over to interview Sheridan about being on a transatlantic flight on that day of all days, and mentioned that her husband was a chef at Mad Dogs and Englishmen, Wil's bar and restaurant. 'Please,' begged Sheridan, 'could you call your husband and let him know I'm stranded here until someone comes for me?' The reporter contacted the chef, the chef contacted Sheridan's son, Hugo, Hugo contacted Wil, and somehow Sheridan and Wil got together.

In the meantime, I had arrived in Aspen and I was frantic. Becca had emailed with the news about the hold-ups at Gatwick but, when I called her, had no idea when Sheridan's flight was supposed to have arrived. I couldn't reach British Airways, I couldn't reach Wil's bar, I couldn't reach Wil at home, I didn't have his current cell number and it was, of course, hours after the plane should have landed. When I finally reached him, Sheridan sounded as though he'd been hit over the head. If I could have got a flight out of Aspen that night into Tampa I would have gone and rescued him.

It was a good thing I didn't. The trip proved traumatic but cathartic. As he later said, Sheridan arrived at his brother's new house and thought he'd walked into his parents' home in Berkshire. When their mother had died, the siblings – Sheridan, Annabel and Wilton – had amicably split the contents of the house between them but whereas Annabel and Sheridan already had homes that were full of furniture, art and memorabilia, Wil and his wife, Olga, were in the process of divorcing and the house in which they lived belonged to Olga's mother. Thus, Wil, with the full agreement of his sister and brother, effectively stripped Fairmans of its contents and relocated them to South Florida. There, according to Sheridan, were his parents' dining table, the sofas, the rugs and the bed in which his mother died. On the walls and tabletops were paintings, cartoons, framed telegrams and photographs devoted to the Morley and Cooper families. He was stunned by it all.

Our own house was something of a Morley museum but this reproduction of the Berkshire house shocked Sheridan into dealing with the death of his parents, and, by extension, the deaths of mine, to whom he had been even closer. Three of these four deaths had occurred since Sheridan's stroke and the onset of his depression, and he had therefore never really mourned for any of them.

But there wasn't time for mourning then. Wil had two small children who live with him and their needs naturally came ahead of Sheridan's. Sheridan found being with toddlers a bit of a strain. He loved his grandchildren in his fashion but never really wanted to come when I went places with them, preferring them to enter his world rather than trying to enter theirs.

From what he told me, he spent the very hot days (this was Florida in August) in Wil's swimming pool avoiding the children, lunchtimes with Hugo, trying to avoid talking about anything that mattered, and his evenings in Mad Dogs and Englishmen, avoiding his child-centred brother. As the fortnight wore on, Sheridan began to recognize the endless patter that Hugo maintains from four in the afternoon until two in the morning as the practised monologue of a circus barker, but also to admire him as the worthy successor to a dynasty of actors. He entertains the customers, said Sheridan, the same way his grandfather, Robert Morley, did, only he does it behind a bar and not on a stage.

Meanwhile, in Aspen, I was having a glorious fortnight, full of friends and laughter and good music. The only fly in my ointment was that I couldn't get Sheridan to talk to me. His brother sent me emails insisting that he was better and happier than he'd seen him in years but I knew that, if he wasn't talking with me, he wasn't better – he was just giving a performance for his brother and son. I left a number of messages. I knew he was getting them, but he never returned any of them.

I was constantly worried, but his brother emailed to say that I should buy him a house in Tampa and allow him to retire there. As you know, wrote Wil, he wants to retire here and stop writing. 'And do what?' I enquired. Sheridan had never had any hobbies. He wasn't really interested in anything outside the theatre and show business in general. As it happened, Sheridan, once he had got over the shock of seeing his childhood home reproduced in South Florida, perked up considerably, at least enough to know for sure that the last thing he wanted was to retire to Tampa, which he referred to as 'a ghastly hole'.

I felt better after my Aspen fortnight, so much so that I was able to convince myself that Sheridan's holiday was having the same effect on him. Maybe it was, at any rate it didn't do him any harm because, to my and everybody's amazement, something wonderful was in store for us when we got back.

Chapter Forty

*O*n 21 November 2002, Sheridan was in London, waking
up alone because I was in New York. As usual, he was wide
awake immediately, ticking off what he had to do that day before
throwing back the covers and padding off to his shower. Sheridan's
showers were conducted with the speed of light. He would stand
in his enormous enclosure (I'd had all the bathtubs in the house
removed to make space for his room-size shower with its complicated
system of water jets from all angles), soap himself all over and be
back in the bedroom, still soapy, before I had even opened my eyes
properly.

Still in the towelling robe that was his uniform when in the house
– Sheridan never got dressed until he went out – he went downstairs
to pick up the newspapers from the special box he had affixed to the
front door and climbed the stairs again to feed Byline, the cat. In the
kitchen, he inhaled two croissants, lots of butter and marmalade, and
two large mugs of instant coffee while he dissected five morning newspapers. He read only the arts pages, trawling for any news of theatre
or film and any good bits of gossip to tell me when he called me in
New York later in the morning.

Peter arrived and the two of them went through the morning
mail, decided what needed to be dealt with and what could wait,

and together they 'did the desk', answered the routine enquiries and opened the press releases that flowed in by the dozen. Although it was still very early in New York, they knew I'd be up and Peter called me to check on something. He said they were running late, that Sheridan was going to Bath to make a speech at a literary luncheon but he was still not dressed and they needed to get on the road if they weren't to miss it. He was no more than usually exasperated with Sheridan's habitual lateness. He rang off hurriedly in order to chase Sheridan away from his desk, a normal occurrence.

On this morning Sheridan dressed carefully in a suit with white shirt and a tie, knowing the ladies of Bath would appreciate his making an effort on their behalf. He phoned me from the car and we talked about our day ahead. It was easy, ordinary, full of details. He had realized, rather belatedly, that the following day would be Thanksgiving in the United States, and that he wouldn't be able to get there because he had a cabaret engagement this evening with Michael Law. He asked me to make his apologies to our friends Stephanie Cooper and Howard Weinberg, with whom we had planned to share the Thanksgiving celebration. Sheridan gave me a run-down of what he and Michael would perform that night and told me what was in the morning papers. He also thought he might drop in and see his mother on the way back from Bath.

I reminded him of where his clean dress shirts were hanging, told him not to forget a comb, and begged him to leave enough time to get back to the house so he could rest and change before his evening activities. The call ended as it always did: 'Talk later, darling, I love you.' 'Love you too.'

By the time Sheridan and Peter returned to the house it was later in the afternoon than either of them intended and they were both tired. Sheridan gave Peter the evening off saying he'd drive himself to Knightsbridge. Peter said that when he left Sheridan was his usual self, just a bit weary, and he assumed he'd have a short nap before dressing for his date with Michael. He was due at the venue at 8 p.m. but the cabaret wasn't scheduled to start until an hour later.

I don't know exactly what happened next. Sheridan's version of it was inevitably disjointed. He said that he woke up to find himself on the floor of the dining room with the telephone ringing. He assumed he had fallen asleep in his chair and been sleeping so heavily he had fallen off without waking. Those who knew Sheridan well and knew how heavily he slept had no trouble believing this. He found that his body wasn't working properly but he didn't question it, and just crawled to the ringing phone.

On the other end was Michael. 'Where are you?' he asked.

Sheridan was befuddled but put it down to not being fully awake. 'I must have fallen asleep. Still not quite with it. But I know I'm supposed to meet you at eight.'

'Sheridan, it's after nine. Just dress and get here. I'll start the show without you. You can join me as soon as you arrive.' Being Michael, dear sweet Michael, he didn't waste any time yelling at Sheridan for being late, and just got on with the job.

Somehow, Sheridan got himself dressed. Peter said that when he arrived the following day the house looked as though a burglar had turned it over looking for something small and valuable. 'It was a wreck,' is how he described it. 'There was broken china, upturned furniture, smashed ornaments. I couldn't believe one man could have wreaked that much havoc all by himself.'

Amazingly, he was sufficiently in control to find his car keys and set off. In less than a block he had hit another car. The other driver, not surprisingly, assumed he was drunk and called the police. When they arrived, they recognized Sheridan and breathalysed him. When they found out that he wasn't, in fact, drunk they merely ruled that he couldn't drive his car and asked him where he was going. Sheridan was, by this time, being held upright only by leaning on the car and the policemen, without enquiring further as to what was wrong with him, decided to give him a lift to his gig.

Only when he arrived at the party and lurched through the tables, pulling several of them over in his effort to get to the stage to join Michael, did it occur to anybody that something serious had happened. Michael stopped mid-song and made an announcement to the audience that the show was over as he needed to take Sheridan to hospital. 'I'm not drunk,' put in Sheridan, from where he was sprawled on the floor, 'I think I must be ill. I'm so sorry.'

Michael and his partner Alan drove Sheridan to the Chelsea and Westminster, the nearest hospital with an emergency room, and then, because the hospital wouldn't tell them anything, they went home to Kent and called me.

It was the end of the last day of our marriage, the end of our lives as we had known them, the end of everything we had. Our marriage was the best thing that ever happened to either of us. And, cut cruelly short though it was, I wouldn't have missed a single moment.

And yet, it wasn't over. It's never over.

Chapter Forty-One

It was 28 August 2006. Sunday morning. Leaving Sheridan asleep, I went off on this glorious English summer morning to play tennis at Hurlingham with all the usual suspects. I didn't stay for lunch as I usually do because I was committed to an afternoon concert at the Proms in the Royal Albert Hall. The American pianist Kevin Cole, whom I met while I was writing my biography of George Gershwin, was to be the soloist for 'Rhapsody in Blue', and I was looking forward to a break from my usual weekend activity of watching Sheridan sleep.

Weekends were always harder than weekdays in the years after Sheridan's stroke. During the week I could sometimes get him out of bed and occasionally coax him to work a little. But weekends were hard. My friends were wonderful, inviting me to all kinds of social events but the only ones I accepted regularly were tennis dates, with Silvana and Molly, usually at Hurlingham, followed by an alfresco lunch. Even though Sheridan stayed in bed throughout most weekends, I still felt he shouldn't be left alone for long periods and I needed to look in on him regularly to make sure he was still breathing and to give him his medication. If I had it to do over again I think I would invite people to the house rather than sit alone watching him sleep but at the time I felt strange about hosting a

Sunday lunch or casual supper, knowing that he was upstairs asleep and ill.

I wasn't a hermit and sometimes, as on this particular Sunday, I went to a concert or took myself to a local movie or went for a walk in Battersea Park, just to get out of the house. But my social life, apart from work and tennis, went out of the window when Sheridan's did and although we were invited to the same number of events we always had been, we only went to the ones we felt were work-related and essential. Other than those, the several Sunday lunches with Sheridan's best friend Christopher Matthew and his family were about the extent of it. Sheridan didn't want to go anywhere, begged me to let him stay in bed and too often, to avoid the effort involved in rousing him, I let him. The Matthews were unfailingly gentle with Sheridan, pretending that he was participating in the conversations and not minding when he sat at their table silently, with his head bowed, so that their only view of him was the top of his head. I was used to that view, they were not, but they coped magnificently, displaying that curiously English kindness in which nothing kind is actually said but just done.

On this particular Sunday, I really had something to look forward to as I sped home from Hurlingham to shower and change quickly. Kevin had kindly given me his performer's parking pass at the Albert Hall so I knew I'd have no problem disposing of the car but as I came up the stairs from the front door something seemed different. Not wrong or bad, just different. The house wasn't asleep and the quiet was an occupied quiet, not a deserted one.

Sitting at the dining table in the conservatory was Sheridan. He had a mug of coffee in front of him and he was reading the Sunday papers. He looked up, smiled at me, and enquired casually, 'Had a good game, darling?' It was as though the whole of the preceding four years had never happened. He was entirely himself, entirely present in the moment. His eyes were clear, he looked straight at me, his voice – that wonderful beloved voice that I had missed so much – was there again. He himself seemed unaware of the change in him, as though he were Rip Van Winkle waking up from his 100-year sleep, oblivious to the fact that yesterday he had been a sleeping zombie, and today he was the Sheridan Morley, husband, who had been away for years. Sheridan was back.

What had caused this? The most likely explanation is that the neural pathways that Tipu had reconnected were finally working again. Belatedly, nine months after the operation for deep brain stimulation, it had kicked in. But the truth is, even now I don't know exactly why he came back. It was sufficient on that particular Sunday that he had.

Still standing on the stairs, tennis racquet in hand, mouth agape, I tried to take in what was clearly a new situation. I didn't want to frighten him by screaming, 'You're back!' which is what I wanted to do. I didn't know whether to mention it at all. In the end, I didn't. I pretended I always came back to this scene of domesticity which, until his stroke, I always had.

'Oh, you're up,' I said, redundantly, grinning inanely. 'That's good. Would you like me to make you some breakfast?'

'No, thanks, darling, I got myself some coffee and a croissant.'

'Good,' I responded, stupidly. 'Perhaps you'll be hungry later.' Sheridan, you see, hadn't been hungry for four years and would only eat if something was set before him on a plate and often not even then. If you asked him what he had eaten he would not have been able to tell you. He merely ate because it was there, not because he wanted to. So that croissant had more significance than just breakfast. It was another sign of the return to a normality he didn't realize he had lost.

'I, er, well,' I stumbled, trying to seem normal, 'I'm in rather a hurry. You see, I was going to Kevin's Prom and I've cut it a bit fine on the time. But since you're up I think I can reach him and explain why I'm not going and we can spend the afternoon together.' In my mind there was no question of my leaving him at home alone. This was so exciting but it could disappear at any moment or perhaps I was having a lovely hallucination and I wanted to enjoy it as long as possible.

'No, don't do that,' he said. 'Perhaps you could get another ticket. I'd rather like to go with you.'

Again, I stared at him. I explained that it was an orchestral concert, Sheridan's least favourite form of entertainment. American music, I told him, but still, instrumental. 'I like "Rhapsody in Blue",' he said, 'and since you write about Gershwin I always feel guilty that I never take an interest.'

I decided on a no-nonsense approach. 'I'm going up to take a shower and then we'd better get going so if you're coming you'll need to get cleaned up and dressed fast.'

'Fine,' he said, cheerfully.

I didn't believe it. I thought that when I came downstairs again he would at best still be sitting at the table reading the papers and would at worst have returned to bed. While I dressed I weighed the odds. When I returned, fifteen minutes later, this man who could sometimes take four or five hours to get out of bed on a day when he had to work, was showered, dressed and waiting for me. This can't last, I told myself, but let's see what happens. I drove us to the stage door of the Albert Hall, listening to him chattering away about what a lovely day it was and about various items of theatre news he'd read in the Sunday papers. I tried to keep my joy in check, not wanting to scare him with how thrilled I was to have him back, and stole little glances at him to be sure it was actually him and not some hologram made in his image.

'Rhapsody in Blue' was the last item on the first half of the programme, which Kevin played beautifully. 'I'll just pop backstage and say "bravo", to Kevin and then we'll go home,' I told Sheridan.

'You just stay here in your seat and I'll be back before the second half starts.'

'Why can't I come, too? I'd like to see him again,'

'Well, you can, I just thought you wouldn't want to handle those stairs.' Access to backstage at the Albert Hall is down a precipitous flight of stairs. Kevin had been to our house for lunch during the previous week. I thought Sheridan hadn't even noticed.

As we went out of the auditorium, we bumped into another friend, the American singer, Kim Criswell, and her new boyfriend. She was on the same mission – to go downstairs to congratulate Kevin. On the way, we were introduced to Brett Kahr, a name that meant nothing to me at the time but would come to have considerable significance in both our lives.

The usual crowd of backstage well-wishers surrounded Kevin and somebody suggested that we abandon the rest of the concert and repair en masse to the pub across the street. I said, gently, to Kim that I didn't think Sheridan was really up to all those strangers and we looked over at him, in the middle of the knot of people around Kevin, perfectly happy and at home. I asked him.

'Good idea,' he said, warmly. 'I'd love a drink and frankly, darling, I've had enough of all this classical stuff.'

Sheridan, through and through. So off we all went to the pub and, by the time I'd bought a round for the assembled throng, I came out into the mews to see Sheridan holding forth, telling stories and regaling them with anecdotes. His voice was strong and completely his own, his delivery impeccable, his timing perfect.

We stayed there, on our feet, listening to Sheridan's stories until dusk. By now the company was somewhat smaller and Kim sensibly declared she was famished and what about the nearby Gore Hotel for dinner. I said, again, that I didn't think Sheridan could quite handle that and I'd rescue the car from the Albert Hall and take him home. Again, Kim and I looked at Sheridan. Kevin and several of his supporters were looking a bit tired and fraying at the edges but Sheridan was fine and announced that he too was starving and dinner at the Gore would be just what he needed. Finally, we were, I think, a party of eight at dinner which was endlessly jolly and celebratory. It was the best time I had spent with Sheridan in more than four years. Everybody, especially him, was in good form, producing their best stories, their most sparkling repartee.

Ego-driven, as all show-biz folks are, we had talked through drinks and dinner about music and theatre, newspapers and plays, the daily gossip of people accustomed to living their lives in public. Finally, as coffee approached, someone thought to ask Brett what he did. Although American, he turned out to be one of Britain's top psychotherapists, and author of a number of well-respected academic books and of several intended for a general audience about fantasy and psychology. To my surprise, although Sheridan never wanted his illness to be generally known and always had to be bullied by me into writing about it, he told Brett about it immediately, with a number of details I'd never heard him describe to anyone but me and his doctors in private.

Kim and I went off to the ladies' room together. 'You do realize Sheridan's trying to persuade Brett to take him as a client,' she said (clients are what shrinks call patients).

'Nonsense,' I answered. 'Sheridan hates and mistrusts all kinds of "talking therapy" and that's surely what Brett does.' Well, I was wrong again, and not for the first time. The following morning I hardly dared open my eyes in case the previous day had been a dream or figment of my imagination. Sheridan's head was not on the pillow next to mine. When I went downstairs, again, as yesterday, Sheridan was up and reading the paper. He looked straight at me, said a cheerful 'Good morning,' and returned to the arts pages. He was definitely back.

Without being pushed, he took his medication, showered and

dressed himself and was downstairs at his desk before I made it to mine. A little later, Becca said to Sheridan, 'There's a Brett Kahr on the phone for you.'

I heard him say, 'Thank you for calling me back,' and then he took the telephone into his own study and I couldn't hear the rest of the conversation. Sheridan, convinced he had met the only therapist he could actually talk to, was trying to persuade Brett, one of the busiest psychotherapists in London, to take him on. Good though Brett undoubtedly is, he was no match for a Sheridan determined on a particular course. Much as he respected Guy Goodwin in Oxford, Sheridan felt that Brett really understood him. Brett was the only 'talking' therapist Sheridan had ever met that he couldn't dazzle, outperform or bamboozle.

For a number of weeks following that Sunday, Sheridan was himself again. He was calling around, touting for work, putting himself about as of old. We went to the movies, we went out to dinner, we had fun together. He was a little 'high' in the afternoons, a little low in the mornings, and he still didn't want to see his family or go out with other people but he'd do it if I insisted. He wrote his own script for Radio 2's 'Melodies for You' that week, I remember, and blew me off when I offered to rehearse it with him as we had done ever since he'd been presenting that programme, 'I don't need to rehearse, darling, it's a perfectly straightforward show.' I was delighted. It couldn't last and it didn't, but it was so much better than what we'd been living with for years that I walked on air.

The next few months were magic. I called Guy immediately on that Monday morning to report developments and we went to Oxford to see him on that Thursday. He warned us not to expect miracles, that this upturn could be the long-hoped-for result of the DBS operation or it could be a temporary remission. As usual, he was right. As the days passed it became clear that Sheridan was not well but he was much better. He was depressed but he was functional. It was no longer an all-day job to get him out of bed and, while he was fairly low in the mornings, he perked up by theatre time and could once again write his reviews himself. It was all as good as it was going to get.

Guy encouraged Sheridan to engage with Brett Kahr. He thought it would be extremely good for Sheridan if Brett would take him on as Guy had always wanted him to have regular therapy which he couldn't provide himself for geographical reasons and because he was a psychiatrist and an academic, rather than a psychotherapist. His team adjusted Sheridan's stimulator, changed the settings and tested the results. They warned us that the battery was running down. Tipu said that, although there existed a battery that could be recharged externally, it hadn't been tested sufficiently and he would replace the battery when it ran out in the traditional way, by removing the stimulator from under Sheridan's skin.

As the euphoria wore off, I began to see the telltale signs of depression taking hold again. Sheridan was better, no doubt about it, but he was deteriorating again, this time quite slowly. But there were enough moments of Sheridan being Sheridan to make it possible for me to return to being, from time to time, me.

Things got worse rapidly when he was fired from his job as principal drama critic of the *Daily Express* in a cost-cutting move. Sheridan thought, and with no little justice, that the *Express* was lucky to have him and was horrified that they could dismiss someone like him with a polite letter. Then he became really upset when Lesley Douglas, controller of Radio 2, fired him from his 'Melodies for You' radio show in favour of Alan Titchmarsh, the gardener. A lifetime at the BBC and, 'Thanks, Sheridan, you're through.' (Subtext: you're too old.)

In the space of two weeks, most of his income and all of his self-esteem had been hammered. In October 2006, we took a long-delayed trip together to New York and all the friends who hadn't seen him since the depth of his depression were thrilled that he was once again able to go out to dinner and tell his stories. As people made a fuss of him and he began to see how the transportation problems which plagued him in London disappeared in New York, where our apartment is on the main bus route to theatrical Broadway, he suddenly decided that he could, indeed wanted to, live there. I made plans. I called forty-one insurance companies in one day to try to get him medical insurance because you can't contemplate a life in the States without it. It was decided. We would live and work in New York, keeping a small flat in London for visits.

When we returned to London, we put the house on the market. Sheridan, still furious over his twin firings and despairing of the country he loved so much having lost its values, wrote a brilliant piece for the *Independent* about why he was abandoning England.

But he was losing the battle with his depression. As Christmas approached, the time of year he loved above all others, he showed no interest in preparations and presents. We decided to hold our annual party but this was a somewhat subdued version and Sheridan was pretty miserable throughout.

This last Christmas wasn't particularly festive but it wasn't horrible and we had Christmas dinner at our house with my family. My cousins adored Sheridan, cherished and respected him, so that even when he was severely depressed they were happy to be with him and his last Christmas was, after all, as happy as he was able to be.

Meanwhile, at the end of the summer, Becca had given her notice. She was interested in finding herself a new challenge. We understood completely. She kindly said she was in no hurry and would give us six weeks' notice. But when we came back from New York in October with our new plan to move to the United States permanently, we asked her if she'd stay with us until April 2007, helping us over the hump of packing up and moving. She agreed, saying she'd never have given her notice if she'd known about this plan first.

We got an acceptable offer for the house almost as soon as we put it on the market. The putative buyers, a GP and his family, asked if we would mind delaying completion until June. This suited us perfectly as we had to find a home for our library which I subsequently discovered contained 22,000 books, CDs, videos, manuscripts, etc.

I knew from bitter experience that Sheridan reacted badly to any kind of change and, although he was much better and as functional as he would ever be, this was going to be change on an industrial scale. I was worried that he might not be able to handle it. I knew we would have to take it very slowly and this eight-month gap before completion would give us that breathing space.

He got increasingly depressed, as I had feared, with every new indication that we were moving. In some ways, it was just a repeat of the way he had behaved when we left Chelsea Harbour but he was much sicker now and more fearful. Everything about the move frightened him. Away from the stimulation of New York and the encouragement of his American friends and colleagues, he was doubting the wisdom of the move.

Disposing of the library was another trauma. He had been offered real money by the University of Texas at Austin, an institution that specializes in collecting the papers of British writers, to sell his archive and he was tempted. We were, as usual, broke – both of us had lost key jobs that autumn – and the money from Texas would have been very welcome. I argued against it, though, because he had no connection with Austin and I thought that, if his archive were to go to an American university, it should be either Yale or Juilliard. Both institutions have strong drama departments where the library could be used in the same way it had been in our house – as an inspiration for generations of theatre students and scholars.

Although Sheridan understood intellectually that we couldn't keep the library if we were to move out of Plantation Wharf, and subscribed in theory to the need to let it go, emotionally he couldn't get his head around it. This collection was much more than a bunch of books and papers, it was who he was and he felt that giving it away or selling it would, in some way, diminish him. Every single book and disc was an artefact as well as a bearer of information and had been bought, pursued or collected by him individually. They were his friends, far more faithful than most, always there when he needed them, reliable and solid. He couldn't bear to let them go.

I wanted to keep the entire library together, giving or selling it as an entity – the Sheridan Morley Theatre Collection – to whichever institution was lucky enough to be the recipient. My plan was to take with us to New York only those thousand or so items that we used every day as reference, a copy of each of our own authored books, and the books that had been written by our friends and inscribed to us. It soon became clear to me that the trauma of stripping our enormous working space would be too much for him so, undaunted, I came up with an alternative with which, initially, Sheridan agreed. Instead of a wholesale clearout, he would go through the shelves book by book so he could decide what he really wanted to keep and we would dispose of the rest, either to a library or a saleroom.

As the weeks passed, I realized that this wouldn't work either. He wouldn't, or couldn't, bring himself to dispose of a single book. I would pull a book from a shelf and say, 'Look, darling, we've got two copies of this, we could certainly do without one of them.'

He would become terribly agitated. 'Oh no, darling, not that, it's one of my favourites. And suppose the other copy becomes damaged?'

In fact, one of our long-time jokes was that we knew we were irrevocably married when we integrated the two libraries, his and mine, knowing that we could never separate them again. We had more than a few duplicates with most of the overlap in the theatre and cabaret sections of the collection. In addition, he had a number of film and, of all things, interior decoration and design books, while I had a fairly extensive working collection of dance, ballet, opera and music books. I knew I had to do something about this quandary but what? I wish I'd known that the decision would never need to be made.

We had a good meeting with the late David Stagg about selling the non-essential books via his company, Bloomsbury Book Auctions. This was fine with Sheridan as long as it remained theoretical. As it turned out, he still wasn't ready to dispose of a single book.

As November became December, Sheridan became increasingly uneasy about the New York plan. Too many of his friends, shocked that he was actually leaving the country, made impassioned speeches about his undoubted Englishness and insisted that he would never be happy anywhere else. These well-meant comments from people who couldn't imagine a London arts scene without him began to take root and, always easily swayed, he began to believe that he couldn't bear to leave.

At about this time, something went wrong with the sale of the house and the estate agent, a family friend acting for us, couldn't get the buyer to complete. I had to deal with this alarming state of affairs on my own because Sheridan's fears were getting the better of him and he couldn't hear about any setback without a terrible anxiety setting off yet another circular riff about the potential problems of moving to New York.

Finally, on the day before they were due to complete, the buyers said they were perfectly willing to go ahead but only if we would take £100,000 off the price. This was shocking. My father taught me that a deal is a deal, and once you've made it, you stick to it. I said 'No', just not so politely.

A few days after this, Lady Something-or-other, whom Sheridan had known in another life, came to look at the house and asked to come back with her architect. It was clear that she intended to buy it but she hadn't yet made an offer and time was flying past.

We were back to square one. We were planning to move in April 2007, it was now the end of January. We hadn't shifted a single book, we hadn't sold our house, we hadn't started packing up and Sheridan was in an almost permanent state of panic. I told myself that he would improve once we got to the States and he was once again energized by the city of New York. We never got there.

On 15 February 2007, Sheridan's grandsons, Barnaby and Tom, were staying with us. I say 'us' but, actually, with me. Sheridan made few efforts to reach out to his relatives until it was too late. I, who came from a close and loving family, was determined that he would have a relationship with his grandchildren and, in an effort to foster it, I made sure he saw as much of the babies as possible.

It wasn't easy. By the time they were born, he was already ill. His interest in small children and his ability to relate to them, never good at best, was by now zero. Almost by accident, the relationship I had hoped for between Sheridan and his grandchildren grew up between his two oldest grandsons and me. We couldn't spend much time together because these two little boys had social schedules to rival that of Paris Hilton. But I loved them and I persevered.

I have always believed that the most valuable present an adult can give a child is not toys or things but undivided attention. Barney and Tom, when they were with us, had me body and soul. As they got older, we had a wonderful time together. At Christmas, the only time we could rely on having them for a week, we'd have floor-to-ceiling activities. Before they came, I'd scramble to finish the work that had to be turned in before Christmas and turn down any radio or magazine work that would have to be done while the boys were with us. Sheridan couldn't possibly cope with both boys but could occasionally be left with one while I did something with the other and would, under duress, go with us to a movie sometimes.

I used to scour the press releases for plays, museum exhibitions, gallery openings, circuses, events, children's operas, jousting on Clapham Common and other activities which were age-appropriate. We ran from one to another from morning till night. The boys learned how to behave in theatres, what to look for in books and plays, how to discuss what they'd seen and how to criticize without trashing. They met actors, directors and writers, and got to ask questions about their jobs. Barnaby became a full-blown theatre addict. Tom liked it but preferred the cinema and really would have given the whole lot up for one good football game. They were wonderful fun and I learned to love them both dearly.

One of our regular outings was a trip to a large local bookshop that has an exceptionally good children's department. I would find a quiet place to read and an available chair where I could see them. The boys were allowed to browse, without me, through their own age and interest sections and, when they found a book they wanted, they would bring it back to me to look after until each had a pile they could barely carry. We spent hours doing that, the boys as enchanted by the stricture, 'Go where you like as long as you stay in this department,' as they were by the books themselves.

By the time we got back to the house we were usually, all three of us, exhausted, hungry and excited. The boys loved it, I loved it and even Sheridan loved it when we all returned to tell him where we'd been.

On Wednesday, 14 February 2007, Valentine's Day, I had the chance to have the boys for just a couple of days. They arrived in the late afternoon and Becca was to drive them back to Berkshire on Friday morning. For some reason – rugby, hockey, a party, whatever – they couldn't stay for the weekend so I determined that we would make the most of the twenty-four hours we had together. My diary for Thursday, 15th reads: 'Boys in London, Science Museum (spying), Tate Modern (slides), Guy Goodwin to call.'

There was a hands-on exhibition of espionage techniques at the Science Museum. The boys loved it – getting into disguises, breaking into safes, writing in code, etc. – and raced around the museum, enjoying every exhibit. We went to the boys' favourite restaurant, Pizza Express near the National Theatre, for lunch, and then to Tate Modern which then had a temporary set of curly slides like helterskelters from each level of the towering building to the floor. The boys were up and down uncountable times. I checked that there were sensible gallery employees at the top of each slide making sure that the kids were properly tucked into their little sacks for descent. I slid down the shortest slide with them once and then contented myself with standing at the bottom applauding their multiple arrivals.

On the way home we went to our favourite bookshop for reading material and then, the boys having opted for sausages, bought the raw materials for supper and made our way back to the house. The boys were somewhat deflated when Granddaddy wasn't up to receive their account of where they'd been and what they'd done, but he'd had a bad day and was asleep. I cooked the sausages, gave them a lick and a promise instead of a proper shower, asked halfheartedly if they'd brushed their teeth, and tucked them into their separate beds. They were both asleep before I left their rooms.

Sheridan came downstairs at about 9 p.m., hungry and upset. The woman who was planning to buy the house had arrived with her interior decorator after the boys and I had left in the morning. They had gone round the house for hours, proclaiming loudly about what was wrong with it and what they were going to change, which rooms they would demolish completely, which walls had to come down, etc., all carelessly within Sheridan's hearing.

While he had been less than enthusiastic about leaving Chelsea Harbour some eight years earlier, he was now used to our house, knew where everything was and could function within the space. This woman, whoever she was, and her designer had exacerbated his fears, and his resentment at her boorishness sent him into a depressive fury. I, of course, was out and he had nobody to vent his anger on so he did what he always did when depression got the better of him: as soon as she left, he wrote me a long and furious letter and went back to bed. Not wishing to engage with the exuberant small boys, he had waited until I had put them to bed before emerging from our bedroom. I wasn't very welcoming. I had just sat down and picked up a book. It had been a long day.

I thought, but fortunately didn't say, that it would have been nice if he'd come down earlier to talk to the boys while I made supper, and perhaps listened to tales of their day for a bit, but all I said was, 'Are you hungry?' When he said he was, I dragged myself off the couch and made him dinner, while making no secret of my weariness.

I sat with him while he ate, too tired to eat myself and wishing he'd hurry up so I could have a few minutes to myself before bed. He was tearful. He said he didn't want to move to New York because he had a great new scheme for staying in the house.

'Did you know, darling, that we could take all the equity out of this house and go on living here?'

Not this one again, I sighed to myself. 'Yes, it's called a reverse mortgage.'

'Well, then we wouldn't have to move, we could live on that.'

'No, because the equity in the house would keep us for maybe three years, if we were lucky, and then we'd have to sell the house anyway. Only then we'd get much less for it because we'd first have to pay the bank back before we saw a penny and that would not be enough to keep us for two more years. What are we supposed to do after that?'

This was not the first, nor the fifth, nor the twentieth time we had had this conversation. He repeated the reverse mortgage scheme again, louder this time, as though I hadn't heard him the first time. Perhaps he thought that, if he shouted it at me, the whole daft machination would suddenly make sense. And then, when I tried to deflect him, he started all over again.

'Go to bed, darling,' I said, heartsick and fed up and not even trying to hide it. 'You're not making any sense.'

He set off up the stairs and stopped halfway up, looking down on me. For a moment, his eyes were clear and I had the impression that he was, unusually, really seeing me. 'Don't you think I know I'm not making sense?' he said, slowly. 'I love you. Don't leave me. Goodnight.'

When I got into bed he was fast asleep on my side. Grumbling, I pushed him over just far enough to make space for myself. His head was on my pillow and I didn't want to wake him so opted for sharing. I opened the book I was reading but I don't think I got through a paragraph before falling asleep.

Tom, always first up, was sitting on top of me when I woke. It was just after 8 a.m on Friday, 16 February. Barnaby, who can sleep for Europe, was nowhere to be seen.

'Come on, wake up,' Tom urged. 'I want to show you a joke on the computer.'

'Shush, you'll wake Granddaddy', I moaned, as I dragged myself in the direction of the bathroom, fully aware that nothing short of an earthquake could wake Granddaddy when he didn't want to be woken.

Life in our house, without the boys and before Sheridan had his stroke, always started slowly. Unless one of us had a radio show or some other early morning event, there wasn't much conversation before about 10 a.m. I would get up quietly and pad off to the gym or an exercise class or, more likely, to the breakfast table where, in solitary state, I'd drink a couple of hundred cups of tea and, depending on which diet I was on at the time, enjoy my breakfast with the newspaper.

Since his depression had settled in permanently, of course,

Sheridan didn't get out of bed voluntarily at all. The best I could do at those times was to wake him for long enough to take his pills, which I always gave him with milk as a substitute for 'take with food', before he went back to sleep.

That morning, that 16th day of February in the year 2007, I slid out of bed. I think I must not have even looked at him, just been aware of his bulk turned on his side towards me, his head on my pillow, in exactly the same position he had been in when I got into bed last night. I just wanted a few more minutes of quiet before the day began.

'Go and get dressed', I whispered to Tom, 'then go downstairs, wake your brother and start getting your stuff together. You're going home this morning so try to remember where you left everything, and gather it up so I can pack it. I'll be down in a minute.' A vain hope, I knew, but it would keep him busy while I took my shower and woke up properly.

The next couple of hours were filled with normal family activity, lost toys, mislaid books, breakfast, teeth-brushing, clearing up, a couple of phone calls, Tom's computer jokefest. I was anxious to get the boys and Becca on the road and return them to Berkshire in good time because I had promised they would be back by lunchtime and because I had an appointment of my own.

When my mother, the youngest of her generation of our family, died, my cousins and I decided that there was a good chance we would lose touch if we didn't make a real effort to see one another. Although we all live in or near London, we are pretty far-flung so, at her funeral, we decided to institute an irregular get-together for lunch. Our 'cousins' lunches' are important to us all no matter how far we have to travel, and we had organized one for that day, miles away from Battersea, at my cousin Mildred's home in Finchley. My plan was to get the boys organized and packed up, wave goodbye and set off for North London.

The first part of the plan worked fine. By about 9.45, every lost sock had been retrieved and was packed. The children had break-fasted – Tom on some disgusting chocolate cereal, Barnaby on one of Sheridan's croissants – everybody was more or less clean and we were ready to go. I realized I hadn't given Sheridan his morning medication so I tipped the pills out of the container and poured him a glass of milk.

I was shouting as I came in the bedroom door. 'Come on, dar-ling, wake up! The boys are leaving and want to say goodbye to you.' No response. I hadn't really expected one. 'SHE-RI-DAN,' I yelled, 'at least wake up long enough to take your pills.' Nothing. I got cross. Usually, he would at least stir in response to all this noise. 'For God's sake, darling,' I complained, loudly, 'it's nearly ten o'clock, the boys have to leave, everything's ready and you won't even open your mouth and take your pills. I can't stand here all day!!!' Nothing. But I still had no sense of doom, no premonition that something was any more wrong than usual. I put the pills and the milk down on to the windowsill so my hand would be free to shake him awake.

Only when I touched him did I understand that something irrevocable had happened. I knew immediately that he was dead but my mind refused to process the information. I went on tugging his arm while I looked at his face. Having lain the entire night on his right side and, having died at some time during the early hours, the blood had drained to the bottom of his body and face so the right side of his face, the only part of him that was visible above the bedclothes, was stained a dark red. Had I looked at him earlier I would have seen it. So, of course, would Tom when he came to wake me. But we were both so accustomed to a heavily sleeping Sheridan that nothing had seemed amiss. He was, by now, completely stiff. I was overwhelmed by the thought that I had lain next to him all night, his head two inches from mine on the same pillow, and I had noticed nothing. I was completely panicked, not by Sheridan's death, but by the idea that I was alone in the house with two small boys who had to be protected, and a dead husband.

The panic didn't last. I knew I had to do something or the boys would come galumphing up the stairs to wake Granddaddy and I didn't want them to discover him dead.

I went downstairs to the boys who were in my study. It was my best ever piece of acting. I was calm, reassuring and sensible. 'I'm very worried about Granddaddy this morning, boys,' I said. 'He's very poorly, I'm afraid. I think I'd better call an ambulance so don't be scared when the men arrive. And I'd like it if you'd stay down here. I'm going to call your Mum.'

Tom, ever practical, asked, 'Do you think Granddaddy would mind if we watched a movie?'

I seized on the idea immediately. 'No, of course he wouldn't,' I said, 'what would you like to see?'

By the time I got back to the living room I was shaking so hard I didn't think I could make it upstairs. I heard a sound from the office. Becca had arrived for work.

'Becca,' I called in a voice I didn't recognize, 'Becca, could you come up here, please? Now.' It wasn't a request.

She came. It must have been frightening to see this jelly shaking in front of her. 'What is it? Is it Sheridan? Is he ill?'

'I think it's worse than that, I think he's dead.' What was I saying? I knew he was dead but, still, my mind wouldn't process it.

She was great. 'Sit down here.' I sat. She ran upstairs and by the time she came down, herself the colour of the white staircase, I was no longer shaking. She wasted no time in sympathy and, like me, went immediately for the practical. 'What do you want me to do?'

'I want you to look after the boys, don't let them come upstairs, I'll deal with Sheridan.'

I didn't know what to do next. Were the emergency services only for the living? Should I call them when I knew there was nothing they could do? What else was there? I went upstairs and, using Sheridan's bedside phone, dialled 999.

'Which service, please?'

'Er, ambulance. I think.' I explained the situation.

A very kind woman on the other end said, 'Are you alone in the house?'

I can't imagine why I said, 'Yes,' as Becca was right downstairs with the boys.

'Would you like me to give you some resuscitation techniques to try?'

'No,' I replied, politely, 'it's much too late for that.'

'Well, dear,' she said, 'you're not alone. There will be someone with you shortly and I'll stay on the line until they arrive.'

'There's no hurry,' I heard myself say. 'He's dead.' But I didn't believe it.

From this point on, everything followed as the night follows day. In fact, the day happened without apparently any input from me. I called Alexis, and told her what had happened and what I had told the boys. I asked her to tell her brother and sister. She said, 'We'll be there as soon as we can.' She and her husband, Reg, and baby Evie arrived within the hour. Juliet, her husband, Stefan, and their toddler, Max, also arrived quickly.

But I needed my own family. I called my sister, Adrienne, always my first recourse in times of joy and trouble. I needed her, right then and there, but she was on her way to Finchley for the cousins' lunch, and had, as usual, not taken her mobile. I called Mildred, and asked her please to get Adrienne to turn around immediately she arrived there and come to me. I meant 'immediately, if not sooner'. For reasons I've never understood, instead of coming to my house, she decided to go all the way home to her place to drop off cousin

June and pick up her husband David so it was mid-afternoon before she arrived and by then I had a houseful. I called my friend, Silvana, and she came at once.

I didn't realize that death has a protocol. A very few minutes after calling 999, two nice ambulance men arrived. They ventured into the bedroom with me and peered at Sheridan, still lying on his side and looking, from the doorway at any rate, fast asleep. I said, 'My husband is dead.' It was a statement, not a question. They went over to the bed and did whatever they do with the pulse in the neck.

The younger of the two men came over to me. 'Yes, madam, life is extinct.' The phrase was so pompous that I burst out laughing. From that moment I think they believed I had murdered my husband.

They called the police and the next time I went down to the living room there were four policemen drinking my tea and eating my digestives. The ambulance man told me that the police are always called in cases of unexpected death but I maintain that if I hadn't laughed . . .

I noticed on one of these trips upstairs that the day's medication and milk were still sitting on the windowsill. It occurred to me that Sheridan, who had so often said he didn't want to go on living with the depression and the misery, could possibly have taken his own life. To my surprise, this possibility didn't shock me at all. It seemed a perfectly logical outcome to a life which was too often bounded by pain. When I could do so without being observed, I went downstairs and counted the remaining pills. They were all there.

Anyway, the police called the local GP, she called the coroner, who called the undertaker. What with the children and the officials, we were running out of biscuits.

I discovered that my default when in crisis is Jewish Mother mode. 'Would you like a cup of tea?' I asked fifty times that day, as though I were hosting a rather odd party. 'There's the pizza

Tom likes in the freezer. I can heat it for you . . . Barney, you've got peanut butter on your nose. Go and wash your face . . . Who's hungry? . . . I'll feed the baby.' There was a conspicuous lack of alcohol. I hardly drink and it never occurred to me until later to offer booze, but the sons-in-law discovered the beer in the fridge and sensibly relieved me of it.

This rather peculiar 'party' continued, people arrived, nobody left. I was empty, feeling nothing much except that I wished they would all go away, until the coroner said there would have to be a post-mortem examination since Sheridan had died suddenly and unexpectedly. The cause of death, said Dr O'Reilly, was far from obvious. She couldn't tell from looking at the apparently-sleeping Sheridan whether he had had a stroke or a heart attack or whether there was another underlying cause. All she could tell was that he was dead and I could have told her that. It was also obvious from his peaceful expression and lack of movement that there had been no sudden pain during the night. I was sure about this, at least.

Several times during his bipolar episodes and again when he was so depressed he was sleeping for months at a time, I had banished him to the spare room, separated from our bedroom by his smart red, black and gold bathroom, or he had remained in the bedroom while I slept in the spare room. Able at last to get some sleep, I was still awake on the instant when Sheridan so much as turned over. Since he had, when depressed, a mild case of sleep apnea (where the patient stops breathing for moments at a time) I must have checked him four or five times a night, so conscious was I of his movements, even two rooms away. Thus I knew that, in bed with me, sharing a pillow, if he had stirred, felt any kind of pain or moved more than a little, I would have known. He died in his sleep and never knew a thing about it.

Many times since then, I have been grateful for this. It is, of course, how we all want to die, in our sleep after a good meal, alongside the person we love. But that wasn't the whole story, it wasn't even part of it. Sheridan was a tortured soul. When he died he was terribly unhappy, his depression having become an integral part of his nature.

While the operation had lifted the demons slightly, they were merely pushed back, not eliminated. He had lost so much – his off-the-wall sense of humour, his prodigious memory, his intellectual judgement and, above all, his confidence. He had lost his jobs, his mentors, his sense of who he was and where he fitted into his world. He felt himself unappreciated and undervalued by his friends, his children, his employers and his peers.

He loved me with a kind of desperation, couldn't contemplate life without me, but one of the tics of his depression was a conviction that he was making my life so difficult that I would leave him. No amount of reassurance would convince him otherwise and eventually I stopped trying. I concluded that as long as I was there with him I was living proof that his fear was groundless. It never went away. And perhaps I didn't do enough to assuage it.

Knowing that the undertaker would be coming late in the afternoon focused my wandering wits. I suddenly realized that soon Sheridan would leave his house and I would never see him again. I said to his daughters, 'I am going upstairs to sit with Daddy. Feel free to join me if you would like.' I made it clear that nobody else was invited.

I sat on my side of the bed and looked at the man I had liked, loved, admired and respected more than any other. He was still there. That strange transition that the religious call the soul departing the body had not yet happened.

I felt so sorry for him, so sorry that he had never regained the supreme confidence and pleasure he used to have in just being Sheridan Morley. So sorry that the stroke and the depression had robbed him of himself and that he had found nothing to replace what he had lost. So sorry that he'd had to live with that crushing sense of loss. There can be nothing worse than losing yourself and knowing yourself to be irredeemably lost.

And so sorry for myself, too. I suddenly saw the many ways I had been saying goodbye to the man I loved over the preceding four years. I had accepted that there would be no more sex, no more holidays, no more shared trips to Venice for a stolen weekend, no more sudden decisions to try a new restaurant or invite a new friend to dinner. No more birthdays and no more impromptu parties. No more spur of the moment decisions, no more lightning changes of mind, no more insights and no more jokes. Worst of all, no more shared laughter. One by one, without really noticing, I had given up on all these.

I knew that never again would anybody love me as he had. I knew that, no matter what he had put me through – the moods, the mania, the depression, the bankruptcy, the damage, the pain – he had been worth it. He had been worth it for the life, the laughter, the joy and the fun that he had brought me. I hoped that, if our situations were reversed, he would have felt the same about me but I could not come to a conclusion about that. We had been friends, lovers, spouses for nearly half a century and I would willingly have taken him on, damage and all, for another half. Sheridan once heard someone he didn't know (and there weren't many people he didn't know) refer to us as the Golden Couple. He loved that. It justified in his mind the decision to leave his first wife and marry me. That Golden Couple soubriquet convinced him that he had made the right choice, that he was destined to be with me and that our marriage was, somehow, inevitable.

I sat there on the bed thinking about a marriage that had gone far more right than it had gone wrong. Even taking into consideration an illness which has destroyed many millions of relationships, and which certainly drastically changed ours, I wouldn't have missed it for the world and I knew he wouldn't. In theory, it was over. He was over.

And yet somehow I knew it wasn't. We were, to the extent that any successful marriage is, the product of the two of us. Although we married when I was fifty and he was fifty-three, theoretically fully formed, we did in some inchoate way complete each other. He could not have been what he became without me; my life was formed by being with him.

His body of work was so extensive that it would live long after him. I resolved then and there to ensure that his name would be celebrated long after he had died because that would matter to him. I didn't know at the time how to do it but I knew that I was going to do it for him. He would live, not in some graveyard or memorial park, but in what he loved and what he was. He would be remembered.

It wasn't over.

Sheridan on Sheridan:
Living with Depression

When I was asked to write this book I showed Sheridan the proposal, outlining what the book would be about and why it needed to be written. I talked about his illness from the perspective of a wife who was confused and ill-equipped to take care of her chronically sick husband. I explained that I wanted to help others in a similar situation and that our story seemed to be a perfect vehicle.

Sheridan read it and, although he was enthusiastic about the project, said, 'That may be how this illness looks to you. It looks very different from inside my head.' He thought about it overnight and then asked whether I would mind if he contributed essays, to be peppered throughout the book, which might clarify how he felt and how the illness affected him. I was thrilled that he wanted to be part of this difficult process and ever after have thought of it as *our* book.

He managed to write three of these essays. And then he died.

Sheridan for Ruth's book –1

Depressives Anonymous, 2003

The fashion journalist Sally Brampton's courage in 'coming out' recently about a nervous breakdown and a suicide attempt ought to be the wake-up call most needed by us depressives, though I fear it will not be, and for good reason. So too should the heartbreaking account by Jane Lapotaire of her brain haemorrhage: but the jury is still out on whether or not memoirs of such painful honesty are really a good idea for the writer, even if (as in my case) the thought of an autobiography which did not deal with home truths was a non-starter. Having insisted on telling the truth about twenty or so other people in a long series of biographies written across thirty years, I could hardly create new rules of engagement for myself. Besides, in the current tabloid climate, if you don't out yourself some other bloody hack will do it for you and get paid. Somehow that was the clinching thought: I'd rather in my book tell you that I have been a near-lifelong depressive with several weeks as a clinical in-patient than wake up to read it in somebody else's words, just in case it is a very slow news day (always beware bank holidays) and some gossip columnist is sufficiently desperate for a paragraph. 'Morley has been in a clinic more than once' is admittedly not a headline likely to sell extra papers to any outside my immediate and long-suffering family, but having spent much of my life in print and broadcast newsrooms I know just how desperate it can get around deadline time. As a critic and a director, as a writer and a reader, I have always believed in crossing the line; the only trouble is that it can lead to schizophrenia, one of the few causes of mental breakdown I have not encountered either in myself or in wandering around specialist breakdown clinics.

But here's the thing: on the one hand, as Aids victims in America discovered (and no, there is no other similarity, and you don't even get Sir Anthony Hopkins as your AA buddy), publicity alone can bring support from government and well-meaning but bored and angry relatives and friends, all of whom too often see this, like Aids, as 'all our own fault', thus classifying us like cancer victims who still smoke or alcoholics who can't give up the bottle. But this is more than a Lost Weekend: it's a lost life, even though I still don't think you are supposed to 'out' yourself, not if you are, like me, sixty-one years old and hoping that your career in arts journalism will see you through: pensions seem not to be a part of the freelance life, and employers get nervous if they think you have gone barking mad while pursuing your calling. The fact that some of the greatest writing of the last century, from Eugene O'Neill to Scott and Zelda Fitzgerald, came out of a clinic is interesting but, then again, they were seldom if ever on deadline. I have always asked my editors whether they wanted it good or by tomorrow, and have seldom, given that choice, been told they wanted it good. Just as well, my enemies will tell you.

But, then again, writing beats screaming at the walls or your loved ones, it beats the belief that you have fallen down a black mineshaft into which you are digging yourself more deeply with every second of every minute of every hour of every day, and if you are a writer then writing is probably what you should do, even through the mental fog. They always tell budding novelists to stick to the familiar and the experienced, and someday please God this too shall end. Besides, what if I had been born a tightrope walker? There is at least not a lot you can do to yourself while writing, and somehow it keeps the suicidal depression at bay, but for an ever shorter time. Sleep might be a better idea, but you wake up feeling worse, and with all the after-effects of sleeping pills, even if you take them as sparingly as I do and then lie awake for an hour or two wondering if you dare swallow the bottle (no, sorry, just the contents) and whether, if you are the size I am, even that would do the trick: Hamlet's 'bare bodkin' has always seemed to me wildly inefficient, unless, of course, he was already skeletal.

The only truly magical moment of the day occurs when you are just about to fall asleep and realize that, with luck, for the next eight hours or so you are not consciously going to have to live with yourself or the job-lot of terrors, real and imagined, that come with depression itself.

I am what is known to medical science as a depressive diabetic, possibly even a diabetic depressive. There now. I've come out and you are still with me, or at least I fervently hope you are. Already you are doing better than I managed when in my right mind: one glimpse of the word 'depression' and I would go off into an anti-*Guardian* rant about journalism not being the same as therapy, and how I didn't buy a paper to learn of other people's troubles, unless of course they were Iraqi terrorists or transvestite comics.

So how did I get to be a serial depressive and why the hell should you care? We'll get to the caring bit later: just stay with me. Usually you get William Styron doing all this (poetic, not bad, not much practical use). But I've also just had to read Kirk Douglas's maddeningly optimistic hospital-bed memoir, *My Stroke of Luck*, bloody useless to me except for hurling at patients snoring happily in nearby hospital beds. Who'd want to stay healthy if all it meant was acting like Kirk Douglas in the first place? Once a critic, thank God, always a critic.

First depressions first: you are not depressed, oddly enough, when a loved one dies or you get fired: that they call unhappiness. Depression comes and goes of its own sweet will: psychiatrists often quote the case-history of a man who spent his entire long life, all eighty-five years of it, in clinical depression. Luckily I never had to meet him. Or he me, come to that.

And here's another curious fact: depression arrives from nowhere and leaves for nowhere. You naturally assume that whatever you were doing when it first kicked in is the cause, and that, equally, whatever you happen to be doing when it leaves, whatever pill you are on, or work you are doing, is the magic fix. Not true: it just comes and goes of its own bloody accord. Try getting that into an already damaged brain.

In my case, I know exactly when it all started, but I still have no idea why: one morning towards the end of my first marriage, at a guess about twenty years ago, I was watching my younger daughter running through our Berkshire garden, and thinking how bloody lucky we were to have her and her brother and sister, when my first and then wife suddenly threw a cup of coffee all over my newly pressed suit. I was shaken but not surprised: I was already trying to leave that marriage for my second and present wife, who has, it could be said, drawn the short straw. As she also has a home in and loves New York, she gets about half of me half of her time, let's agree on about a quarter all in, what with the gaps for mental incompetence (me), and the newly truncated transatlantic airline schedules (her). Depression gets the rest: oh yes, and then there's the diabetes, though that is relatively new to me, and already shows every indication (like the depression) of taking up residence for fucking ever in my already-overcrowded body. Sorry, I should have explained, the language gets worse along with the health, mental or other.

Where was I? Back in Berkshire, covered in coffee. Or so I recall: what my then wife had realized was that I was in no fit state to drive up the M4 to the office at *Punch* where I was, for the last decade of what we still call 'the real magazine', a blissfully happy arts editor and drama critic. I was also trying to make some sort of name in radio and TV, and to have a vaguely familiar-looking man roaming the streets of EC4 looking frankly barking, and talking to or rather at himself, would not have been exactly career-enhancing. My wife called our local doctor, who said that it was a mental breakdown and that there was a lot of it about. When my father died a few years later, he said there was a lot of that about, too.

The GP found me a psychiatrist: like me he was a big man, jolly and bearded, and I seem to recall him also trying for a second marriage through great gulfs of guilt about children and home-breaking. I have always had the terrible feeling that, finding in me a looking glass instead of an altogether different type of patient, may have driven him over the edge. At any event he checked me into the Cardinal, a brilliant clinic near Windsor which is like the Priory in Roehampton but mercifully without the rock stars or the madness reporters from *Hello* magazine: 'But, darling, depression is the new anorexia and, besides, you look wonderful in white with straps.'

Like all the great country-house hotels, the Cardinal wraps you in kindness and safety but also in psychiatric care until you feel strong enough to make it back down the M4 to the real world, which is of course where all the trouble starts again. We depressives are like John Osborne's Archie Rice, dead behind the eyes: but, like Mormons, we can spot each other across crowded rooms, and we don't even have to roll up our trousers or join the CID. It's all in the eyes, or rather it isn't.

Are there any advantages to being a depressive drama critic? Oddly enough there are, though actors probably disagree. I suddenly recognize Hamlet and Uncle Vanya and especially Ivanov and the aforementioned Archie Rice (if we're on to Osborne, how about Jimmy Porter and the dramatist himself?) as polar depressives: all their ostensibly bizarre behaviour at long last makes total sense. Even so, for me it has been a bipolar sort of life these last twenty years: fly high, take on all assignments, wait for the crash to come (I neither smoke nor drink nor drug, by the way, my own addictions are eating and reckless shopping, just thought you'd like to know), and then get into the Cardinal as quickly as the nearest loving relative can drive you there and away from the Barclaycard tracker dogs or even my own accountant, the wonderful Mark Gold, whose major headache I fear I am.

Even my own wives and children tell me I am the most ludicrously improvident person they have ever met, and that's in show-business circles. Like the diabetes and the depression, it is all my father ever left me. Not that his legacy, or rather the lack of one, was exactly a surprise. 'Lunch now, or a legacy later?' Robert would enquire over the Garrick bar, and I always went, of course, for the lunch.

Shamefully, I now feel about the Cardinal the way food critics must feel about a favourite restaurant: for God's sake don't tell the world it's there, or you'll never get a bed when you most need it. Get better, get back to work, and get to learn that there's not a lot you can do about being a bipolar depressive, though apologies to all those you love seem to me a minimal requirement. And so here they are, with especial thanks to my Aunt Sally for the exercise bicycle, which I really do use most mornings. The ones I manage to make downstairs at any rate.

But the problem of 'outing' remains: a broken leg can usually be advertised by crutches or a stick; people know at once either not to ask so daft a question as 'How are you?', or else not to be surprised when you fall on them, a painful experience for them if it happens to be me, since I am (as I may already have noted) not exactly light of body.

It was at the end of last November, though it feels like a century ago that, driving to host a cabaret, I wrote off the front of my car and was taken by the police for a drunken driver; by the time they got there I was leaning against what was left of the bodywork, gibbering gently; thank God no human or animal got hurt, as they now say at the end of Hollywood movies. When an understandably perplexed policeman saw no change in his breathalyser, he courteously asked me where I would like to be driven: 'To the nearest hospital' might have been a sensible answer, but I gave instead the address in Pavilion Road where I had agreed with my cabaret partner, the brilliant pianist and singer Michael Law, to provide a birthday-party show for a long-time client. By now, even I had noticed that I was falling over roughly once a minute and, when standing, not entirely making sense; deciding that honesty would be the best policy, I opened the show by solemnly telling the black-tie audience that despite all appearances to the contrary, I had not been drinking, merely having a diabetic stroke. It was, said Michael memorably from behind his keyboard, not perhaps the best or jolliest way to open a birthday cabaret.

Another curious problem is the pills: one of the few advantages of being massively overweight (see under Diabetes) is that you can drink for hours, get breathalysed regularly if you are as bad a driver as I am, and have nothing to show disbelieving traffic cops. The alcohol must somehow sink instantly into the feet, a doctor writes. By trial and error over several weeks at the Cardinal, my psychiatrist Dr Leslie Morrish (we agreed on first meeting that talking was unlikely to do the trick, but a shift in my chemical balance just might) found a mix of pills that lifted the depression: I took them for many years in what, I was secretly rather proud to note, were known medically as 'heroic' dosages. When I went to chemists in Chelsea to renew prescriptions, they would routinely ask for how many people these drugs were intended: when I told them 'Just me', they would ritually phone the Cardinal to double-check.

What else about the diabetes/depression double whammy? Does it make you suicidal? Yes it does but that, curiously enough, is the least of my problems. I am blessed with a loving and tolerant family: when I wrote a biography last year of the late John Gielgud which one or two critics were kind enough to call definitive, I was most endeared by something he recalled about his 1953 arrest for homosexual soliciting: 'Of course,' he said to me once, 'I thought of killing myself that night, but I couldn't find the bloody kitchen scissors. I couldn't even find the kitchen: O God, how do people manage it? I fear I must be very clumsy,' and that is what thankfully saves me too. Peter Coller, who works with us, points out in his languid way that I am the only driver he knows who can open the car roof regularly while searching for the ignition. I am not, thank God, a likely do-it-yourself death merchant.

I am also blessed by several magazine, Teletext and newspaper employers, all of whom have been far more tolerant than I deserve, and above all by Jim Moir and Judy Elliott and Tony Cherry and Gillian Reynolds who have kept my desk warm for me at the 'Radio 2 Arts Programme', which I have hosted every weekend for more than ten years; I have been more than lucky to spend virtually all of my BBC Radio life with a network that, thanks to Jim, maintains a strong sense of family. When I started out, there were a lot of those 'families' around magazine journalism and the arts and broadcasting: now they are all too bloody rare. Me, I blame the computers and Docklands in roughly that order. Probably also the Japanese.

Loss of work, loss of pride, loss of cash, loss of friends, above all loss of nerve and marriage and identity, are all what depression is really about. In that context, I am however blessed; nobody has actually left me, yet, even when I have idiotically tried to leave them and restart a life abroad – not an entirely sensible project if you happen to have no money and enough trouble negotiating Battersea. Then again, I am blessed with a cabaret partner in Michael Law who puts up with several lost and lucrative engagements despite my alas-untested conviction that he would do rather better with a show which promised its audiences neither sight nor sound of me; and, talking of audiences, the Bill Kenwright organization protected its actors and its investment but characteristically refrained from firing a visibly sick director from *The Chalk Garden*, a play I have long yearned to revive, while the cast graciously and kindly pretended not to notice that I was in some danger of 'losing the plot', one of the remarkably few occasions when that phrase could have been used as fact rather than metaphor. Anyway, I told myself hopefully, if Hamlet, the most depressed of all Shakespeare's heroes and clearly some turrets short of a castle even in Elsinore, could get his act together to instruct the Players, then maybe I should try for it. Actors, producers, other journalists and stage directors and producers seem almost alone to understand our curious and mentally crippling condition: my father Robert would simply fly to Le Touquet and lose money at the casino there, returning invariably poorer but infinitely happier.

But now we get to the real problem: secrecy and shame. One of the many reasons (her parents, her work and, happily, me) Ruth Leon came back home to London was that, at the height of the Aids crisis in New York, she couldn't bear another funeral. Because we are both arts writers, we would find ourselves all too often writing obituaries for the same American actors or dancers, and the same scenario would have to be played out across the Atlantic: the dead man's partner, also male, would urge us to print 'He died of Aids' so as to encourage a then-recalcitrant Nixon or Reagan government to commit more funding to research. But then, almost invariably, we would hear from the deceased's mother: 'We never told his children/the neighbours/his father', and we would allow the secret to go to his grave.

The importance of what Sally Brampton and Jane Lapotaire have done recently is to expose a secrecy which I hate and fear even while subscribing to it. My beloved wife and two distinguished journalists, both old *Punch* friends and colleagues, have indeed told me I might as well be writing a professional suicide note instead of this: but if one of the prime causes of depression is a feeling of worthlessness, coupled with a futile desire for secrecy and a desperate inability to get back to work, all in the belief that your brain has literally closed down, then this is my sole claim to having tried to make at least one thing better in forty years of journalism – critics don't usually get to do that.

While I was in his Cardinal, Leslie Morrish and I and several others began talking about the large number of classical musicians who, unable to pay for private insurance, were finding their careers cut short in midlife by physical or mental illnesses not of their making: we have therefore founded Octave, a charity which will exist solely for their recuperative physical or psychological benefit in the clinic. Details can be had from the Cardinal Clinic, Oakley Green, Windsor, Berks, and yes, we really do need your help. We are already extremely fortunate in that the great and good BUPA, whom God preserve, remains among a very few other private health insurance schemes still willing to support depressive care, but even there are signs that we may soon have to look after ourselves financially as well as in all other ways, and while still trying to walk on broken legs – the drugs are there, but they can take a month or more to click in and an equally long time to click out, while understandably most hospitals have other priorities.

I cannot ever recall feeling more ashamed than when, in a general accident ward (I had fallen on a first night and cut my forehead wide open on a Barbican staircase; I like to think of it as RSC revenge for several of my notices, but it was probably just the bloody pills), surrounded by people with 'real injuries' instead of just a broken brain, my best friend from our student days at Oxford came to visit me, valiantly cheering me up before noting as he left, 'Oh yes, by the way, I seem to have cancer. Do get well soon.'

The actors I have been working with (albeit briefly) for Kenwright are generous and patient, but all in all, I think I'd rather not have become a diabetic depressive at sixty-one. Watching your wife, indeed any of your family, slowly but surely finding you unbearable, becoming terrified of going anywhere you might inadvertently run into someone who wants to know how you are, would be hard enough were I not a compulsive party-goer, better always, as my family tells me repeatedly, in public than in private.

So what would you suggest I do at sixty-one? Press on in the hope that someone somewhere will finally get the magic pill right, or jog back to the comparative safety of the past as a theatre historian? Try to find a teaching job somewhere near a beach and away from the Congestion Charge? I even once had one of those, at the University of Hawaii, and this very year was a visiting professor at the University of South Florida: and they say the critical life is uneventful. I even discovered Bette Midler on a beach: I mean, before she was Bette Midler. The beach was just where we happened to be at the time, if you're still with me. If you're not, that's another problem of depression: my mind has always wandered, but now it gets totally lost coming home.

They seem to have rearranged London in my enforced absence, let alone where they used to put theatres. Since when has the Globe removed itself from Shaftesbury Avenue to the South Bank, and what happened to make it circular? When I was a child haunting my father Robert's West End home, nobody told us of any connection to Shakespeare. Then again, John Gielgud once told me that he had declined to have the Queen's Theatre renamed in his honour, for fear that theatregoers would demand to be taken to the old Queen's: but now there is a Gielgud, so what was that? And where is the Mermaid and since when did the Mayfair stop being a theatre and become a hotel? If there is an Olivier and a Gielgud, where is the Redgrave and where the Richardson? I feel like the character in a celebrated 1930s parody of *Hamlet* who returns after a few months abroad to ask if he has missed anything of any significance at the Elsinore court.

Oh yes, and while we are at it, where is the Almeida and how come that the National, built with three stages, now boasts of five?

But I guess the real terror is to do with age: it may now be illegal to discriminate against anyone in their sixties, but how about a depressive in his or her sixties?

Yet I am still among the lucky ones: I may lack a retirement plan but I still have an amazingly tolerant and long-suffering partner, three children, two grandsons, a long-living mother and employers in newspapers and magazines who seem to understand a condition

I still find inexplicable. Bill Kenwright still allows me to direct the occasional play, a long-held dream, and recently I even managed to play a corrupt judge in a BBC TV crime series called 'Judge John Deed'. Many are a lot less lucky, and already far too many of them are dead. That is fundamentally what matters about Sally Brampton's breakthrough as well as her breakdown: it tells us there are others out there in the dark, dark wood, even if we can't see or hear them. Believe me, we didn't become depressives for the fun of it. Or to annoy those we love; or even our employers. We got stuck with it, and the trouble is that just as you can't be a little bit pregnant, you can't be a little bit depressive either. It really is like having to live underwater in a sea of black ink, with brief gulps for air on the surface where all the unaffected swimmers are happily frolicking.

Thank you, on behalf of all of us, one in six people in this country, who are still slowly drowning, for your attention and hopefully your cheque. Oh yes, and for those of you as obsessed by random statistics as I am, there are more diabetics in Britain who don't know they have anything wrong with them, let alone anything life-threatening, than there are of us who know we have it. Would I rather have been left ignorant? Guess.

As the great and good Dr Stuttaford of *The Times* (and I have always secretly thought that if we had enjoyed our very own doctor during my time at *The Times* in the 1970s, we'd have been a lot more able to cope with the office, let alone our lives) has recently noted in that paper, mental illness of any kind from depression to violence is far better catered for now than it was even twenty years ago; the problem for us depressives is that there is still no sticking plaster for the mind, no way of walking on crutches to advertise the chemical imbalance. All we can do, as yet another crash into black tar looms, is to fail again, and much better. 'We can't go on, we must go on'; that was Samuel Beckett, one of the great depressive heroes, and even he had to wait forever for Godot. Maybe there is a Godot after all; if so, could he please pick up the phone? An answering service isn't quite the same, and I have this terrible feeling, Dr Stuttaford, that if I ever did reach a Samaritan on the phone at current Telecom rates (never mind the mobiles, though I do – once only us depressives were allowed to talk out loud in the street), I would probably bore him or her into far too early a grave: I once drove a psychiatrist raving mad, and there are not many of us who can boast of that.

Sheridan for Ruth's book –2

2006

By the summer of 2006 I had got as close to suicidal as I ever wanted to get. Despite the pills, and by now I was up to a dozen a day, despite the pacemaker which now seemed a vast and useless battery cut into my chest and likely to provoke unwanted queries on beaches, I was less able to function than I had ever been. Suddenly overwhelmed by the recent deaths of my parents and Ruth's, and the subsequent loss of what I still idiotically thought of as my family home, by fears that in my sixty-fifth year I was no longer in type or character the kind of critic or broadcaster they were hiring, and by the realization that although I had no mortgage I also had no pension, the money having gone into real estate, I began quite seriously to see no hope and no future.

That way lies serious trouble: facing every new day becomes a major problem, as does facing the world. You suddenly start feeling surplus to requirements and wondering what it feels like to drown, especially if you live as we do on a river bank.

Sustained work becomes difficult, if only because a critic who briefly loses faith in his own judgement has precious little to write about; equally terrifying, I noticed that my radio voice had lost some of its confidence.

My employers at the BBC and the *Daily Express* were more than kind: nervous breakdowns are nearly as common in journalism as they are in show business, but they do terrible harm to a marriage and a family, and through the fog I dimly became aware that without a cure I'd be likely to lose my darling Ruth and damage an albeit distant family of children and grandchildren.

To think about all this, and work out how to get fixed given that the stroke had rendered all the old miracle pills inoperable, I went to stay with my brother and son, who run a highly successful restaurant and bar in, surprisingly, Tampa, Florida. It was curious, so far from home, to find my brother's new house so full of our shared past – pictures and photographs, posters and furniture all going back to our parents' and grandparents' time.

That kind of focuses the mind, as did what my brother and son now do: they run a highly successful business which although undoubtedly hard work and long hours, remains unquestionably their own. Nobody can hire or fire them, tell them they are too old, or unfashionable, or that they have thought of someone more suitable for the job: it is an enviable kind of freedom and, of course, a place in the sun.

It was difficult to deal with any of this while trying to maintain a cheerful front, not least in the bar in front of strangers, and it wasn't until I got back on the plane to London that something truly broke: I wept all the way home, unnerving a stewardess and realizing finally that this couldn't go on. There are advantages to being vaguely familiar in public but there are also disadvantages, and one of those is that you can't really be seen in tears, not at least if you want or have to continue to be suitable for employment. When I got home I slept for two days, which is basically how you escape depression or fear or major decisions without resorting to drugs or drink, and when I woke up I realized this couldn't go on. I either had to rejoin the real world, Ruth's world, and deal with all the problems out there before they got any worse, or I had to get out forever. But I can't face death, and exile is vastly more complex professionally and financially than I had first thought. So that left living through it, desperately trying to fight the demons, even though they are getting stronger and I am getting older: no one ever tells you how physically and mentally exhausting depression can be, or the time it takes away from relationships and career.

***

I'm not exactly sure what I felt about all of this: relief certainly that I was no longer actively suicidal and had found the courage, if that's what it is, to face every new day. But alongside that, an aching sense of loss: loss of freedom and independence of movement, in that denied a car I either had to beg for lifts or deal with a public transport system which for half a century, since starting to drive at eighteen, I had managed to avoid in all its vagaries and crowds and maddening inefficiency. Loss too of my own space in a newspaper or magazine, which again I had enjoyed and rather taken for granted since my late twenties.

Ruth tells me not to tilt at windmills, that the world has moved on without me, and that I have simply to live with the way things are now. But what if I can't: what if I see the way things are now as an utter denial of all I have spent my life working towards?

Yes, I feel an aching sense of unfairness and bad timing: that the generation of journalists and publishers and critics and actors just ahead of mine was not thrown on the scrapheap or forced to accommodate themselves to changing times and machinery. They were celebrated and looked after, paid and pensioned, for who they were and what they did: not asked to behave at sixty-five as if they were twenty-one with no track record, eager for employment and willing to do whatever it took to stay in the good graces of employers who seem now to want far more for far less, without really understanding who they are employing or why, or what they need in return.

I know with the pills and the pacemaker and the psychiatrists to whom I seem to talk endlessly, that I have at all costs to avoid another depression – I am still exhausted from the last, and I am well aware that another could cost me my marriage and my job and my life. But how to avoid the urge just to get out from under a business and a city that is no longer mine, but filled with alien authority? How to avoid the despair that rackets around in my head when I hear what my employers now want of me? How to find the money just to bow out gracefully in the face of changing circumstances?

Everywhere I look, I am being replaced by others if not younger then certainly tougher than me in my present state – Toby Young, Matt Wolf, Barry Day – all doing jobs I thought were mine not as of right, but by years of hard work. I have let opportunities, such as the Coward Letters, slip through my fingers and the thought paralyses me for an entire weekend: how could I have been so stupid, so ill, so otherwise occupied? I spent months searching for a book project when the Coward Letters were there all the time for the taking; I just didn't think they were that good after we'd done the Diaries, and I am about to be proved wrong. I think. The issue is not how good they are but that they exist and have never been published: they will serialize and sell in this country and America and as literary executor I should have edited them and would have done, had Gra (Graham Payn, Coward's long-time lover and heir) not died and had I been thinking clearly after Gielgud and the memoirs . . . So much changes so fast, and I have fallen way behind . . . I have effectively dropped off the edge of my own universe, and I don't know how to climb back . . .